Gnosticism &
the Early
Christian World

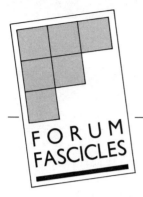

FORUM
FASCICLES

PUBLISHED VOLUMES

GNOSTICISM & THE EARLY CHRISTIAN WORLD

IN HONOR OF JAMES M. ROBINSON

EDITED BY
JAMES E. GOEHRING
CHARLES W. HEDRICK
JACK T. SANDERS
WITH HANS DIETER BETZ

SONOMA, CALIFORNIA
POLEBRIDGE PRESS
1990

Design & composition: Polebridge Press, Sonoma, California
Cover: Helen Melnis Cherullo
Printing & binding: McNaughton & Gunn, Inc., Saline, Michigan
Display & text type: Plantin

Library of Congress Cataloging-in-Publication Data
Gnosticism and the early Christian world : in honor of James
   M. Robinson / edited by James E. Goehring, [et al.].
      p.   cm. — (Forum fascicles)
   Includes bibliographical references.
   ISBN 0-944344-16-X : $29.95
   1. Gnosticism. 2. Nag Hammadi codices—Criticism, interpretation,
etc. 3. Gnostic literature—Relation to the New Testament.
4. Bible. N.T.—Criticism, interpretation, etc. 5. Robinson, James
McConkey, 1924– . I. Goehring, James E., 1950–
II. Robinson, James McConkey, 1924– . III. Series.
BT1390.G4945   1990   89–77940
                                          CIP

Printed in the United States of America

Contents

Tabula Gratulatoria

IN HONOR OF JAMES M. ROBINSON

★

LUISE ABRAMOWSKI

Universität Tübingen

★

To a scholar from whom I have learned much, and to one whom in calling friend I honor myself.

PAUL J. ACHTEMEIER

Union Theological Seminary in Virginia

★

KURT UND BARBARA ALAND

*Institut für
neutestamentliche Textforschung
Münster*

★

On your 65th birthday let me extend to you my sincere appreciation for your great contribution to the editions of Nag Hammadi texts.

PROF. DR. SASAGU ARAI

University of Tokyo

★

Floreat magister gratia auctoritate.

MR. JON MA. ASGEIRSSON

The Claremont Graduate School

★

★

I wish to extend my personal congratulations to Dr. James Robinson for a timely and well deserved Festschrift. His indefatigable pursuit of high scholarship standards has opened to a wide public the knowledge of a phase of Christianity hitherto unknown.

LOLA ATIYA

Salt Lake City, UT

★

NH II 82:26–29

... ⲛⲓⲙ ⲡⲉ ⲉⲧⲛⲁⲣ̄ ⲛⲟϭ ⲉϨⲣⲁⲓ̈
ⲉϫⲱⲛ ...
... ⲡⲙⲁ ⲛ̄ⲧⲁⲧⲉⲧⲛ̄ⲉⲓ ⲙ̄ⲙⲁⲩ
ⲉⲧⲉⲧⲛⲁⲃⲱⲕ ϣⲁ ⲓ̈ⲁⲕⲱⲃⲟⲥ ...

TJITZE BAARDA

*University of Utrecht
The Netherlands*

★

HEINRICH BAARLINK

*Theological University, Kampen
The Netherlands*

★

vii

★

Congratulations and best wishes, with sincere appreciation for your friendship and scholarly contributions.

PROF. WILLIAM BAIRD

Brite Divinity Schoool
Texas Christian University

★

With best wishes and thanks especially for all you have contributed to the work of Studiorum Novi Testamenti Societas.

ROBIN BARBOUR

University of Aberdeen

★

S. SCOTT BARTCHY

University of California
Los Angeles

★

To that preeminent scholar of the Biblical world to whom so much is owed by so many.

ROBERT BATER

Queen's Theological College
Kingston, Canada

★

THEOFRIED BAUMEISTER

Johannes Gutenberg-Universität
Mainz

★

H. KEITH BEEBE

Occidental College

★

Meine Glück– und Segenswünsche für den weiteren Lebensweg des Jubilars verbinden sich mit Hochschätzung für das umfangreiche wissenschaftliche Werk sowie mit einem herzlichen Dank für alle Hilfe und die Möglichkeiten fruchtbarer Zusammenarbeit.

DR. HANS-GEBHARD BETHGE

Humboldt-Universität Berlin
Sektion Theologie

★

CONGRATULATIONS
to one whose surpassing
passion for integrity of text
has moved countless others
to no end of enterprise:
archaeological, semiotic,
exegetical, philologic,
hermeneutical, heuristic,
sometimes downright mystic.

EDWARD F. BEUTNER

Santa Clara University

★

BIBLIOTHÈQUE D'HISTOIRE
DES RELIGIONS

Collège de France

★

Congratulations on your academic enterprise and your work in gospel studies and Coptology.

EMER. PROF. J. NEVILLE
BIRDSALL

University of Birmingham
England

★

Many thanks.

STERLING BJORNDAHL

Camrose, Alberta

★

★

Beste Wünsche für Sie und Ihre weitere Forschung.

PROF. DR. DR. ALEXANDER
BOEHLIG
Tübingen

★

My congratulations and best wishes to you as scholar, pioneer, and international organizer of research.

PEDER BORGEN
*University of Trondheim
Norway*

★

Reçois, cher ami, mes félicitations et mes vœux à l'occasion de ton soixante-cinquième anniversaire.

FRANÇOIS BOVON
University of Geneva

★

DR. WILLIAM BRASHEAR
*Ägyptisches Museen
Berlin*

★

PROF. DR. INGO BROER
Wilnsdorf, West Germany

★

In multos annos floreas, crescens in scientia dei.

F. F. BRUCE
*University of Manchester
England*

★

CHRISTOPH BURCHARD
University of Heidelberg

★

★

PROF. DR. ULRICH BUSSE
Universität Duisburg

★

RON CAMERON
Wesleyan University

★

Lieber Jim, zu Deinem Geburtstag gebe ich Dir zurück, was Du mir bei Deinem Letzten Besuch in Dein Exemplar von "De resurrectione" schriebst: ". . . in appreciation for all you have done for me over the years."

CARSTEN COLPE
Free University of Berlin

★

καὶ ἐδικαιώθη ἡ σοφία
ἀπὸ πάντων τῶν τέκνων αὐτῆς

WENDY J. COTTER, C.S.J.
*University of St. Michael's College
Toronto*

★

Congratulations not only on your own publications but for having established, with the Nag Hammadi Codices, the publication standards for all such future discoveries.

JOHN DOMINIC CROSSAN
De Paul University

★

Dem ausgezeichneten Basler Schüler, dem hervorragenden Kollegen und Forscher, dem treuen Freund, mit guten Wünschen für seine Weiterarbeit. En souvenir des bons moments passés à Bâle, Paris, Strasbourg, Chamonix, Emory, Clermont.

OSCAR CULLMANN
Universities of Paris and Basle

★

★

To a bridger of aeons.

FREDERICK WILLIAM DANKER

St. Louis, Missouri

★

Happy to enlist among your admirers

DAVID DAUBE

School of Law
University of California
Berkeley

★

GERHARD DAUTZENBERG

Justus Liebig-Universität
Gießen

★

It is hard to recall any scholar in the last generation who has done more than James Robinson both to develop his own research and to foster that of others on the actual historical sources of early Christianity. We thank him for pointing the way past many an impasse.

JON F. DECHOW

Portola Valley, CA

★

With deep appreciation and respect for your creative and pioneering leadership in the field of New Testament studies.

KARL PAUL DONFRIED

Smith College

★

I've only found your work pathbreaking for the last twenty-five years: I so look forward to more.

WILLIAM G. DOTY

The University of Alabama

★

★

Bardaişan of Edessa sends you his congratulations in great admiration for the way you have used your free will and borne your scholarly fate serving students East and West of Antioch.

PROF. HAN J. W. DRIJVERS

Dept. of Semitic Languages
University of Groningen
The Netherlands

★

JAMES D. G. DUNN

University of Durham
Great Britain

★

It is a specific and signal honor for all of us that we should have the privilege to honor you, Dr. James M. Robinson. You are the epitome of scholarly integrity, courage, vigor, ingenuity, and endurance. We are better scholars because you have been among us.

PROF. J. HAROLD ELLENS, PH.D.

Institute for Antiquity and Christianity

★

To Jim, always on the front lines of scholarship, leading a cadre of younger colleagues in an effectively organized campaign to achieve the next important objective. May the future of your scholarly past bring still more victories—for you and for us.

ELDON JAY EPP

Case Western Reserve University

★

★

In herzlicher Verbundenheit durch den gemeinsamen Dienst am "Buch der Bücher."

Ihr

PROF. DR. JOSEF ERNST
Theologische Fakultät Paderborn

★

Your seminars were the best. Thanks for making biblical scholarship so rewarding and so fun.

CRAIG A. EVANS
Trinity Western University

★

Forsan et haec olim meminisse juvabit.
Vergil, *Aeneid I*, 203.

CHRISTOPHER FARMER
San Marino, CA

★

JOSEPH A. FITZMYER, S.J.
Catholic University of America

★

Thank you for your long and valuable contribution to the scholarly world. We are greatly indebted to you.

H. J. FLANDERS, JR.
Baylor University

★

ROBERT T. FORTNA
Vassar College

★

PROF. DR. HUBERT FRANKEMÖLLE
Universität Paderborn

★

★

SEAN V. FREYNE
Trinity College, Dublin

★

You have brought honor to your profession and to your academic colleagues everywhere. We share the hope that many more productive and enjoyable years lie ahead.

ROBERT W. FUNK
Polebridge Press &
Westar Institute

★

WOLF-PETER FUNK
Université Laval

★

LLOYD GASTON
Vancouver School of Theology

★

The New Hermeneutics et Trajectories ont profondément marqué ma vision du Nouveau Testament pendant mes études et influencé mon activité universitaire postérieure. Je vous en suis fort reconnaissante.

PROF. OLIVETTE GENEST
Université de Montréal

★

אַשְׁרֶיךָ וְטוֹב לָךְ:

ERHARD S. GERSTENBERGER
Philipps University
Marburg

★

*

Not only for rediscovering SOPHIA, both ancient and modern, but also for having lived into our SBL the ancient triad of PISTIS-ELPIS-AGAPE, and for having persisted in all this against opposition, I salute you and give thanks.

JOHN G. GIBBS
Westminster/John Knox Press

*

Εἰς πολλὰ ἔτη
PROF. DR. JOACHIM GNILKA
Universität München

*

JAMES E. GOEHRING
Mary Washington College

*

Greetings and best wishes from the Mother Country.

LESTER L. GRABBE
*University of Hull
England*

*

DR. HENRY A. GREEN
University of Miami

*

PR. PIERRE GRELOT
Institut Catholique de Paris

*

Greetings and best wishes.

WILLIAM C. GRESE
Bloomington, Illinois

*

May your personal quest for continued success and happiness mirror your scholarly and professional quests. My memories of our excavation at Nag Hammadi are especially pleasant. With best regards.

(Dein) Wachstum heißt, von immer Größerem besiegt zu werden
—Rilke

C. WILFRED GRIGGS
Brigham Young University

*

ROBERT G. HAMERTON-KELLY
*C.I.S.A.C.
Stanford University*

*

May I join in congratulating you, Jim, and wishing you all the best in the years to come. I cherish many happy memories of our times together.

REV. CANON DR. RAYMOND J. HAMMER
*22 Midsummer Meadow
Inkberrow, Worcs. WR7 4HD
United Kingdom*

*

HERMANN HARRAUER
*Papyrussammlung der
Österreichischen Nationalbibliothek*

*

Congratulations upon reaching this milestone in your career. I appreciate your friendship and the contribution you have made to the field of New Testament study.

CLAYTON K. HARROP
*Golden Gate Baptist
Theological Seminary*

*

★

pro studiis de natura deorum reli-
gionumque
optime scriptis fautis auctis
omnes amici discipuli conlegae
gratias tibi JMR maximas agunt.

PAUL B. HARVEY, JR.
Pennsylvania State University

★

My congratulations and best wishes!

GÜNTER HAUFE
Universität Greifswald
Sektion Theologie

★

Esteemed teacher and colleague, I am
deeply grateful for the standards you set
for your students and colleagues with
the honesty and integrity of your scholarship, and for teaching us by your
example the "art of the possible."

CHARLES W. HEDRICK
Southwest Missouri State University

★

DAVID HELLHOLM
University of Oslo
Norway

★

JAMES D. HESTER
University of Redlands

★

RONALD F. HOCK
University of Southern California

★

Mit guten Wünschen in herzlicher Verbundenheit.

PAUL HOFFMANN
Universität Bamberg

★

★

INSTITUTE FOR
ANTIQUITY AND CHRISTIANITY
Claremont Graduate School

★

Thanks for your leading role in getting
the Nag Hammadi texts published.

WESLEY W. ISENBERG
Concordia College
River Forest, IL

★

DR. ARLAND D. JACOBSON
Concordia College
Moorhead, MN

★

To my Doktorvater
Who is admired and respected
Who challenges and frustrates
Who drives students toward excellence,
 yet
Who remains a friend
I extend my congratulations,

RONALD L. JOLLIFFE
Walla Walla College

★

Ad multos annos!

MARINUS DE JONGE
University of Leiden

★

τοῖς ἐγρηγορόσιν ἕνα καὶ κοινὸν κόσμον
εἶναι

EBERHARD JÜNGEL
Universität Tübingen

★

CHARLES KANNENGIESSER
University of Notre Dame

★

★

Nach wie vor bin ich für die religions-
und traditionsgeschichtlichen Arbeiten
des Jubilars sehr dankbar. Ad multos
annos!

PROF. DR. KARL KERTELGE

Universität Münster

★

Congratulations on your 65th Birthday.
I have always appreciated your work and
advancement of New Testament
scholarship.

PROF. CHAN-HIE KIM

School of Theology at Claremont

★

In gratitude for the stimulus you provided American New Testament
scholarship at a time when it was still
searching to find its own identity.

JACK DEAN KINGSBURY

*Union Theological Seminary
Virginia*

★

JOHN S. KLOPPENBORG

*Faculty of Theology
Univ. of St. Michael's College*

★

To James M. Robinson, A superior
leader in modern scholarship, in
abiding appreciation of his loyal
collegiality and friendship, and with my
best wishes for a long life in good
health, constructive endeavors, and a
happy mind.

ROLF P. KNIERIM

*School of Theology and
Claremont Graduate School*

★

Τῷ ἀδελφῷ καὶ συνέργῳ

HELMUT KOESTER

*Harvard University
The Divinity School*

★

With appreciation, admiration, and all
best wishes!

ROBERT KRAFT

University of Pennsylvania

★

Floreas in multos annos!

PROF. EDGAR KRENTZ

*Lutheran School of Theology
Chicago*

★

PROF. DR. J. LAMBRECHT

*Dean, Faculty of Theology
K. U. Leuven*

★

Mes félicitations à mon cher collègue
James M. Robinson.

XAVIER LÉON-DUFOUR

*Centre Sèvres
Paris*

★

PROF. DR. ANDREAS
LINDEMANN

Kirchliche Hochschule Bethel

★

Grüße an den, der die Q-Forschung so
stark gefördert hat.

PROF. DIETER LÜHRMANN

Philipps-Universität Marburg

★

★

Mögest Du jung bleiben wie bisher.
Herzlich

PROF. ULRICH LUZ
Universität Bern

★

J. LOUIS MARTYN
Union Theological Seminary

★

My deepest appreciation to you for your
many contributions to my understanding of early Christianity. Your
many stimulating works have not only
been pivotal in their field, but even
foundational for all further research.
Thank you and best wishes to you on
this special occasion.

LEE MARTIN McDONALD
*First Baptist Church
Santa Clara, CA*

★

With deep appreciation for your
Erasmian call *ad fontes*.

LANE C. McGAUGHY
Willamette University

★

ANNE M. McGUIRE
Harverford College

★

EDGAR V. McKNIGHT
*Furman University
Greenville, SC*

★

★

EDWARD McMAHON
Texas Christian University

★

Hoping that you will achieve the facsimile edition of the Manichaean Coptic
texts as you did with the Gnostic papyri.

REINHOLD MERKELBACH
*Institut für Altertumskunde
Universität Köln*

★

Thank you, Jim, for dismantling and
reassembling the categories.

PAUL ALLAN MIRECKI
University of Kansas

★

ⲧⲉⲭⲁⲣⲓⲥ ⲛⲁⲕ ⲁⲩⲱ ϯⲣⲏⲛⲏ·
ϫⲉ ⲟⲩⲛ ⲟⲩⲛⲟϭ ⲛ̄ⲣⲁϣⲉ ϣⲟⲟⲡ
ⲛⲁⲛ ⲉⲃⲟⲗ ϩⲓⲧⲟⲟⲧⲕ̄.

FRANÇOISE MORARD
Fribourg, Suisse

★

J. MURPHY-O'CONNOR
*Ecole Biblique
Jerusalem*

★

Herzliche Glückwünsche! Ad multos
annos!

FRANZ MUSSNER
Universität Regensburg

★

F. NEIRYNCK
Leuven University

★

★

My congratulations and best wishes.

REV. ROBERT F. O'TOOLE, S. J.

St. Louis University

★

Congratulations and deep appreciation from all of us to whom your dedication made available the discoveries at Nag Hammadi.

ELAINE PAGELS

Princeton University

★

To my teacher and friend, congratulations and best wishes.

STEPHEN J. PATTERSON

Eden Theological Seminary

★

JOHN J. PILCH

Biblical Theology Bulletin
Catonsville, MD

★

FR. IGNACE DE LA POTTERIE, S.J.

Pontificio Istituto Biblico

★

PROF. MARTIN RESE

Evangelisch–Theologische Fakultät
Münster

★

THE REV. PROF. JOHN REUMANN

Lutheran Theological Seminary
Philadelphia

★

★

With congratulations and gratitude always for making the Nag Hammadi Library and the Institute for Antiquity and Christianity available to us.

VERNON K. ROBBINS

Emory University

★

TONI ANN ROBINSON

Claremont, CA

★

Congratulations

WILLIAM C. ROBINSON, JR.

Andover Newton Theological School

★

EUGEN RUCKSTUHL

Lucern

★

Mit herzlichem Glückwunsch und Gruß.
Der nächste ThR-Gnosisbericht ist Dir gewidmet (im Druck).

KURT RUDOLPH

Philipps-Universität Marburg

★

PROF. MAURITS SABBE

Theology Faculty Library
K. U. Leuven

★

Hearty thanks for all you have done for biblical studies—and for all you yet will do.

JAMES A. SANDERS

Ancient Biblical Manuscript Center

★

★

Mit den besten Wünschen für Ihre
weitere Tätigkeiten.

AKIRA SATAKE

Hiroshima

★

Πολλὰ χρόνια καὶ εὐλογίαι.

ERNEST W. SAUNDERS

Mt. Vernon, ME

★

Best wishes and thanks for a long friendship and a fruitful collaboration.

TORGNY SÄVE-SÖDERBERGH

Uppsala University

★

May God bless you with time and
further inspirations for Q research and
related fields.

WOLFGANG SCHENK

Eppstein, Germany

★

With gratitude for your many, many
contributions.

DAVID M. SCHOLER

*North Park College and
Theological Seminary*

★

DAVID SCHROEDER

Canadian Mennonite Bible College

★

Multos in annos!

PHILIP SELLEW

University of Minnesota

★

★

Gratias tibi ago, Magister.

JOHN H. SIEBER

Luther College

★

וְצִיר אֱמוּנִים מַרְפֵּא
Proverbs 13:17

LOU H. SILBERMAN

Vanderbilt University

★

Χάρις σοι καὶ εἰρήνη πληθυνθείη ἐν
ἐπιγνώσει τοῦ θεοῦ καὶ ᾿Ιησοῦ τοῦ
κυρίου ἡμῶν (2 Peter 1:2)

DR. STEPHEN S. SMALLEY

Chester Cathedral

★

DENNIS E. SMITH

Phillips Graduate Seminary

★

With warm gratitude for years of
instruction, help, and friendship. May
you have many more productive years to
share with us.

EDGAR W. SMITH, JR.

Grand Rapids, MI

★

For Jim, in whom wisdom has found a
resting place.

JONATHAN Z. SMITH

University of Chicago

★

ⲁⲕⲟⲩⲱⲛ ⲘⲠⲢⲞ ⲁⲕⲟⲩⲱⲛⲅ ⲈⲂⲞⲗ
ⲚⲦⲈⲅⲒⲎ

RICHARD SMITH

*Institute for Antiquity and Christianity
Claremont Graduate School*

★

★

DR. GRAYDON F. SNYDER
Chicago Theological Seminary

★

REV. PERE SPICQ, PROF.
EMERITE
*Université de Fribourg
Suisse*

★

Heartiest congratulations and all good
wishes. I hope you will continue to ask
probing questions for many years to
come.

PROF. GRAHAM N. STANTON
*King's College
University of London*

★

The Toronto School of Theology con-
gratulates you on this festive occasion
and expresses its appreciation for your
significant scholarly contributions and
wishes you a fulfilling future.

MICHAEL G. STEINHAUSER
Toronto School of Theology

★

GEOFFREY L. STORY, JR.
Illinois Wesleyan University

★

PROF. DR. GEORG STRECKER
*Georg-August-Universität
Göttingen*

★

In gratitude for your scholarship, your
insights, your perseverance, and your
diplomacy.

PROF. WALTER F. TAYLOR, JR.
Trinity Lutheran Seminary

★

★

Συγχαρητήρια καὶ εἰς ἀνώτερα
TONI TRIPOLITIS
Highland Park, NJ

★

Pour scruter l'évangile et lire les gnostiques, James M. Robinson a guidé
l'Amérique. Pourquoi cesserait-il quand
viendra l'an deux mil?

ETIENNE TROCME
University of Strasbourg—2

★

Herzliche Segenswünsche und liebe
Grüße zum Jubuläumsgeburtstag in
kollegialer Verbundenheit.

PROF. DR. KARL-WOLFGANG
TRÖGER
Humboldt Universität zu Berlin

★

DR. C. M. TUCKETT
*University of Manchester
United Kingdom*

★

Νείλου μὲν ποταμοῦ ῥόος χθόνα οἶδε
ποτίζειν, Σχολαστικοῦ δ' αὖ τούτου
λόγος φρένας οἶδεν ἰαίνειν.

ERNEST W. TUNE

★

Sydämelliset onnittelut–
Warmest congratulations!

RISTO URO
University of Helsinki

★

★

Hartlik geluk met jou suksesvolle loop-baan.

WILLEM S. VORSTER
Unisa, South Africa

★

PROF. DR. FRANÇOIS VOUGA
Kirchliche Hochschule Bethel

★

Congratulations and warm appreciation for a long and distinguished career of service to the world of scholarship and to the profession! Keep up the good work!

WILLIAM O. WALKER, JR.
Trinity University

★

Vir Ingeniosus
Et Eruditus

ROY BOWEN WARD
Miami University

★

Remembering long associations with homage and appreciation.

AMOS WILDER
Harvard Divinity School

★

★

Congratulations to a fine scholar and a big man. My thanks for many favors.

FRANK WILLIAMS
*University of Texas
El Paso*

★

ⲓⲁⲕⲱⲃⲟⲥ ⳨ⲧⲙⲁⲉⲓⲟ ⲛⲧⲉⲕⲇⲓⲁⲛⲟⲓⲁ
(NHC V 29,4–5)

MICHAEL A. WILLIAMS
University of Washington

★

En signe de reconnaissance pour votre esprit d'innovation dans le domaine scientifique et votre ouverture humaine.

PROF. DR. JEAN ZUMSTEIN
*Université de Neuchâtel
Switzerland*

★

A young and promising James M. Robinson
(Photograph by A. Blankhorn)

James M. Robinson

A BIOGRAPHY

Prepared by Stephen J. Patterson

James M. Robinson has on occasion described his own theological career as a programmatic attempt to follow up all of the various strands pulled together by Rudolf Bultmann, whose synthesis of the data from the previous generation's work provided the foundation upon which the next generation might begin to build its own future. When one traces the course of Robinson's tenure in our guild through early studies in Wilhelm Herrmann, to the new quest of the historical Jesus, the later Heidegger and the New Hermeneutic, the Nag Hammadi library and the study of Gnosticism, and most recently the redis-covery of Manichaean texts in the museums of Europe and the revival of interest in the problem of Christian origins through research on Q, one may say that his career has indeed been, in the best sense, post-Bultmannian. But more than that, in following up and clarifying these various strands inherited from the previous generation, all the while involving not only himself, but always also large teams of young and eager colleagues, he has served to pass along to the next generation his own legacy, a wealth of scholarship to which many have contributed, inspired by the questions, issues, challenges and dilemmas first brought to clarity in Robinson's work.

James McConkey Robinson was born in 1924. His father, William Childs Robinson, was an orthodox Presbyterian, thoroughly Calvinist, who taught Ecclesiastical History and Polity for many years at Columbia Theological Seminary in Decatur, Georgia. Though Robinson began his theological education within the parameters of this traditional conservatism, he soon began his pilgrimage away from these roots. Shortly after receiving a B.D. from Columbia in 1946, he traveled to Basel to study with Karl Barth and Oscar Cullmann. Later he would describe Cullmann's book *Christ and Time* as a kind of theological halfway house away from orthodoxy,[1] but in retrospect this could be said of his work with Barth as well. For although his eventual Basel dissertation, entitled *Das Problem des Heiligen Geistes bei Wilhelm Herr-*

---

1 "How My Mind Has Changed," 486.

mann,[2] was written under Karl Barth, and with a decidedly Barthian slant, his progressive migration to the left did not find its end point in Basel. For even while putting the final touches on this dissertation in 1950–51, Robinson spent a semester in Marburg attending Bultmann's lectures on 1 Corinthians and his seminar on Hellenistic Religions. It was during the latter, in which Bultmann applied his demythologizing technique to a variety of Hellenistic texts, that Robinson began to see the sense of Bultmann's controversial methods. Ultimately Robinson would find his theological future not in the Barthian side of Neo-orthodoxy, but with Bultmann on the left. Years later he would write: "By now I have come to recognize in demythologizing the only form in which I can believe, and, what is more significant, what makes believing important."[3]

In 1952 Robinson was called to a post at the Candler School of Theology of Emory University in the area of Biblical Theology, where he taught until 1958. While there he resumed work on a New Testament Th.D. at Princeton Theological Seminary, which he had begun in 1948, but soon thereafter had abandoned in favor of contemporary theology and Barth. When he resumed the Princeton doctoral program in 1953, he worked with the German transplant, Otto Piper. His dissertation under Piper on the concept of history in the Gospel of Mark was published in 1957 as *The Problem of History in Mark.* The influence of Bultmann and the post-Bultmannians, particularly with respect to the discussion of "history" then current on the continent, is to be seen especially in the opening chapter of this, Robinson's first bonafide monograph. Its acceptance by the faculty at Princeton is no doubt as much a tribute to Robinson's diplomatic skills (so much in evidence throughout later endeavors) as to their tolerance for new thinking.

In 1957 Robinson was invited to deliver a lecture to the Oxford Congress on the Four Gospels. The resulting paper, entitled "The Kerygma and the Quest of the Historical Jesus," became the basis for what is arguably Robinson's most lasting theoretical contribution to the field of New Testament, *A New Quest of the Historical Jesus.* In offering his own synthesis of the Jesus question Robinson managed not only to make his own statement on the issue, but also to give definition and nomenclature to an entire theological movement: the new Quest.

In 1958 Robinson was called by Ernest Cadman Colwell to come to Claremont together with John Cobb and join the faculty of the School of Theology at Claremont. Robinson's continuing interest in European trends in theology produced a collaborative effort with Cobb in the editing of a three volume set New Frontiers in Theology including *The Later Heidegger and Theology* (1963), *The New Hermeneutic* (1964), and *Theology as History* (1967). During this period Robinson also served as editor of the English edition of *The*

---

2 The reader may refer to the complete bibliography of James M. Robinson in the companion volume, *Gospel Origins and Christian Beginnings,* xiii–xxvii.
3 "How My Mind Has Changed," 483.

Beginnings of Dialectic Theology (1968) and *The Future of Our Religious Past: Essays in Honor of Rudolf Bultmann* (1971). In 1965 he helped to found and edit the *Journal for Theology and the Church,* which produced seven volumes of the latest theological work from the German academy in translation. This long list of titles pays tribute to the enormous amount of energy Robinson has invested over the years in encouraging dialogue between American and European—especially German—scholarship. This too must be counted as one of Robinson's enduring contributions to the modern study of the New Testament.

It was during this period that Robinson became involved with another "service project" with which his name has been associated perhaps more than anything else. In 1965 Robinson traveled to Jerusalem to serve as Annual Professor at the American School of Oriental Research. In the course of his stay there he visited Cairo to inquire about the *Apocalypse of Adam,* a tractate from the as yet little known collection of texts from Nag Hammadi commonly referred to now as the Nag Hammadi Library. When he found that access to the manuscripts was restricted to a small group of Europeans, whose work to date had placed only a small fraction of the texts in the public domain, Robinson responded with a combination of espionage and diplomacy. With transcriptions based on photographs of a small number of texts supplied by the German Archaeological Institute in Cairo, Robinson assembled a group of young American and European scholars willing to learn Coptic, and started the Coptic Gnostic Library Project. Later he acquired photographs of the rest of the collection through UNESCO, which had acquired photographs in view of a facsimile edition, and had draft transcriptions and translations prepared of all the codices, so that outsiders could have pre-publication access to them. When the original cartel charged with publishing these materials discovered what had happened, they lodged a protest with UNESCO. Happily for the academy, UNESCO responded by creating the International Committee for the Nag Hammadi Codices, and making Robinson its Permanent Secretary, ruling that it was in the best interest of UNESCO to disseminate the texts entrusted to it rather than protect the rights of a monopoly by restricting access. As a consequence, between 1972 and 1977 the International Committee under Robinson's leadership was able to publish the eleven volumes of *The Facsimile Edition of the Nag Hammadi Codicies,* thus placing all of the Nag Hammadi texts in the public doman in a relatively short period of time. (A twelfth volume, the *Introduction* appeared in 1984.) The value of this service can only be measured against the fate of a similar manuscript collection discovered near the shores of the Dead Sea at about the same time, a portion of which has yet to see the light of day!

The Coptic Gnostic Library Project was one of the first projects sponsored by the Institute for Antiquity and Christianity, founded as an institute of the Claremont Graduate School in 1967 by Robinson, under the patronage of Colwell, its founding Director. Robinson, having been called to the Graduate

School as Arthur Letts, Jr. Professor of Religion in 1964, became its Director in 1968. The Institute for Antiquity and Christianity, which has flourished under Robinson's leadership, is illustrative of the ethos of cooperative and collegial scholarly pursuit Robinson has sought to encourage in American biblical scholarship. This model for doing the work of scholarship is evident today not only in the many cooperative projects the Institute for Antiquity and Christianity has sponsored over the years, but also in the structure of the Society of Biblical Literature, whose current health and scope owe much to the efforts of Robinson and others to open its doors and expand its membership in the 1960s.

In many ways Robinson's most recent projects continue the interests he has pursued over the course of his career. With the Nag Hammadi Codices safely in the public domain, he has begun to assemble a group of scholars to make yet another papyrus collection available to a scholarly public, the Manichaean Codices of Medinet Madi, recently rediscovered after a long period of obscurity following World War II. More central to the New Testament issues Robinson has doggedly pursued for almost forty years is the International Q Project, sponsored jointly by the Institute for Antiquity and Christianity and the Society of Biblical Literature, which aims to reconstruct as nearly as possible a critical text of Q. With the Q projects, Robinson is returning full circle to many of the issues which dominated his early career, prior to his immersion in the Nag Hammadi project: the quest of the historical Jesus, early Christianity's (and modern theology's interest in the "word," and the problem of Christian origins in all its diverse aspects. It may well be that the most significant of Robinson's contributions to the study of the New Testament and Christian origins is yet to come.

Robinson, a member of the Religion Faculty of Claremont Graduate School since the inception of that program in 1959, becomes Chair of that Faculty as of 1990.

Gnosticism
& the Early
Christian World

Ridicule and Rape, Rule and Rebellion

THE HYPOSTASIS OF THE ARCHONS

Karen L. King

1. Introduction

The problem of how we are to understand the use of gendered imagery in gnostic myth and mythology[1] is both fascinating and complex. Rather than attempt to contribute further to the research on the background and hermeneutics of Gnostic myth or attempt a speculative move from the symbolic world (of myth) to the social world (of community), this study will attempt to trace the movement from social construction of gender and gendered social roles in Late Antiquity to the symbolic application of gender in gnostic myths. The example I have chosen to use is *The Hypostasis of the Archons*.[2]

---

1 I use the term "mythology" here to describe the narrative accounts that describe theology, cosmology, anthropology, and soteriology. My meaning is essentially the same as that of Hans-Martin Schenke's term "system" but avoids the difficulty of that term, which might seem to imply something logically systematic. (See Schenke's own elucidation of his use of "system" in "Phenomenon and Significance," 684–85.) "Myth" is here used with emphasis upon its basic meaning of "a narrative account" and to refer to specific extant narratives.

    Jacob Neusner's use of the term "system," which I find compelling ("The boundaries of a system are drawn by the coincidence of the lines of a particular literary document with the lines of a particular, clearly defined social group" [*Method and Meaning*, 83]) is difficult to employ in the study of Gnosticism precisely because we know so little about its social description. See below n. 2.

2 *The Hypostasis of the Archons* was discovered in Codex II (text 4) near Nag Hammadi in Egypt (NHC II,*4*). The best edition and translation of the text are by B. Layton ("Hypostasis of the Archons"); this edition and translation are used here.

    The text has been classified by H.-M. Schenke as belonging to the "Sethian" type of Gnosticism (see "Das sethianische System," 165, and "Phenomenon and Significance," 588).

    H.-M. Schenke has argued that the existence of this distinctive type of Gnosticism, which he calls "Sethian," has a base in a distinct group (see especially, "Phenomenon and Significance," 590–93). F. Wisse has questioned whether one may in fact talk about a distinctive community of Sethians (see "Stalking Those Elusive Sethians"). Wisse's objections, however, have not found widespread acceptance (see especially, M. A. Williams, *Immovable Race*, especially 186–209, and J. Turner, "Sethian Gnosticism").

2. The Cultural Construction of Gender in Antiquity

Images of gender rely upon cultural constructions of social gender roles and sexuality for meaning. The resonance and tenor of "female" and "male," "mother," "father," "whore," "virgin," "daughter" and "son," etc., are shaped by social instruments that vary across culture and across time. Such terms gather nuance as much (or more?) from cultural ideals as from lived experience, the two most often defining each other in complex exchanges and mingling of signification. The use of gender imagery in Gnosticism shows a similar complexity in the relation between cultural constructions of gender in antiquity and mythic narrative.

Because gnostic myth trades on metaphors drawn from Mediterranean culture, a model of how gender is socially constructed should enable us to understand better what connotations gendered language and imagery carry into the mythic context.

Here a note of caution is required: such models identify only the *ideal* cultural construction of gender, from which the social *reality* of men and women may depart widely.[3] What is important for our purposes, however, is not a description of social reality, but a model of ideal gender definitions current in the Mediterranean world in Late Antiquity. It is against these ideals of social behavior that the actions and motives of the myth's characters are evaluated.

Before beginning, let me emphasize that work describing the social construction of gender in antiquity is only beginning and has been pursued primarily in the context of the history of women in Western culture. The model—and thus the results—proposed here are therefore provisional.[4] In

---

3 Exceptions to the standard tend not to obviate the general validity of the rule but only demonstrate the flexible way in which ideal constructions of gender may be ascribed to real persons. For example, though women in certain cases became rulers (Queens), owned land and farmed it, became philosophers, fought, etc., when they did so they were considered to have become in that regard "male." Similarly a man who had "female " characteristics could be called a "woman." In Xenophon's dialogue *Oeconomicus,* the husband Ischomachus is praising his wife's domestic virtues, and Socrates replies, "Upon my word, Ischomachus, your wife has a truly masculine mind by your showing!" (X.1; trans. E. C. Marchant, 447) The clear implication is that if a woman fulfills the duties demanded of her well, she is said to be masculine. That is, "masculine" implies perfection—even perfection of woman's duties. It is also true that while ideal cultural constructions of gender generally defined women out of the public, political sphere, this does not mean that they were unable to have any effective influence upon public decisions. Real women played political roles most usually as objects of dispute in conflicts of male honor, pawns in political alliances, etc., or they wielded power through the manipulation of men, especially sons (see J. F. Collier, "Women in Politics").
4 The following description of the cultural construction of gender in antiquity draws heavily from anthropological work on honor-shame cultures and gender divisions between public and private spheres, especially Malina, *New Testament World;* Pitt-Rivers, "Honour and Social Status"; Campbell, "Honour and the Devil"; Rosaldo, "Woman, Culture, and Society"; and Torjesen, "Controversies" (draft manuscript).

addition, I will describe here only those aspects of the ancient ideals which have a direct bearing upon the interpretation of *The Hypostasis of the Archons*.

The basic unit of social organization and economic production is the familial household, headed by the father. The household includes also his wife and children, dependent relatives, and servants. Roles in the household are determined by gender, as well as by age and status (family member, freeborn, or slave).[5] Gender roles in the household sphere can be summarized as follows:[6]

Male	Female
without/outdoors	within/indoors
gaining wealth	preserving wealth
acquisition	distribution
command	obedience
instruct	nurture/serve
face adversity	endure adversity
more courage	more timidity
stronger	weaker

The pattern of organization outside the household sphere replicates these household categories for division of moral, economic, and manual labor. Because ideally women are to be indoors, the public sphere of life in the polis is essentially a male sphere even when women are present.[7]

Women therefore are defined primarily by their roles in the household in relation to men as mothers, wives, and sisters (or potential mothers and wives, i.e., virgins), or negatively as whores. Men on the other hand are defined within a complex system of differentiated roles in public sphere activities as well as by their familial roles as fathers, husbands, and heads of households.[8]

These categories imply that the ideal moral divisions of labor in society tend to be defined by gender. Women (being weaker and more timid) are charged with the duties of nurture and service. This means they are to be concerned for shame, to be shy, submissive to authority and deferential, passive and restrained. In Mediterranean society, shame is symboled by the female maidenhead and expressed by virginity and sexual exclusiveness.[9] Men (being

---

5 For a short summary of the vexed issue of class in Roman society, see MacMullen, *Roman Social Relations*, 88–120, 183–202.

6 These categories are derived from: Aristotle *Politics* I; Xenophon *Oeconomicus* VII–IX; Ps. Aristotle, *Oeconomicus* III.1; Columella, *Res Rustica* XII preface–1.

7 M. Z. Rosaldo has suggested that these differences may fundamentally be a result of the split between domestic/private (female) and public (male) spheres. See "Woman, Culture, and Society," and "Use and Abuse of Anthropology."

In addition, we must not presume that the situation of urban social organization is replicated in the rural sphere; there is nonetheless evidence that the same *ideal* standards hold. See, for example, studies of small village life in the contemporary Mediterranean world, such as Peristiany, *Mediterranean Family Structures*.

8 Rosaldo discusses this point in "Woman, Culture, and Society" in terms of ascribed and achieved status (see esp. 28–31).

9 See Pitt-Rivers, "Honour and Social Status," 45; Malina, *New Testament World*, 46.

stronger and more courageous) are charged with the duties of fighting and ruling. They are to be concerned with gaining and defending honor, to be bold and daring; male honor is symboled by the testicles and sexual aggressiveness.[10] They are concerned with precedence and prestige. Unlike female status, which is ascribed, male status must be achieved.[11]

The male sphere is one that is sharply hierarchical and agonistic. Male virtues therefore tend to regulate and promote harmony in such a highly competitive and aggressive arena. "Moderation" ($\sigma\omega\phi\rho\sigma\sigma\acute{v}\nu\eta$, especially regarding sensual desires), "understanding" ($\sigma\acute{v}\nu\epsilon\sigma\iota s$), and "self-control" ($\acute{\epsilon}\gamma\kappa\rho\acute{a}\tau\epsilon\iota a$) are valued as highly as courage and strength.[12] Note here the contradiction in the construction of masculinity: On the one hand males are understood to be sexually aggressive; on the other hand they are to keep this aggressiveness under control in order to be socially virtuous. To be a "man" means to share in those qualities which elevate one above the beasts: reason and language. To be male (sexually active) means in some sense to participate in bestiality. The ideal is of course for the "man" to control the beast. Uncontrolled bestiality, i.e., sexual immoderateness, means a loss of one's humanity. In art, the contrast appears in the fact that generally ideal men are portrayed rationally (in mathematical proportion); male sexuality is often portrayed in caricature, as in the portraits of satyrs and oversized phallic objects.

According to Karen Torjesen,[13] male virtues of moderation, understanding, and self-control function to increase cooperation in the state and to promote personal excellence; these virtues thereby enhance functioning in the public sphere. Virtue can be seen from one angle then as a kind of social control, in this case to control aggressive male behavior that would disrupt the community. Female virtues, according to Torjesen, are also used for social control. In this case, however, female virtues of chastity, silence, and obedience are not aimed at enhancing functions in the household sphere; instead these virtues function to keep women from disrupting or threatening male power. Moreover, Torjesen argues, for a woman to enter the public sphere and to assume voice and leadership would imply a loss of female virtue.

This pattern of ideal gender roles is supported by the way power relations (i.e., the hierarchy of command and obedience) are rationalized for both the household and the public spheres. Ideally the naturally superior rule the naturally inferior; rationality and moral virtue are the criteria for excellence that are to determine status, i.e., the hierarchical order of society is to be determined by the quantity of reason and moral virtue that a group or individual possesses.

---

10 Malina, *New Testament World*, 46.
11 See above, n. 8.
12 See for example, Plato *Symposium* 196C; *Laws* IV.710A; *Phaedo* 68C; *Republic* 430E–431B; Aristotle *Politics* II.5 (1263.10–12); *Nicomachean Ethics* III.10–12. Secondary materials: see G. Luck, "σώφρων."
13 The following materials are summarized from an unpublished paper by Torjesen titled, "Women's Virtues and Vices."

The same line of justification for hierarchy in the male sphere can be used to rationalize the "natural" subjection of classes of persons,[14] such as women and slaves[15]: the superior are to rule the inferior for their own benefit and for the good of the master. The classic example is Aristotle.[16]

These ideal social standards influenced views about matters as seemingly unrelated to social status as biological reproduction. Aristotle, for example, based his theories of political status on his biological classifications. He saw the male as the ideal of perfection for the species; females are biologically inferior to males, an aberration from the male norm of perfection.[17] Apart from such "sophisticated" biological theories, however, it was generally held that a son "inherited" the moral as well as physical characteristics of his father, and a daughter those of her mother ("like father, like son"; "like mother, like daughter").[18]

In the sphere of religion, these gender constructions appear mythically as the story of the Father Sky God and the Mother Earth Goddess. The former represents power that can be used either positively to overcome Chaos and establish order, harmony, and beauty, or negatively to destroy and pollute. The Mother Goddess in her positive aspects is associated with life (growth and productivity) and nourishment, or in her negative aspects with death by ensnaring and rejecting. The male is associated with mind and reason, the female with matter and passion. As in the household and public spheres, so in the body itself, the superior is to rule over the inferior: reason over passion. The male thus represents mythically the transcendent sphere, the female the material world.

3. Images of Gender in *The Hypostasis of the Archons*[19]

The purpose in turning now to *The Hypostasis of the Archons* is to analyze how these presuppositions about gender and gendered social roles are em-

---

14 The fact that groups of persons can be treated in a collective manner illustrates the important notion of collective honor (see Malina, *New Testament World*, 39–42). That this social presupposition is assumed in our text is shown by the fact that individuals are not distinguished. Characters, like Adam or Norea, represent not individuals but classes, such as psychics and pneumatics; and groups, such as the Archons, can be treated as though they were a single unit, sharing the same ideas, motives and characteristics.
15 "Barbarians" are another example, though the reasoning shifts from "natural superiority" to "cultural superiority."
16 See for example, *Politics* I.5; I.2, 12–13.
17 See for example, the excellent study of the relation between Aristotle's politics and biology by Horowitz, "Aristotle and Woman." See also the discussions by R. Smith, "Sex Education," and Castelli, "A Response to Sex Education."
18 See Malina, *New Testament World*, 44.
19 The analysis that follows demonstrates how much I have learned from the work of Gilhus ("Nature of the Archons"), McGuire ("Virginity and Subversion"), and Perkins ("Sophia and the Mother-Father" and "Sophia As Goddess"). My results stand in sharp contrast to the analysis of M. A. Williams ("Uses of Gender Imagery," 211–20) though my considerations of method have been greatly stimulated by his essay, "Gnostic Perspectives."

ployed in the text. What this analysis wants to get at is the unique way in which this particular text understands gender and employs gender imagery. The study should illumine something about the inner dynamic and meaning of the text[20] that was invisible before. Since the text both presupposes a shared cultural view on gender and at the same time reveals its own particular reflections about that shared cultural construction, we should expect to learn something too about one perspective on gender as it was constructed in Late Antiquity.

Specific images or mythic motifs do not come into gnostic myths with a predetermined mythological function; rather, that function is determined by the use of any given image or motif in a particular myth. On the other hand, these images or motifs *do* come heavily laden with meaning, meaning that is largely determined before it enters the mythic context. Indeed a motif is undoubtedly chosen precisely because of the specific contents it already carries— though once removed to a new mythic context it can be manipulated to a variety of ends. The rest of this paper is concerned with uncovering what those ends are regarding gender imagery in *The Hypostasis of the Archons* and what this presupposes about the text's understanding of gender and religion. The following discussion will consider the use of gendered language regarding (1) the nature of the world below, (2) the situation of the Gnostic in that world, and (3) salvation.[21]

3.1   The nature of the world below

In *The Hypostasis of the Archons,* the nature of the world below is described consistently in gendered terms. On the one hand, Matter (and Abyss) are personified as a mother,[22] following the ancient association of the earth and materiality with the feminine. This motif, however, is not highly developed. Rather the main representatives of the world below are the Archons. There are three important elements in their presentation: the caricature of (1) illegitimate male (political) authority and (2) the lack of male "moderation" ($\sigma\omega\phi\rho\sigma\sigma\acute{\nu}\nu\eta$), especially (3) moderation and "self-control" ($\acute{\epsilon}\gamma\kappa\rho\acute{\alpha}\tau\epsilon\iota\alpha$) in sexual desires.[23]

The Chief Archon (Samael, Sakla, Yaldabaoth) is characterized as blind, ignorant or mistaken, and arrogant, the source of Envy[24] and the Father of Death. He is androgynous and formed like a beast; his mother is the Abyss; he

20 It should also be noted that the thorny questions of sources behind *The Hypostasis of the Archons* are being ignored here. The goal of this study is to understand the meaning of gendered language in the text as it now stands.
21 Due to considerations of space, the topics of the nature of the divine world and the origin of evil will not be considered in this paper.
22 *Hyp. Arch.* 87,7; 92,16–17.
23 Though the terms $\sigma\omega\phi\rho\sigma\sigma\acute{\nu}\nu\eta$ and $\acute{\epsilon}\gamma\kappa\rho\acute{\alpha}\tau\epsilon\iota\alpha$ do not appear in the text per se, the actions of the Archons make it clear that they do not possess these important moral characteristics, as will be shown below.
24 Yaldabaoth becomes envious when Sabaoth ascends and is given charge of the seventh heaven (*Hyp. Arch.* 96,3–8). The pervasiveness and evilness of envy in a contemporary honor-shame culture is described by Campbell, "Honour and the Devil," 157–58.

derives from Matter—no father is mentioned. Though he himself has no father, he is the world creator: the creator of a fatherless world like its fatherless father.

Among his creations are his seven offspring, the Forces of Chaos (Archons, Authorities of Darkness, Rulers of Unrighteousness). They too are androgynous, arrogant, lustful, blind, and ignorant. They are described as weak and powerless, for they possess only soul, not spirit. They lack understanding and are easily agitated. Their intentions are consistently wicked: they try to trap the light and defile it, and when they fail, to obliterate humankind and beasts.[25] In all this they fail. Moreover their eventual rape of the sarcic Eve makes them liable to condemnation. Though they try to curse the beings of spirit, it is they themselves who are accursed.[26] All these wicked acts and failed intentions show their true characters: They are wicked, ignorant, and powerless.

A comparison of this presentation with the model of gender described above makes it clear that the Chief Archon and his offspring are being portrayed here as caricatures of ideal masculinity.[27] As was described above, the ideal of masculinity presented in classical art is the beautiful and beautifully proportioned, rational, and abstract male figure. Males as sexually aggressive beings are often portrayed as only partially male: Like the satyrs, they are really beasts, not "men." The visual description of the Chief Archon as "an arrogant beast resembling a lion"[28] immediately places a considerable distance between this ideal rational male and his caricature, the satyr-like Archon.

That he is arrogant demonstrates a lack of honor, moderation, and social understanding: He does not "know *himself*," i.e., his place in the sociopolitical/cosmic order. This ignorance is fully demonstrated when he cries out: "It is I who am God; there is none [apart from me]."[29] The Voice from above unmasks this falsehood, but that does not stop him from wickedly trying

25 The Archons make six obvious attempts: (1) They try to lay hold of the image of Incorruptibility that appeared in the waters (*Hyp. Arch.* 87,11–20). (2) They attempt to seize the Image by attracting it to the form of Adam that they modelled (*Hyp. Arch.* 87,33–88,3). (3) They next attempt to steal the Spiritual Principle by removing it surgically, so to speak, and in the process form the Woman (*Hyp. Arch.* 89,3–11). (4) The Archons then attempt to rape Eve, in an attempt to possess the Spirit by sowing their seed in her (*Hyp. Arch.* 89,17–31). (5) They expel humankind from the Garden and throw them into a life of turmoil (*Hyp. Arch.* 91,3–11). (6) When despite all this, humankind begins to multiply and improve, they decide to destroy it in a deluge (*Hyp. Arch.* 92,4–8). (7) Their final attempt to defile the Light is by raping Norea and leading her astray (*Hyp. Arch.* 92,18–31).
   The language of desire here connotes simple attempts to possess, pollute, degrade, and destroy. The Archons' erotic strategy to gain the Spiritual Element is thoroughly condemned. Perhaps there is an implicit critique here of views such as that of Plato that the rise of the soul can begin by "begetting upon the beautiful" (*Symposium* 206B and following).
26 *Hyp. Arch.* 92,23.
27 Perkins has made the same point: "These writings mock verbosity, boasting, combativeness and aggression on the part of the gods, all typical characteristics of male language and behavior" ("Sophia as Goddess," 182).
28 *Hyp. Arch.* 94,16–17. See also 87,27–33.
29 *Hyp. Arch.* 86,27–32; see also 95,4–5.

to exert illegitimate authority by capturing, polluting, or destroying what is superior to him, i.e., the Spiritual Element.

That he is a beast and androgynous illustrates the fact that his inferiority is based in nature. He is an aberration far removed from the model of male perfection.[30] Richard Smith has shown how the gnostic portrayal of the Archon's bestiality is linked to contemporary notions about reproduction. As a product of the female Sophia working without her male consort, the Chief Archon must be weak and ill-formed.[31] This natural inferiority is stressed further by distinguishing him as a solely psychic and material being;[32] he lacks spirit and therefore the capacity for the highest illuminations of gnosis. Moreover his leonine form points toward an association with excessive passion,[33] stressing even more strongly his incapacity for the proper social virtues of moderation and self-control.

The story seems to delight in this caricature. The text's use of mockery, wit, and ludicrousness show a strong sense of play and a talented penchant for narrative entertainment. The Chief Archon, together with his offspring, again and again play the buffoon. The portrayal of the Archons is the perfect stuff of bawdy, slapstick-style comedy. As soon as he boasts that he is the only God, a Voice challenges his claim and puts him to public ridicule. One child even deserts him! (The readers snicker.) Trying to regain his stature by capturing and degrading the Spirit, he only makes a greater fool of himself. He and his offspring make a human form, but they can't get it to awaken, no matter how they exhaust themselves blowing wind. (One can picture the scene: The buffoons blowing and blowing fruitlessly over a mud man!) Then they try to shape a pretty woman and rape her, only to be left the laughingstocks. And by whom? A woman!! (This is really funny! Being overpowered and outwitted by *women* is surely a significant part of the joke!) So they try again. They get Noah to build an ark. Orea burns it up. So they try to rape her; it seems to them (wrongly) that this is the only strategy they have had that worked! (Notice how again—amusingly—they had never seemed to understand that the Female Spiritual Principle had outmaneuvered them by entering the tree.) But again they fail and this time entirely disappear from the story.

The exception to this caricatured presentation is Sabaoth. When he hears the voice of Zoe from above, he recognizes that his Father, the Chief Archon, is a fraud, renounces him and his mother (Matter), and turns instead to praise Sophia and her daughter Zoe. As a result of this repentance, he is placed in charge of the seventh heaven.[34] Sophia sets Zoe (Life) on his right hand and

30 See Aristotle *On the Generation of Animals* 773.
31 See "Sex Education," esp. 349–51.
32 *Hyp. Arch.* 87,17–18.
33 See Jackson, *The Lion Becomes Man,* esp. 175–213, where he argues that the lion as a symbol for the passions is a Platonic element found widely in early Christian and Gnostic ascetic writings.
34 *Hyp. Arch.* 95,4–25.

the Angel of Wrath on his left hand.[35] The right represents his repentance and praise of the spiritual Sophia; the left represents the condemnation of the world as the unrighteous realm of absolute power.[36]

Sabaoth succeeds in social virtue where his Father and siblings failed. He accepts his proper place of submission and obedience to higher authority and power; as a result, he is invested by his new "patron" with legitimate rule; and in so doing, he provides a model for the salvation of the psychic element in the world below. (We will discuss this further in section 3.52 below.)

3.2 The situation of the Gnostic in the world below

The situation of the Gnostic is often described as entrapment (especially in matter) and oppression (especially by the powers that rule this world). The proper response is always rebellion. This rebellion can take two directions: (1) rejection of the physical body and (2) rebellion against worldly authority.[37] Both are quite typical of ascetic patterns in Gnosticism.[38]

The Hypostasis of the Archons contains two extremely pointed examples of rebellion against the powers that govern the world; they are portrayed in the Rulers' attempts to rape Eve and Norea[39] in 89,17–31 and 92,8–93,13. The point of these two accounts is to express through mythic narrative the situation of the Gnostic in the world and to give a pattern for how to respond with hope. The use of the metaphor of attempted but unsuccessful rape to elaborate this theme is an excellent choice. Here the feminine clearly represents the Gnostics; her plight is their situation in the world; her success is a model for theirs. The stories offer two patterns for success: the division of the self and paternal intervention.

3.2.1 The division of the self.

The first option is presented in the story of Eve's rape.[40] The Authorities have quite unknowingly created a woman of considerable attraction.[41] Their character is described by their actions. Upon seeing her they become agitated[42] and enamoured; they want to "sow their

35 *Hyp. Arch.* 95,26–96,3. Layton sees this as a representation of the God of the Hebrew Bible as seen by gnostic exegetes. See "Hypostasis of the Archons," 75 n. 175.

36 *Hyp. Arch.* 95,35–96,3.

37 A third possible alternative is libertinism, but since there is no room for this alternative in *The Hypostasis of the Archons,* it will not be considered here.

38 For other discussions of asceticism and gender language, see M. A. Williams, *Immovable Race,* 99–102, and Wisse, "Flee Femininity," 297–307.

39 Norea appears in ancient literature as the sister or wife of Seth and as the wife of Noah. The definitive studies of this figure are by Pearson, "Figure of Norea" and "Revisiting Norea."

40 As Gilhus notes in her discussion of the relation of *The Hypostasis of the Archons* to Genesis ("Nature of the Archons," 32–62), there are two themes in the text that have no basis in Genesis: the seduction of Eve (*Hyp. Arch.* 89,17–31) and Orea's destruction of the ark (*Hyp. Arch.* 92,14–18). There are, however, precedents in Jewish haggadah (see "Nature of the Archons," 34–36, 73–74).

41 Gilhus states that the attraction of the Authorities to Eve and their desire to rape her is due to their desire to capture the spirit for themselves and produce children of light. See "Nature of the Archons," 184.

42 This motif of agitation is often contrasted in gnostic texts with the theme of stability. It

seed in her." They do not even try persuasion; they simply run after her. On the one hand, their attempt is a success. They catch her and engage in gang rape. The text condemns the action thoroughly. It is called a foul defiling and they are themselves liable to condemnation. On the other hand, however, the rape is not successful at all; quite the contrary. We are told that the Spiritual Woman laughs at them. She knows them to be witless and blind. At the moment when she is in their clutches, she becomes a tree, leaving behind only her body, which is described as a "shadowy reflection resembling her."

Now, on the one hand, this narrative makes good storytelling. The Female Spiritual Principle is powerful and good; the Rulers are ignorant and wicked. They are chasing her, intending to do her harm. The readers are worried about what will happen to her, outraged at the Rulers' effrontery, terrified for what may happen. Then, just as she falls into their clutches: a miracle! She becomes a tree and they—like idiots—don't notice! Good overcomes evil. Happy ending—presumably. But let's look a little closer.

She becomes a tree.[43] Her body—that shadowy resemblance—remains. It is not turned to wood; only the Spiritual Principle becomes a tree, not the modelled form that had been stamped in her likeness.[44] The story reminds us too of another woman, Daphne, who became a tree in a desperate attempt to escape from a would-be rapist.[45] A comparison may be instructive.

The account that I have chosen for comparison is that of Ovid from the *Metamorphoses* (I.450–567). In his portrayal, the trouble is caused by the mechanations of Cupid, who shoots Phoebus (Apollo) with an arrow that kindles love and shoots Daphne with an arrow that puts love to flight. When Phoebus sees Daphne, he falls in love with her; but Daphne, when she sees him, begins to flee. As he pursues her, Apollo attempts persuasion. He even tells her that he's afraid that she will hurt herself running so quickly; if she slows down, he promises to pursue less swiftly! The final result is clear,

refers in general to the unstable nature of the lower, created realm in contrast with the stability of the higher, pleromatic realm. See M. A. Williams, *Immovable Race*.

43 The motif of female transformation into a tree has parallels in ancient literature and art (Cant 7:6–8; see Tardieu, *Trois mythes gnostiques*, 165–74). Layton interprets this tree as the Tree of Life from Gen 2:9 ("Hypostasis of the Archons," 57, n. 60). Pearson adds that this interpretation of Jewish scripture may also draw upon a pagan mythological motif, that of the tree-nymph, or "Hamadrayad," escaping from the attempted rape of Pan (see "She Became a Tree"). Gero has suggested that the use of the tree motif may be linked to older tradition, preserved in a fifteenth century catalogue, that interpreted the tree as a symbol of female sexuality (see "Seduction of Eve").

44 The obvious Platonic imagery need not be considered for the moment, though without it the clear dualism of body and spirit would not be comprehensible. This split between image and reality is, however, central to the theme of the text: This world is ontologically lower, less real, than the pleromatic World Above. Gilhus emphasizes the difference between this split woman (the Spiritual Woman and the sarcic Eve) and Adam (see "Nature of the Archons," 112–13). For a different perspective on the split of the Spiritual Woman and her Shadow, see Bianchi, "Docetism."

45 There are examples in addition to that of Daphne. This example is chosen to exemplify one feature of the story here that differs from all the others: the split of Eve into the shadowy image and the Spiritual Woman.

however, from the fact that he is a god and she a mere maiden. The longest part of the narrative is taken up with describing the flight, with Apollo's ardor and Daphne's terror. At last, tiring from the flight, Daphne calls out for help to her father Peneus, a river spirit, to transform her and ruin the beauty which she sees as the source of her troubles. She is transformed into a laurel tree, and Apollo makes her branches sacred, quipping that if she cannot be his bride, she will at least be his tree.

This single account in Ovid of Daphne's attempted rape by Phoebus Apollo contains elements found in both of the two rape accounts in *The Hypostasis of the Archons*. In the rape of Eve, there are elements paralleling Ovid's description of Daphne's flight and transformation; in the attempted rape of Norea, there are parallels to Daphne's call for help to her Father and his response, which saves her from the intended rape. The transformations of Eve and Daphne into trees have both striking parallels and differences.[46] Leo Curran notes in his study on "Rape and Rape Victims," that

> rape does worse than undermine a woman's identity; it can rob her of her humanity. Change from human to non-human is a constant occurrence in the *Metamorphoses,* and the majority of instances of course have nothing to do with rape. However, transformation into the non-human is uniquely appropriate in the case of rape, for the process of dehumanization begins long before any subsequent metamorphoses of the woman's body. The transition from human to sex object and then to object pure and simple proceeds by swift and easy stages, its onset being simultaneous with the decision to commit rape. The final physical transformation of so many rape victims is only the outward ratification of an earlier metamorphosis of the woman into a mere thing in the mind of the attacker and in his treatment of her. The identification of rape and dehumanization is intimate and virtually immediate in Daphne, where the heroine begins to lose her humanity as soon as the chase begins. . . . After her transformation, Daphne as tree is an exact analog of a victim so profoundly traumatized by her experience that she has taken refuge in a catatonic withdrawal from all human involvement, passively acted upon by her environment and by other persons, but cut off from any response that could be called human.[47]

In this light, the use of a tree as a metaphor for the state of a person traumatized by rape seems particularly apt. In our story of the Spiritual Woman, however, things end somewhat differently than with Daphne. Daphne, withdrawn to wood, nods in silent consent at Phoebus's insistence that she be his tree; the Spiritual Woman laughs in derision at the Authorities as they rape her abandoned image. Like Daphne, the Spiritual Woman also becomes a tree, but

---

46 Indeed a comparison of Ovid's account of the attempted rape of Daphne in the *Metamorphoses* with the Woman's escape into the tree in *The Hypostasis of the Archons* provides a good example of a mythological motif that takes its valence from the context in which it is placed.

47 Curran, "Rape and Rape Victims," 277.

her image, the sarcic shadow, remains and is raped.[48] The text quite clearly describes the division of her as a person, especially in the implicit denial that the carnal body is to be experienced as one's true self. In Ovid, Daphne's *body,* her whole self, is transformed, and she escapes the rape itself (though the resultant trauma seems to hint otherwise). Daphne's physical transformation into a tree symbolizes, too, her psychic withdrawal from humanity, from any kind of normal social and sexual life, a complete traumatization of the self. In our text, the Woman's withdrawal is from her own body. It is her denial, not only of social world, but of self (in modern post-Freudian terms). The account in *The Hypostasis of the Archons* describes a severe case of dissociation and psychic disruption.

This strategy for dealing with pain and suffering in the world closely resembles that of the ascetic who also must practice psychic dissociation in the denial of the physical body. What our story makes more clear than most (gnostic) ascetic texts do, however, is the *political* implications of this.[49] The reason for the withdrawal is described as a flight from rape. Curran writes,

> Ovid's habit of reverting to certain themes and motifs suggests that he was on the verge of a realization that rape is less an act of sexual passion than of aggression and that erotic gratification is secondary to the rapist's desire to dominate physically, to humiliate, and to degrade.[50]

Our text stresses this point all along,[51] and we should take it seriously. The existence of self in the body is described as subjection to illegitimate domination, physical brutality, humiliation, and degradation—all terms of considerable poignancy in a culture that so highly values honor and the symbol of female chastity.

But the story has another side, a triumphant side. In the story, the with-

---

48 Gilhus notes that this is part of the Father's plan, but it involves a different evaluation of the sarcic woman, based in my opinion on the moral division of labor in honor-shame cultures. As Malina notes, once a woman has lost her sexual exclusiveness (chastity), it cannot be regained (*New Testament World,* 42–47). The evaluation of the sarcic Eve then is based on her sexual function in relation to the men who rape her; once they have possessed her, her status becomes embedded in theirs. Gilhus makes a similar point, though from a different perspective: "From her origin woman has the same possibilities as man, she is even nearer to the pneumatic ideal and not created by the archons like Adam. Formally she is granted the same possibilities for salvation. But she is not evaluated primarily on the basis of her origin and formal possibilities, but on the basis of her function; and her most important function was to bear the mixed seed of the archons. By this act she became *sarcic* and the female counterpart of the archons. The archontic rape of Eve was necessary for the salvation of the lost light, but nonetheless woman is defiled thereby. The sexual act becomes a symbol for involvement with the archons, and it is by this involvement with the archons that Eve is sullied" ("Nature of the Archons," 120–21; see also 124).

49 For a consideration of the variety of models for ascetic behavior and self-understanding in Graeco-Roman antiquity, see Wimbush, "Renunciation." His essay makes it clear that rejection of the world is not necessary for asceticism.

50 Curran, "Rape and Rape Victims," 283.

51 For example, see *Hyp. Arch.* 86,27–31; 91,4–11; 92,4–8, 18–19, etc.

drawal from the body goes hand in hand with the acknowledgement of superior power on the part of the Gnostic. The myth limits the power of exterior authority over the (inner) person.

In so doing it offers a biting critique of illegitimate power. Pheme Perkins writes in reference to the Rulers' attempts at rape,

> The gnostic stories have worked an emotive twist on this theme by discovering that the "powers" of such gods are to be ridiculed. Such mockery takes place from a position of "hidden superiority" that shows up the violence, aggression, boasting, folly, rape and domination of the forces which claim to rule the world as ignorant posturing and pretending to divinity. The truth to which the Gnostic comes by repeating the Sophia stories is not the pathos of a suffering victim but the appropriation of a new identity that is not given in the stablished, social, religious and symbolic world that he or she shares with the rest of humanity.[52]

The description of the Spiritual Woman's success points in two directions: (1) an acknowledgement of the power and superiority of the Spiritual and (2) a sharp and biting critique of male authority, violence, and aggression. Both of these elements are lacking in the account by Ovid.[53]

3.2.2 Paternal intervention. The second pattern for rebellion is paternal intervention.

The second story, the attempted rape of Norea,[54] resembles the first story in that the wickedness and ignorance of the Rulers are exposed by their own actions; similarly the Spiritual Principle, present in the figure of Norea, again shows its superiority. The way in which the Rulers are foiled, however, differs considerably in this account. In this case it is the intervention of a (male) hero who rescues the distressed heroine from the ignorant and wicked Rulers. The form of the rescue is the reception of saving gnosis.

These differences between the two rape accounts in *The Hypostasis of the Archons* are important in terms of the expectation of the Gnostic. In the rape of Eve, the Authorities were simply acting out of their foul desire. This time the motive of the Rulers is more spiritually perverse and subtle: they intend to lead Norea astray.[55] Rather than simply overpower her, they begin by trying

---

52 Perkins, "Sophia as Goddess," 101–2.
53 Yet Curran notes, "For him [Ovid] it is no contradiction to present rape simultaneously as both an outrage committed upon a woman and as a grotesque caricature of masculinity" ("Rape and Rape Victims," 267).
54 According to Gilhus, the rape of Norea is an original invention of the author ("Nature of the Archons," 151).
55 Gilhus too has noted a shift in the Archon's motives in the rapes of Eve and Norea, though her analysis differs from mine: "In contrast to the episode of Eve which was characterized by lust for the light and desire for children by the light, the episode of Norea is characterized by the desire to defile her and her light. The reason for this difference is that in Eve's case the archons were on the offensive and were—at least in their own view—powerful; but after men ate from the tree of knowledge, the archons were on the defensive and their very existence was endangered. The motive for the attempted rape of Norea is different from the motivation for the rape of Eve and arises from this shift in power. The seduction of Norea is a necessary, defensive stratagem on

persuasion[56] as Apollo does with Daphne. Like Daphne, Norea is not deceived for a moment. Unlike Daphne, however, Norea turns the tables on her attackers, naming their true nature: darkness and ignorance.[57] Now the Rulers get really angry and demand that she "render them service." At this point, Norea does not perform a transformation, as her mother did, but she cries out for help to the true deity above, the Holy God of the Entirety, even as Daphne called out for help to her Father, Peneus the water spirit.[58] Both received the help that thwarts the immediate aims of their attackers. Rather than performing a transformation, however, the Father of the Entirety sent the Great Angel Eleleth. He appears and the Rulers quietly withdraw. Eleleth has come to save her, however, not simply by scaring off her attackers, but by teaching her about her Root. This knowledge, he says, will save her from the grasp of the Lawless.

Up to this point, the form of the story follows the typical Hellenistic romance where the attacked heroine is saved by the hero.[59] That topos itself relies on deep-seated cultural constructions of gender. The description of ideal female behavior given above provides a useful model to analyze the dynamic underlying this scene. Malina has written,

> The honorable woman, born with the proper sentiment of shame which she inherits from her mother strives to avoid the human contacts which might expose her to dishonor. She cannot be expected to succeed in this endeavor unsupported by male authority and control.[60]

Norea is in a position of clear danger to her honor as a woman. The Rulers intend to lead her astray, and they do so in a particularly sly way. They appeal to her mother's behavior. Since a daughter is considered to have inherited her mother's sense of shame, and since the Rulers still ignorantly think that they

the part of the archons. Its purpose was to defile the light and prevent its escape, for the final escape of the light means the total ruin of the archons" ("Nature of the Archons," 184). Rather than seeing their actions as a sign of increased perception of weakness on the Archons' part, however, I think that the point is to show increasingly the treachery and wickedness in their characters. They never did perceive that their attempted rape of Eve did not succeed; indeed as I have argued above, there is a real sense in which it did succeed.

56 Curran notes a similar "theme of the seducer who is ready to turn to rape if persuasion fails" in Ovid ("Rape and Rape Victims," 268).

57 I am heavily indebted on this point to A. McGuire's essay on "Virginity and Subversion." She writes, "From the perspective of gender analysis, the Rulers' demand that Norea render them service can be read as an attempt to submit the female spiritual power to the Rulers whose nature (*hypostasis*) is manifested overtly in their presumptuous claims to sexual dominance. Their encounter exposes their authoritarian "power" as illegitimate and ultimately powerless tyranny. At the same time, it reveals Norea's power as virginal and superior. Norea's response to the Rulers might thus be read as a rejection of false claims to dominate and subordinate the spiritual powers from above" ("Virginity and Subversion," 252–53).

58 *Metamorphoses* I.544–47.

59 See Scopello, "Jewish and Greek Heroines."

60 *New Testament World*, 44.

have in fact defiled her mother, they have every reason to believe that she will submit. Norea, however, knows the truth and is like her true mother, the Spiritual Woman. She possesses true shame and like any honorable woman in a compromising position, calls out for help. No one in antiquity would expect a young, inexperienced girl to be able to handle the situation without male support. The danger she is in of being shamed is made clear by the seemingly enigmatic remark of Eleleth when he appears: "Why are you crying up to God? Why do you act so boldly towards the Holy Spirit?" Rather than *succoring* her, he *reprimands* her; he reprimands *her,* not the Rulers! They are allowed to slink away unheeded into the background while Eleleth reproaches Norea. From his point of view, the fault is *hers* for being in a compromising situation and acting so boldly. We remember the ideals of feminine virtue described above: "Female honor . . . is symboled by the maidenhead (hymen) and stands for female sexual exclusiveness, discretion, shyness, restraint, and timidity."[61] Nothing in her behavior up to now would have led one to describe Norea as discrete or timid. In the previous episode, she blew upon Noah's ark and caused it to be consumed by fire.[62] Thus Eleleth, as her male protector, is quite proper, culturally speaking, to reproach her for her indiscretions. The solution, Eleleth feels, is to instruct her more clearly about her situation.

One is reminded of Ischomachus and his wife in Xenophon's *Oeconomicus.* Ischomachus asked for something from the household stores, and his young wife could not give it to him. She blushes and is ashamed, but he responds, "The fact is, you are not to blame for this, but I, because I handed over the things to you without giving directions where they were to be put, so that you might know where to put them and where to find them."[63] It is the man's responsibility to give proper instructions so that the woman can be properly obedient. Thus Eleleth rectifies the dangerous situation of Norea, not by trouncing the bad guys but by giving her proper teaching, as the situation warranted.

He promises her then that after three generations a male savior, the True Man, will come and "free them (her and her children) from the bondage of the Authorities' error."[64] The text ends with Eleleth's vision concerning the end of the ages.

> Then all the Children of the Light will be truly acquainted with the Truth and their Root, and the Father of the Entirety and the Holy Spirit: They will all say with a single voice, "The Father's truth is just, and the Son presides over the Entirety": And from everyone unto the ages of ages, HOLY—HOLY—HOLY! AMEN![65]

61 *New Testament World,* 43. See also Pitt-Rivers, "Honour and Social Status," 44–45.
62 *Hyp. Arch.* 92,14–18.
63 *Oeconomicus* VIII.2.
64 *Hyp. Arch.* 96,30–31.
65 *Hyp. Arch.* 97,12–21, translated by Layton, "Hypostasis of the Archons," 422–24.

This praise emphasizes an important point: Though the story caricatures the Rulers, it does not expose and reject male authority *as such* but contrasts the proper authority of the Father with the improper authority of the Rulers. This fact should caution us not to read too much criticism of male authority per se into the description of the Archons and the first account of rape discussed above. In protecting Norea, the Father is acting honorably and protecting his own and his family's honor, and he will eventually regain all that has been displaced and restore the family integrity and order.

3.2.3 Rape and rebellion. Rape is used here as a metaphor for the wickedness (excessive sexual desire, agitation, violence, etc.) of the archons and the power of enlightened spirituality to escape. The use of rape as a metaphor suggests the state to which the Gnostic felt subjected in the body: pollution, fear, vulnerability, degradation, pain. The caricature of the archons simply supports this view. The Gnostic in the body was subject to oppression, humiliation, physical abuse, pollution, exploitation. The two stories offer complementary means of escape: the psychological division of the self through the rejection of the body and waiting for the intervention of the Father in the sending of the True Man at the end of time. Both strategies point toward rebellion against the Rulers of the world and their attempts to enslave and degrade the Spiritual Principle.

In conclusion: These two examples, of how gendered imagery, such as rape, is used to express the motif of rebellion, show well how female and male can carry different valences to make similar points. In one case the association of femaleness with materiality leads to its rejection (the sarcic Eve); in the other case, the situation of the Gnostic can be identified with that of the Female Spiritual Principle, and the true self of the Gnostic himself or herself can be described as female. In both cases, the Gnostic is called upon to flee from the world and fight against the enslavement of the Rulers.[66] Similarly, male imagery can express views of both illegitimate (caricatured) and legitimate (heroic) male authority and power.

The text clearly does not have a view of gender that sees "male" or "female" in simplistically negative or positive terms. For modern scholars to frame our

---

66 A. McGuire came to similar conclusions: "In conclusion, I want to suggest that the meaning and power of gender imagery in *The Hypostasis of the Archons* resides in its projection of an image of subversion: Norea stands as a model of spiritual subversion of the oppressive powers that illegitimately claim to rule the cosmos, the social order, the psyche, and the body. That she is female and they are androgynous or male in representation has symbolic significance. This does not mean that spiritual power is almost exclusively female in manifestation. It suggests instead that the unmasking of illegitimate male domination by female figures of spiritual power proved to be a powerful vehicle for the expression of the Gnostic revolt against the powers. As mythic symbol, the gendered representation of Norea and the Rulers does not point to oppressive rule of men. Rather, the mythic symbols of Norea and the Rulers may gain their representational power from a correspondence to the social world of the original audience or the contemporary reader, but their symbolic power resides in their ability to use that correspondence to depict and subvert the reality (*hypostasis*) of false powers" ("Virginity and Subversion," 257).

questions in such terms distorts the complexity—and profundity—of the text's perspective on gender.

3.3 Salvation

The topic of salvation may be considered from two viewpoints, that of saviors and that of those who are saved.

3.3.1 Saviors. There are several savior figures in the text, both male and female: the Father, Son, and Eleleth; the Holy Spirit, Incorruptibility, the Female Spiritual Principle (Spirit-endowed Woman), and Norea. Each will be considered in turn.

Salvation ultimately is achieved by the Father. It is he who sets in process the retrieval of the light; it is he who is really in charge, who has a plan and is in the process of bringing it to completion; it is he who seeks what is good for his children.[67]

The last stage of his plan to unify the Light below with the Entirety above will be effected by the Son, the True Man, who will bring the true teaching and anoint the Children of Light with the unction of Life eternal.[68] He is the eschatological savior.

There is a third male who figures strongly as a savior figure in the text; this is the Great Angel Eleleth (Understanding).[69] Norea describes him as powerful beyond telling: "His appearance is like fine gold and his raiment is like snow."[70] Eleleth describes himself as "Understanding; I am one of the four Light-givers who stand in the presence of the Great Invisible Spirit."[71] He teaches Norea about the Root of Truth, the creation of the lower realm, and the final culmination of the age when the True Man will come. In contrast to the Archons who lack *understanding* (ⲙⲛ̄ⲧⲁⲧⲉⲏⲧ), Eleleth personifies *Understanding* (ⲧⲙⲛ̄ⲧⲣⲙⲛ̄ϩⲏⲧ). They are described as deformities, beastlike and androgynous; Eleleth's appearance is perfect, described in terms of precious metal and pure snow. If the text presents the Archons as caricatures of masculinity and male authority, then Eleleth together with the Father and the Son are the ideals of masculinity and male authority: powerful, true, just and good, beautiful.

The most compelling set of savior figures in the text, however, are female: the Holy Spirit, Incorruptibility, the Female Spiritual Principle, and Norea. Sophia is presented primarily as the cause of sowing the Seed of Light in matter, but her daughter Zoe functions also to bind Yaldabaoth[72] and, with Sophia, to raise Sabaoth up to the seventh heaven.[73]

---

67 See *Hyp. Arch.* 87,22–23; 88,10–11, 33–89,3; 96,11–15, 35–97,1.
68 *Hyp. Arch.* 97,1–5.
69 *Hyp. Arch.* 93,2–22.
70 *Hyp. Arch.* 93,14–16.
71 *Hyp. Arch.* 93,19–22.
72 *Hyp. Arch.* 95,5–13.
73 *Hyp. Arch.* 95,19–22.

The Spirit (or Holy Spirit) inspired the great apostle[74] and descended in order to give life to the psychic Adam.[75] She is the principle of spiritual immanence in human beings.

Incorruptibility acts twice to aid the Light below. First she looked down into the waters, providing an image for the creation of Adam.[76] This is done in order that she might "bring the Entirety into union with the Light."[77] Second, a voice is sent forth from her for the assistance of Adam.[78] Incorruptibility is also described as the abode of the Seed of Light where the Holy Spirit dwells.[79] Her roles, therefore, are essential to the plan of salvation, and she is indeed salvation itself—the home of the redeemed Gnostic.

The voice sent from Incorruptibility takes on a persona of its own: the Spirit-endowed Woman or Female Spiritual Principle. She calls to Adam and in so doing gives him Life.[80] This makes clear the relation of the voice from Incorruptibility that vivified him and the Woman who in calling him gave him life. When the Authorities attempt to rape her, she laughs and escapes into a tree, providing a model of rebellion for the Gnostic (as described above). When she enters the snake, the reptile is named "Instructor" and proceeds to teach the Man and Woman.[81] Again the feminine principle is the agent of salvific activity; she represents the immanence of spiritual power in the world.

It is Norea, however, who more than any other figure provides the image of savior,[82] especially the type of the so-called "saved savior."[83] She is begotten "as an assistance [for] many generations of humankind."[84] She is herself the Mother of the Children of Light[85] and receives revelation from Eleleth. In addition, by her behavior (consuming the ark[86] and naming the archons) she is the model for rebellion against the Forces of Darkness.

3.3.2   The saved.   In addition to the aspect of saviors, those who are saved typify the pattern of salvation. There are four models in the text: (1) the repentance and ascent of Sabaoth, (2) the rescue of the Spirit-endowed Woman, (3) the rescue of Norea, and (4) the eschatological salvation of the Children of Light.

74 *Hyp. Arch.* 86,20–25.
75 *Hyp. Arch.* 88,11–16.
76 *Hyp. Arch.* 87,12–14.
77 *Hyp. Arch.* 87,20–23.
78 *Hyp. Arch.* 88,17–19.
79 *Hyp. Arch.* 93,29–30.
80 See B. Layton for the well-known pun on the Aramaic terms relating life, physician (mid-wife), snake, and instructor ("Hypostasis of the Archons," 54–55).
81 *Hyp. Arch.* 89,31–90,12.
82 For a fuller discussion, see Gilhus, "Nature of the Archons," 170–84. As Gilhus has also pointed out, in *The Hypostasis of the Archons* Norea assumes many of the roles given to Seth in other Sethian texts (see 153–68).
83 For the meaning of this term, see Rudolph, *Gnosis,* 121–31.
84 *Hyp. Arch.* 91,34–92,3.
85 *Hyp. Arch.* 96,19–22. See the discussion in Gilhus, "Nature of the Archons," 177–78.
86 *Hyp. Arch.* 92,14–18.

The raising up of Sabaoth forms an interesting case in this text for two reasons. (1) His repentance and ascent indicate the possibility that the offspring of the Chief Archon are not predestined for damnation but are condemned for their actions and intentions.[87] (2) When Sabaoth receives knowledge of the higher world, he rejects both his mother, Matter, and his father, the world-creator; but he praises only the Feminine Divine (Sophia and Zoe), not the Father of the Entirety. He rejects Sonship and subordinates himself to the Divine Mother-Daughter.[88] In *The Hypostasis of the Archons* the Gnostic is called to reject both female materiality and the caricatured male rule of the world creator, the entraping mother and the ignorant, powerless father,[89] and to turn to the Female Spiritual Principle.

A second model for salvation that resembles rejection of female materiality is the psychic dissociation of Eve. Here too, as with Sabaoth, not only Matter (the sarcic shadow) but also the Archons (male authorities) are rejected. The remaining characters, Adam and Eve, are in the same position as Sabaoth; they are in ignorance, possessing only soul. The Spiritual Principle instructs them, illustrating again the concern of the spiritual for the psychic.

The third example of salvation, that of Norea by Eleleth, portrays the female as a weak heroine in need of rescue by a strong male hero. As stated above this is a common topos in Hellenistic romance.

The final example is the future event of the coming of the True Man who will bring *gnosis* and anointing, allowing the Children of the Light to ascend back to the Light. This event is an eschatological version of the intervention of the Father through an emissary (this time the Son), already seen in the delivery of Norea by Eleleth; now it will occur in the end time to the Children of Light by the True Man. The rescue of Norea thus clearly forms the pattern for the salvation of all the Seed of Light.

4. Conclusion

Let us now return to our initial question: How we are to understand the use of gendered language in *The Hypostasis of the Archons?*

We began by assuming that gendered terms and concepts in Gnostic myth would reflect the social construction of gender in Late Antiquity. Using this perspective, four points emerge.

1. Gendered images and concepts are central to the text's mythology, espe-

---

87 See Gilhus, "Nature of the Archons," 77, 212–13, 219–22; M. A. Williams, *Immovable Race*, 158–85.

88 Worship of the Divine Mother-Daughter is perhaps not so surprising; we see a model for this practice for example in the Eleusinian mysteries. What is surprising is the rejection of Sonship, as though the worshiper were the child of Hades and must first reject his Father in order to worship the Mother, not the Earth Mother Demeter who is also rejected, but heavenly Wisdom and Life.

89 *Hyp. Arch.* 95,13–17.

cially the description of the nature of the world below and the place of the Gnostic in the world. Gender figures significantly in the discussion of salvation as well.

2. The use of gendered language serves to confirm ancient social constructions of gender simply by the uncritical acceptance of these motifs as metaphors. There is no basis in the text for a social program for the overthrow of patriarchy; the ideal of the text is a return to the legitimate rule of the Father and the Son in the World Above. Unlike the apocalypticist, the Gnostic does not conceive the world as the place of a new *creation* but looks forward to escape from the world and to *return* to the place of perfection already under the Father and Son.

Neither does the text argue for a social program toward egalitarianism, since the gnostic view of the equality of men and women on a spiritual level is based in a belief that human beings are essentially non-bodily. Such a view does not imply *gender equality* but *genderlessness*. Equality is here a fact of transcendence, not the basis for social change.[90]

3. *The Hypostasis of the Archons* plays out in full the contradiction between the ancient social definition of a male as (sexually) aggressive and the social demand to overcome and in some ways even to deny one's own sexuality in order to become a "man." Yet this use of gendered language, especially in the caricatured portrait of the Archons and the idealization of transcendent male rule, points toward a non-gendered *social* issue: the critique of *authentia.*

Gendered language in *The Hypostasis of the Archons* is not primarily veiled social criticism of *gender roles.* Yet the gendered language does point to the social world, not, however, to change or redeem it, but to expose it. The primary object of criticism is not the oppression of women by men, but absolute power ($\alpha\dot{v}\theta\epsilon\nu\tau\acute{i}\alpha$) that degrades and oppresses men and women alike. That illegitimate power is shown by caricature to be wicked, blind, and ignorant, and it is contrasted with the Truth of the Father Above whose power is goodness, light, and knowledge.

That the text consciously wishes to express this is made clear by the description of the left side of judgment in political terms as "represent(ing) the unrighteousness of the realm of *absolute power* ($\alpha\dot{v}\theta\epsilon\nu\tau\acute{i}\alpha$)."[91] This image is an extremely straightforward indication of the text's view of totalitarian political power. The title of the text—the nature of the Archons—further emphasizes that exposing the nature of absolute power is the central topic of the text. The text's covert social criticism is aimed directly at (Roman) totalitarianism, not patriarchy, though patriarchy does provide the text's model for the misuse of power. Aristotle had already perceived that ancient political order is modelled on the structure of gender relations in the domestic sphere.[92] What is inge-

90 For an account of why one would not expect revolution in antiquity, see Carney, *Shape of the Past,* 120–21.
91 *Hyp. Arch.* 96,1–2.
92 See *Politics* I.1–2.

nious here is the way in which the text uses the implicit power relations, already present in the social construction of gender in antiquity, to comment on power in the political sphere.

4. The use of feminine language, to represent the Gnostic in the world and to present the image of the saved savior, gives an insightful portrait of the feminine in antiquity.[93]

Norea provides a particularly good example. She is a strong but ambiguous figure. On the one hand, she is powerful; like a goddess her fiery breath consumes the ark of Noah and with it the wicked plans of the world rulers.[94] She is also the model of purity—"the virgin whom the Forces did not defile."[95] On the other hand, she is vulnerable; when faced with the attempted rape of the Archons, she requires the help of a savior, Eleleth. Her conversation with him shows that she is at least in part ignorant—she needs to ask Eleleth about the nature of the Archons[96] and if she too derives from their Matter.[97] She is at once the Savior and the Saved, the representative of salvation and the virgin mother of the Children of Light. She is the prototypical Gnostic, a strong but ambiguous figure.

Though in other gnostic texts the role of the saved savior is played by a male figure, often Adam or Seth, our text has very subtly exploited the fact that male figures do not carry the close association with materiality, immanence, nurture, and life giving that is communicated by reference to the cultural construction of woman. Furthermore since gender construction in antiquity largely expresses a male viewpoint, woman also appears as the other, the incomprehensible, the foreigner—all images that function well to describe the Gnostics in this world, especially over against images of male rulers who simply can't figure them out and repeatedly misjudge their real strength.

The text seems to know that the gnostic soul, which exists in the degradation of entrapment in the material world and yet which is at the same time a most pure spark of true divinity and light, shares a metaphorical ambiguity with woman as she was culturally constructed in antiquity: She is at once associated more closely than man with sexuality and materiality, is considered to be weak and in need of instruction, and is subordinate to male authority, but is also the powerful, life-giving mother and the ideal of virginal purity. This ambiguity made the feminine an extremely attractive image for expressing the gnostic perception of the human condition: caught between death and degradation on the one hand, and a taste for eternity and illumination on the other.

Seen as savior, the ambiguity inherent in the cultural construction of woman is also useful in expressing mediation between these straining poles of

93 Gilhus believes that the primary creativity seen in *The Hypostasis of the Archons* lies in its positive treatment of female mythology and female symbolism ("Nature of the Archons," 42–43).
94 *Hyp. Arch.* 92,14–18.
95 *Hyp. Arch.* 92,2–3.
96 *Hyp. Arch.* 93,31–94,2.
97 *Hyp. Arch.* 96,17–19.

material nature and transcendence.[98] In our texts only the feminine figures are presented as both immanent in the world and capable of ascent from it. As such, feminine figures provide linkage between the worlds above and below. The True Man may ultimately be the savior, but he is distant and abstract; the female savior, Norea, is strong and present. She is the source of life and teaching.[99] Because the female figures of *The Hypostasis of the Archons* are immanent and active in the world below, but are also representatives of the divine world above, they not only transcend the conflict between the two, but in this role they provide a "crucial link between the human in this world and that divinity which constitutes his/her truest identity."[100] Since she stands between the pleromatic home of the Gnostic and his/her current residence in the world below, the Female Spiritual Principle can help the Gnostic transverse the distance between political exploitation and empowerment, between the experience of degradation and the knowledge of infinite self-worth, between despair and peace.

98 Sherry Ortner has expressed this point by describing the symbolic ambiguity that arises from the association of woman with nature. Though identified with nature, women are not simply bodies, but fully human and capable, like men, of culture and the transcendence culture seeks to achieve. See "Female to Male?"

99 Gilhus concludes her book with the statement that in *The Hypostasis of the Archons*, "the male aspect of God is transcendent, his female aspect is immanent and the source of life, love and instruction" ("Nature of the Archons," 241–42).

100 Perkins, "Sophia and the Mother-Father," 107.

Genealogy and Sociology
in the Apocalypse of Adam

Luther H. Martin

At either end of the earth and at both extremes of time, the Sumerian myth of the golden age and the Andaman myth of the future life correspond, the former placing the end of primitive happiness at a time when the confusion of languages made words into common property, the latter describing the bliss of the hearafter as a heaven where women will no longer be exchanged, i.e., removing to an equally unattainable past or future the joys, eternally denied to social man, of a world in which one might *keep to oneself.*
—Lévi-Strauss, *The Elementary Structures of Kinship*[1]

Although Gnosticism has provided a rich trove for psychological analyses,[2] it offers meagre data for sociological inquiry, unless a parallel between mythological metaphysics and social situation is assumed. Such social analyses of gnostic traditions most often employ a general sociology of individualism (for example, that of Marx or Weber) or a sociology of context (Green)[3] that simply reformulates the orthodox judgements of early heresiological literature in terms of social scientific categories of alienation or marginality. Yet the prominence in gnostic myth of kinship categories of relationship, especially that of father to son,[4] and of those based upon claims to a common ancestry suggests an unexplored possibility of social insight. Accounts of descent from a common ancestor represent a conventional strategy of collective identity among peoples of antiquity. The discourse of such inclusion is that of kin relationship, which anthropologists consider "the most central of social processes."[5]

1 Lévi-Strauss, *Elementary Structures of Kinship*, 497.
2 See especially the insightful inquiries of Gilles Quispel informed by the analytical psychology of C. G. Jung after whom Codex I from Nag Hammadi was named; but see Darnton, *The Great Cat Massacre*, 9–72, and Martin, "Artemidorus," who question the historical adequacy of interpreting pre-psychological era texts psychologically, a hermeneutic which assumes the universal as opposed to the contingent validity of psychological theory.
3 Green provides a helpful overview of sociological interpretations of Gnosticism in *Economic and Social Origins*, chap. 1.
4 The father-son relationship in gnostic myth is usually treated as "an expression of spiritual or didactic filiation," see e.g., Peel, "Treatise on the Resurrection," 137.
5 Fox, *Kinship and Marriage*, 3, 13; an excellent introduction and overview of this difficult and often confused subject.

Kinship systems tell us how *people themselves* see their world of kin; from whom they distinguish themselves and on what basis.[6]

Kinship nomenclature systems are social inventions. The criteria for assigning persons to the role of kin vary from culture to culture in ways having little or nothing to do with biology.[7] Rather, systems of kinship represent implicit classifications of an ideal kinship universe.[8] This distinction between idealized kinship systems and actual kin relationship corresponds to the distinction between "culture" and "society," whereby "culture" designates shared patterns of expectations, evaluations, and symbolic meanings, and "society" designates a group of people who share these cultural attributes with some measure of regularity.[9] As summarized by J. A. Barnes,

> It is obvious that many people can think alike without having anything to do with one another, and that many people who come into contact with each other everyday [may] hold radically different views.[10]

While ideal kin classification systems may or may not correspond to real groups or categories, they do give an accurate picture of significant categories of social relationship in a kinship universe. Bruce J. Malina has shown the value of anthropological theory for addressing the meaning of social realities in the world of early Christianity, and Robert A. Oden has demonstrated the usefulness of theoretical kinship analyses for understanding the conventionalized biblical genealogies of Genesis.[11]

In the spirit of Hans Jonas' "experimental vein" of gnostic studies,[12] it might be asked what an analysis of gnostic claims to kin inclusion determined by eponymous descent might disclose about gnostic society, if indeed there be one,[13] and/or about the culture that has produced such a kin system. "Sethian gnosticism," the fixed point of which has been described as "the idea that Gnostics constitute a special 'race' descended from Seth,"[14] provides the ideal case study for an anthropological "demythologization" of a gnostic kinship universe.[15] Because of the relatively early date of the *Apocalypse of Adam*, NHC V,5, hypothesized on the basis of an absence of distinctively Christian

6 Fox, *Kinship and Marriage*, 243.
7 White, *An Anatomy of Kinship*, 6; Fox, *Kinship and Marriage*, 34.
8 Fox, *Kinship and Marriage*, 245.
9 J. A. Barnes, *Three Styles*, 25.
10 Barnes, *Three Styles*, 25.
11 Malina, *New Testament World*; Oden, "Jacob As Father." See also Leach, *Genesis as Myth*; and Donaldson, "Kinship Theory."
12 Jonas, *The Gnostic Religion*, 320.
13 Wisse ("Stalking Those Elusive Sethians," 575) concludes that the Sethian tractates "must not be seen as the teaching of a sect or sects, but as the inspired creations of individuals who did not feel bound by the opinions of a religious community."
14 Epiphanius, *Against Heresies*, 39.2.3, trans. Layton, *The Gnostic Scriptures*, 188; MacRae, "Seth in Gnostic Texts and Traditions," 21; Pearson, "Figure of Seth," 489; Stroumsa, *Another Seed*, 125.
15 As with Gnosticism generally, there is no information about the social makeup or practices of any Sethian group; see Wisse, "Stalking Those Elusive Sethians," 564.

imagery,[16] and because that document belongs to a general class of "charter myths," in which privilege is established through a genealogy that the descendent comes "to know in contrast to others who are excluded,"[17] it will be the focus of the following analysis.[18]

1. Kinship in the *Apocalypse of Adam*

Any cultural system defines two patterns of kin relationship: descent and alliance. Descent groups are defined by a real, putative, or fictive descent from a common ancestor through either the male line (patrilineally) or the female line (matrilineally), or through both sexes (cognatically).[19] Such groups may share common property, ritual, some activity, or, as in the *Apocalypse of Adam*, a name.[20]

According to the *Apocalypse of Adam*, Seth is the descendent of Adam and Eve (64,26; 65,2–3, 12–13; 66,7–8), while Cain (though the name is absent from the corrupt text) is the offspring of Eve and Sakla, the demiurgic deity of this world (66,25–27).[21] The descendents of this primordial *menage à trois* constitute two patrilineally defined descent groups (γενεαί) (65,8; 71,19, 23; 82,19; 83,1), in which the typical father-son-brother constellation dominates:[22] the Sethites and the Cainites. Descent is traced from Adam to Seth and his seed, on the one hand (64,1–3; 67,14–21; 69,9–17; 85,19–24), and from Sakla through Seth's half-brother, Cain, to Noah and to his sons Japheth, Ham, and Shem, on the other (70,10–11).[23] The name of Shem does not recur in the text, but Shem is most certainly the covenanter with Sakla (72,31–73,12). Shem's descendents are the Israelites (73,1–12) who have "done all [Sakla's] will" (74,17–18).[24] By contrast, the descendents of Japheth and Ham

---

16 Klijn, *Seth*, 90, n. 42; Rudolph, *Gnosis*, 135; Turner, "Sethian Gnosticism"; but compare Stroumsa, *Another Seed*, 103.
17 Burkert, *Ancient Mystery Cults*, 76; on "charter myths," see Kirk, *Myth*, 256–57.
18 See translations by MacRae and Parrott in J. M. Robinson, *The Nag Hammadi Library in English*, 2d ed., 256–64; by MacRae in Parrott, *Nag Hammadi Codices V, 2–5 and VI*, 151–95 (includes Coptic text) and in Charlesworth, *Pseudepigrapha*, 707–19; and by Layton in *The Gnostic Scriptures*, 52–64.
19 Fox, *Kinship and Marriage*, 34.
20 Fox, *Kinship and Marriage*, 49.
21 Abel, who according to Epiphanius was replaced by Seth after Cain killed him (39.2.4), is not mentioned in the *Apocalypse of Adam*.
22 Fox, *Kinship and Marriage*, 121.
23 The text has it that Sakla gives "power to his [Sakla's] sons and their wives by means of the ark," thus making Noah a Cainite by descent in contradiction to the account in Genesis, where Noah is a Sethite. MacRae and Stroumsa suggest that the text suffers from a haplography and restore it to read: "and he will give power to *Noah, his wife*, his sons and their wives" (Stroumsa, *Another Seed*, 83 and n. 11). By betraying the requirements of descent through his covenant with Sakla and the Cainites, however, Noah becomes a "sinful Sethite" (Stroumsa, *Another Seed*, 86), allied thereby with the Cainites. From the perspective represented by the *Apocalypse of Adam*, the question seems to be not whether Noah is a Cainite, but whether he is considered to be a Cainite by birth or by alliance.
24 Klijn, *Seth*, 94; Stroumsa, *Another Seed*, 85.

28 • Luther H. Martin

form twelve kingdoms of Gentiles (73,25–27). Four hundred thousand (Gentile) men, who have departed from the descendents of Japheth and Ham, "enter into another land and sojourn with those men who came forth from the great eternal knowledge" (73,13–24; 74,8–16), that is, with the descendents of Seth (73,13–20; 65,5–9).

The *Apocalypse of Adam* employs two kin terms in dealing with descent, "son" and "seed." The Coptic ϢΗΡΕ, or "son" (equivalent to the Greek υἱός) is used to refer both to Seth (67,15; 85,21) and to the (Cainite) sons of Noah (70,10, 21; 71,2, 4; 72,16, 18; 73,1; 74,18), including their sons (76,13). As a man gains complete rights over the possession of his own children in patrilineal systems,[25] so Seth dominates his line as their forefather, even as Cain dominates his.

The kin category "son" is further qualified in the *Apocalypse of Adam* by the use of "seed," for which three words are employed: the Greek loan words σπορά and σπέρμα and the Coptic word ϬΡΟϬ. L. Schottroff has pointed out that σπορά is always used positively in the *Apocalypse of Adam* and refers to the line of Adam/Seth whereas σπέρμα refers to the descendents of Sakla/Cain.[26]

Σπορά characterizes authentic descent from Seth, the sole legitimate offspring of Adam and Eve. His legitimacy is based upon his parents' union in *knowledge* (γνῶσις), which had been taught Adam by Eve (64,12–13) and which is inherited by Seth (65,3–5; 69,11–17). It is into the *seed* (σπορά) of the great aeons that *knowledge* (γνῶσις) entered (65,4) to become the *seed* (σπορά) of the great generation who is Seth (65,8). Σπορά is the equivalent, therefore, of γνῶσις, and three revealers tell Adam that this *seed* (σπορά) of knowledge has passed to Seth (66,3–8). Like angels, those men who work in the imperishable *seed* (σπορά, 76,7) will receive the gnosis that passed from Adam through Seth to that *seed* (σπορά, 85:22).

Cain's illegitimacy, on the other hand, is based on his father's position's being lower than that of Eve (64,16–19). This low "rank" is characterized by his lack of gnosis and by his acting on the basis of an antithetical "desire" (ἐπιθυμία) that he introduced into the world through his union with Eve (67,1–4). This primordial opposition between knowledge and desire defines the separate races of Seth and Cain.

Σπέρμα is used to describe the seed of Noah and his sons (72,24; 73,14, 25, 28; 74,17; 76,12) and that of the four hundred thousand men who are from the seed of Japheth and Ham (74,11). Although the Coptic ϬΡΟϬ can translate both σπορά and σπέρμα,[27] it is used in the *Apocalypse of Adam* to refer to the descendents of Noah (73,2, 6) and thus in the sense of σπέρμα.

There are no further genealogical connections established in the *Apocalypse of Adam* between any of the ancestors and the gnostic Ego. This "telescoping"

25 Fox, *Kinship and Marriage*, 121.
26 Schottroff, "*Animae naturaliter salvandae*," 79 (cited by Stroumsa, *Another Seed*, 125, n. 2).
27 Crum, *A Coptic Dictionary*, 831b.

tendency, whereby "those ancestors whose presence in the genealogy is ines-sential for the reckoning of contemporary relationships" have disappeared,[28] establishes an ancestral ordering for classes of human identity.[29] The genea-logical taxonomy defined by the *Apocalypse of Adam* establishes three such classes: (1) the descendents of Seth, (2) the descendents of Cain, including Noah and his descendents (Jews through Shem and twelve kingdoms of gen-tiles through Ham and Japheth), and (3) the four hundred thousand apostate Gentiles.[30] The kinship universe articulated by the *Apocalypse of Adam* provides authority for this proper order of nature because its genealogy from mythical time can be stated.[31]

The paradigm of identity established by the *Apocalypse of Adam* for the contemporary gnostic Ego is, of course, Sethian descent. Comparative sociol-ogists generally distinguish descent (the transmission of kinship membership rights) from inheritance (the transmission of property) and from succession (the transmission of office), neither of which necessarily requires a kin rela-tionship.[32] Whereas succession, which validates right to an exclusive office,[33] is not an issue in the *Apocalypse of Adam*, the tractate does link inheritance to descent. Descent systems establish the procedure for transmitting inheritance not only of property and position, but also of values and knowledge.[34] The in-heritance of *gnosis* belongs to the race of Seth (65,4–9) and to no other race (71,16–26). It legitimates as heirs of *gnosis* those "sons" who claim Seth as their ascendant.

Although the Sethites and Cainites are differentiated by separate patrilineal ascendants, they share a common matrilineal ancestor. This shared relation in the Sethian kinship universe gives rise to an overlapping grouping of descen-dent kin with membership rights dependent upon additional criteria of eli-gibility involving choice among such alternatives as marriage or adoption.[35] Since intercourse is renounced by the Sethites (72,12–13; 73,23–24; 75,1–4) and by the four hundred thousand (73,20–24), the joining of the four hundred thousand with the Sethites may be understood in terms of the kin category of adoption.

2. Kinship in Roman Society

Adoption is a legal fiction that permits a family tie to be artificially created.[36] The frequency of this practice in Roman society shows that biology was of

28 Goody, "Kinship," 403.
29 Geertz, *Interpretation of Cultures*, 373 and n. 12; Sagan, *At the Dawn of Tyranny*, 146.
30 Layton, *The Gnostic Scriptures*, 52.
31 Kirk, *Myth*, 256–57.
32 Goody, "Kinship," 401–2, following Rivers, *Kinship and Social Organisation*.
33 Goody, "Kinship," 403.
34 J. A. Barnes, *Three Styles*, 139.
35 Goody, "Kinship," 406.
36 Maine, *Ancient Law*, 22.

little concern in the Roman conception of the family.[37] As adoption involved also the assent of the adoptee,[38] it may be considered a practice of kinship recruitment upon which the religious notion of conversion was modeled in genealogically articulated systems.[39] The Greek technical term for legal adoption, υἱοθεσία ("sonship"), is used in this metaphorical sense of conversion most notably by Paul (see Gal 4:5).[40]

Adoption in Roman society was not by legal document but by will or testament,[41] the instrument by which the devolution of an inheritance was prescribed in antiquity.[42] Following the lead of G. MacRae,[43] Stroumsa notes that the *Apocalypse of Adam* "is actually a 'testament' of Adam, for the revelation took place at the time of his death."[44]

Sir Henry Maine, founder of the comparative study of jurisprudence and one of the founders of modern kinship analysis, understood ancient law to be based upon the problem of legitimate inheritance.[45] Because such discursive formations as the canon of law have their own histories—viz., when they emerged, the conditions of their emergence, from which discourse they diverged or merged, etc.[46]—and because "insistence on abiding by shared values and norms was an expression of commitment to the existing social structure,"[47] it is useful to review some of Maine's conclusions concerning inheritance and law as exemplars of the historical boundaries of kinship discourse within which the *Apocalypse of Adam* might have been articulated.

"The original Will or Testament," Maine writes, "was . . . an instrument . . . by which the devolution of the *Family* was regulated."[48] "In the old Roman Law of Inheritance the notion of a will or testament is inextricably mixed up . . . with the theory of a man's posthumous existence in the person of his heir."[49] The Roman notion of inheritance is that "though the physical person of the deceased had perished, his legal personality survived and descended unimpaired on his Heir or Co-Heirs, in whom his identity (so far as the law

---

37 Maine, *Ancient Law*, 107; Veyne, "Roman Empire," 17.
38 Maine, *Ancient Law*, 114–15.
39 *Contra* Stroumsa, *Another Seed*, 86.
40 Betz, *Galatians*, 208–9, also 185–86.
41 Veyne, "Roman Empire," 17.
42 Maine, *Ancient Law*, 147.
43 "Seth in Gnostic Texts and Traditions," 18; and in Parrott, *Nag Hammadi Codicies*, 152.
44 Stroumsa, *Another Seed*, 82.
45 Maine, *Ancient Law*, 1. Maine's work not only remains a classic of comparative jurisprudence but is one of the foundations of modern kinship studies. See, for example, Fox, *Kinship and Marriage*, 18, and Fortes, *Kinship and the Social Order*, 11–12. Morgan's *Systems of Consanguinity and Affinity* is the undisputed foundation for kin term systems.
46 Foucault, *The Archaeology of Knowledge*, 22.
47 Malina, "'Religion' in the World of Paul," 99.
48 Maine, *Ancient Law*, 158.
49 Maine, *Ancient Law*, 157.

was concerned) was continued,"[50]—the elimination, Maine concludes, "of the fact of death."[51]

"The prolongation of a man's legal existence in his heir, or in a group of co-heirs, is neither more nor less than a characteristic of *the family* transfered by a fiction to *the individual*."[52] Ancient society "has for its units, not individuals, but groups of men united by the reality or the fiction of blood-relationships."[53] "All ancient societies regarded themselves as having proceeded from one original stock, and even laboured under an incapacity for comprehending any reason except this for their holding together in political union."[54] All ancient witnesses to testaments in Rome "indicate that what passed from the Testator to the Heir was the *Family*, that is, the aggregate of rights and duties contained in the *Patria Potestas* and growing out of it."[55] Under Roman law, *patria potestas* was the basis of family life.[56] "The life of each citizen is not regarded as limited by birth and death; it is but a continuation of the existence of his forefathers, and it will be prolonged in the existence of his descendents,"[57] whether through agnatic descent or through adoption.[58]

Under Roman law, the line of inheritance was:

1. The *sui*, or direct descendents, equivalent in the *Apocalypse of Adam* to Seth.

2. The nearest agnate. Agnatic descent refers to cognates who trace their connection exclusively through males, as does the *Apocalypse of Adam*. Whereas "Parental Powers proper are extinguished by the death of the Parent . . . Agnation is as it were a mould which retains their imprint after they have ceased to exist."[59] Agnation is not based upon the marriage of Father and Mother, but only upon the "authority of the Father" (*patria potestas*), including those brought under this authority through adoption.[60]

3. The *gentiles*, i.e., the collective members of the dead man's *gens* or *house*, who, on the ground of bearing the same name, were supposed to be descended from a common ancestor.[61] The four hundred thousand descendents of Japheth and Ham adopted by the house or race of Seth establish the primoridal model for those who will inherit *gnosis*. Under Roman law, "the only purpose of *adoptio* is to bring *patria potestas* into existence."[62] Even as Jesus requires

50 Maine, *Ancient Law*, 151, 156.
51 Maine, *Ancient Law*, 157–58.
52 Maine, *Ancient Law*, 154.
53 Maine, *Ancient Law*, 152, see also 104, 213–14.
54 Maine, *Ancient Law*, 106.
55 Maine, *Ancient Law*, 158.
56 Curzon, *Roman Law*, 32.
57 Maine, *Ancient Law*, 214.
58 Curzon, *Roman Law*, 32.
59 Maine, *Ancient Law*, 124.
60 Maine, *Ancient Law*, 123.
61 Maine, *Ancient Law*, 165–66.
62 Schulz, *Classical Roman Law*, 144.

those who will do "the will of my Father in heaven" to reject their natural family (Matt 12:46–50; Mark 3:31–35; Luke 8:21), adoption into the *patria potestas* of Seth requires the rejection of the adoptee's Cainite origin.

3. Kinship Rationales in the *Apocalypse of Adam*

"Whatever else kinship systems do," Robin Fox has summarized, "they divide people into categories of kin and then define marriageability in terms of these categories."[63] Marriage was equivalent in status to adoption under Roman Law,[64] and, like adoption, has been treated by kinship analysts largely in the context of recruitment to kinship groups.[65] Lévi-Strauss, however, has emphasized the importance of marriage alliance over descent as the basis for the social state. For Lévi-Strauss, kinship groups are "units in a system of 'alliance' made or 'expressed' by marriage."[66] In the *Apocalypse of Adam* alliance, based upon desire, is the identifying mark of the Cainites.

Adam/Eve, an androgynous pair who are divided by Sakla (64,20–23), are as much brother/sister as husband/wife. Sakla, the God who created them, created for himself a son (Cain) with Eve (65,25–28), thus establishing exogamous marriage. Exogamy is regarded as equivalent to the prohibition of incest, which, according to Lévi-Strauss, is not so much the prohibition of marriage with mother, sister, or daughter as it is an obligation to give mother, sister, or daughter to others.[67] It "provides the only means of maintaining the group as group, of avoiding infinite fission and segmentation which the practice of consanguinous marriages would bring about."[68] This exogamous bond of alliance with another family represents a tendency to social cohesion[69] and "ensures the dominance of the social over the biological."[70]

Because of the *gnosis* that the Sethian seed contains, Sakla enjoins Noah against mixing his $\sigma\pi\acute{\epsilon}\rho\mu\alpha$ with the alien $\sigma\pi o\rho\acute{\alpha}$ ("no seed will come from you [Noah] of the man who will not stand in my presence in another glory [Seth]" [71,4–8]).[71] In exchange for Noah's pledge not to mingle with the race of gnostics, Sakla offers "power to Noah, his wife, his sons and their wives" (70,10–11).[72] Authority over his newly established exogamous alliance is granted by Sakla to Noah and his sons as a kingly rule over the earth. The

---

63 Fox, *Kinship and Marriage*, 2.
64 Veyne, "Roman Empire," 17.
65 Fox, *Kinship and Marriage*, 22.
66 Fox, *Kinship and Marriage*, 22.
67 Lévi-Strauss, *Elementary Structures of Kinship*, 481.
68 Lévi-Strauss, *Elementary Structures of Kinship*, 479.
69 Lévi-Strauss, *Elementary Structures of Kinship*, 480.
70 Lévi-Strauss, *Elementary Structures of Kinship*, 479. Similarly, in Roman society, marriage was understood primarily as a civic duty rather than as a matter of establishing a family (Veyne, "Roman Empire," 37–38).
71 Stroumsa, *Another Seed*, 83.
72 See n. 23 above.

gnostic sons of Seth, by contrast, are described as a "race without a king over it" (92,19–20).[73] Thus a Sethite kinship system based upon an agamous kin model of adoption is contrasted with a Cainite kingship system based upon exogamous marriage alliances.

Anthropologists regularly distinguish between "kinship" and "kingship" systems as types of social organization.[74] Whereas kinship systems are characterized by a genealogically defined communal authority and a "self-consciousness about their superior place in the world,"[75] kingship systems represent the tendency towards centralized leadership and power.[76]

Whereas sexual license is universally reputed of kings,[77] it is related to the breakdown of kinship systems.[78] In the *Apocalypse of Adam* marriage alliances, mandated by the rule of exogamy, are viewed negatively. They are based upon *lust* ($\epsilon\pi\iota\theta\nu\mu\iota\alpha$, 67,3) which results in pregnancy (80,3; 81,8, 9, 17) and the transmission of $\sigma\pi\epsilon\rho\mu\alpha$. And in the hymnic section of the *Apocalypse of Adam* (77,27–83,3), spokesmen of the twelve kingdoms enumerate various views of the incarnation of the savior "in their own language of lustful beginnings and carnal births,"[79] which had been "imparted to them by their god Sakla (73:3–4)."[80]

The Gnostics, on the other hand, having no such desire (83,16.), are *undefiled* (ⲁⲧⲭⲱⲕⲙ, 75,3–4; 75,6; 82,23), and are protected, therefore, from such $\epsilon\pi\iota\theta\nu\mu\iota\alpha$ (73,24; 75,4). By avoiding $\epsilon\pi\iota\theta\nu\mu\iota\alpha$, ⲭⲱⲕⲙ, and the transmission of $\sigma\pi\epsilon\rho\mu\alpha$, which are characteristic of marriage alliances, the Sethites avoid the social state itself.

The Sethites' inverse reading of Genesis emphasizes the asocial implications of its Sumerian prototype. According to the citation from Lévi-Strauss, which concludes his study of kinship and which opened this essay, the Sumerian myth places a golden age of primitive happiness prior to the time when a confusion of languages made words into common property and established the possibility of alliances between peoples. This possibility is represented in the *Apocalypse of Adam* by the dispersion of Noah's sons and their descendents, who constitute the twelve kingdoms. Before this confusion of tongues, words were the property of each particular group, a privilege of *gnosis* still claimed by

---

73 See Fallon, "The Gnostics."
74 Sagan, *At the Dawn of Tyranny*, 225–42.
75 Sagan, *At the Dawn of Tyranny*, 236, 240.
76 Sagan, *At the Dawn of Tyranny*, 236.
77 Sagan, *At the Dawn of Tyranny*, 320–21.
78 Sagan, *At the Dawn of Tyranny*, 72.
79 Stroumsa, *Another Seed*, 91.
80 Stroumsa, *Another Seed*, 90. It is tempting to explore the relation of this section of the *Apocalypse of Adam* to the Matthean genealogy of Jesus, in which all the women named "conceived Jesus' forebears in illicit sexual encounters," culminating in the virgin birth (Rothkrug, "German Holiness and Western Sanctity," 218–19). Matthew borrows the phrase, $\beta\iota\beta\lambda o\varsigma$ $\gamma\epsilon\nu\epsilon\sigma\epsilon\omega\varsigma$, "book of origin," with which he begins his gospel, from Gen 2:4a (LXX), which introduces the "J" narrative covering the genealogy of mankind from Adam to Seth (Gen 2:4a–4:26! Allen, *Matthew*, 1). But this is another story. . . .

the Sethites (as by "orthodox" Christians following the miracle of tongues reported in Acts 2).

Lévi-Strauss compares the Sumerian denial of happiness to social man with the Andaman myth of the future life, which

> will be but a repetition of the present, but all will then remain in the prime of life, sickness and death will be unknown, and there will be no more marrying or giving in marriage.[81]

Again, an ideal age, set this time in the future, is characterized by the absence of alliance. These two motifs correspond, according to Lévi-Strauss, since both remove to an equally unattainable time an ideal, epitomized also in the *Apocalypse of Adam*, of a world eternally denied social man "in which one might keep to oneself."

4. Kinship and Society in the *Apocalypse of Adam*

Contrary to those who would find within gnostic myth a cultural paradigm for the positive evaluation of women in ancient society, the idealized kinship universe articulated in the *Apocalypse of Adam* is a staunchly patriarchal cultural system.[82] It defines gnostics as those who claim patrilineal descent from Seth.

In the "racial theology" of the *Apocalypse of Adam*,[83] membership in the Sethian descent system is defined as a potential of the descendents of Japheth and Ham, the gentiles; Jews, the descendents of Shem, are considered unregenerate Cainites. Such "antisemitic" gentiles,[84] who nevertheless read the book of Genesis as their "charter myth," could only be a "class" of Christians,[85] the thirteenth kingdom referred to in the *Apocalypse of Adam* (82,10–19).[86]

Membership in this Sethite-Christian descent group is not understood biologically, but rather is based upon the paradigm of the four hundred thousand descendents of Japheth and Ham who join with the Sethites and with whom the primordial genealogical drama of the *Apocalypse of Adam* concludes. Sethites are Sethites not through some literal claim to consanguinity, but by choice: "adoption" in the discourse of kinship, "conversion" in that of religion.

The four hundred thousand converts are a heterogenous people who renounce all alliances, whether based upon desire, which has characterized the Cainites ever since the union of Sakla with Eve, or upon power, which has

81 Man, *Aboriginal Inhabitants*, 94–95, cited by Lévi-Strauss, *Elementary Structures of Kinship*, 457.
82 Malina makes this same point with respect to theological studies of the Bible ("'Religion' in the World of Paul," 94).
83 Stroumsa, *Another Seed*, 86.
84 Stroumsa, *Another Seed*, 85; on "anti-semitism" in the Nag Hammadi documents, see Gager, *The Origins of Anti-Semitism*, 167–73.
85 Layton, *The Gnostic Scriptures*, 20–21.
86 Stroumsa, *Another Seed*, 94–100.

characterized the Cainites ever since the covenant of Sakla with Noah and his sons. From the anthropological perspective of this study, their rejection of marriage should be taken less as evidence for an ascetic life style than as a rejection of alliances, that is, as a rejection of any social definition of identity. Such "keeping to oneself" should not be understood as recommending individuality, a modern notion, but as the embodiment of sacrality. Since birth and death are part of a single process of corruption (70,3–5; 76,15–17), this embodiment of sacrality is not in the corporeal body produced through sexual relations, but in an angelic or resurrected body (76,6, 23–24; 83,14) which "will not perish" (76,21–23). "For," as "orthodox" Christians well knew, "in the resurrection they neither marry nor are given in marriage, but are like angels in heaven" (Matt 22:30//Mark 12:25 and Luke 20:35–36).

The rejection of kingship, or political alliances, by the Sethites in favor of a kinship model suggests a form of social relations characteristic primarily of peoples defined by place. "The first century world," writes Malina, "was marked by geographical and social immobility which resulted in the heightened support and constraint of a closed social network."[87] With the newly bureaucratic urbanization characteristic of Hellenistic civilization,[88] new inhabitants came to cities from the countryside where their ancestors had lived for centuries. Such a move provides the conditions for the creation of alternative social systems. The question then arises of the basis for nonkinship forms of social cohesion or identity inclusion. One option is adherence to the centralized leadership or authority characteristic of kingship systems; another is the formation of quasi-family associations to replace the kinship networks left behind.[89] The Sethite emphasis on kinship suggests a conservative (and "orthodox" [Matt 22:21; Mark 12:17; Luke 20:25]) evaluation of Hellenistic urban life, favoring a previous status quo,[90] rather than the radical posture conventionally attributed to an urbane gnosticism from the interpretative orientation of normative Christianity.[91] Such kin associations do not represent powerlessness, but the absence or rejection of a centralized locus of power in favor of a diffused embodiment of power.

When the four hundred thousand renounced their Cainite alliances, they joined the "kingless race" (82,19–20) and settled in "another place" with the Sethites (73,13–25) who had already rejected such alliances. This "other place" is no geographical place but "heaven," the placeless place of angels (72,10–11; 73,16–20). Here they may "reflect upon the knowledge of the eternal God" embodied in their hearts and attributed to their redeemer, the

---

87 Malina, *New Testament World*, 101.
88 See de Ste. Croix, *Class Struggle in the Ancient Greek World*, 10–11; Martin, *Hellenistic Religions*, 26.
89 Sagan, *At the Dawn of Tyranny*, 72. See also Little, *West African Urbanization*, and Mitchell, *Mishpokhe*.
90 Malina, "'Religion' in the World of Paul," 96.
91 On gnosticism as a "city religion," see Rudolph, *Gnosis*, 291. See also Kippenberg, "Verländlichung."

heavenly Seth (76,24–30), with whom they are now identified by name. A placeless people who no longer bury because they have lost contact with their natural kin,[92] the Sethites are linked through their fictive kinship relations and are "already resurrected" into their legitimate inheritance of gnosis, a cultural system that defines an asocial reality.

92 Rothkrug, "German Holiness and Western Sanctity," 215–41; and Johannesen, "The Holy Ghost in Sunset Park."

Two illustrious statesmen: Henry Kissinger and James M. Robinson (Photograph courtesy of the Institute for Antiquity and Christianity)

iii

The Trimorphic Protennoia
and the Prologue
of the Fourth Gospel[1]

Gesine Robinson

Hardly any other book of the New Testament has posed such extensive and difficult riddles for exegetes as has the Fourth Gospel. It puts New Testament scholarship really "on the spot." The mass of literature, in commentaries, essays, and monographs is so great that it is hard to get an overview. A glance at the surveys of research presented from time to time gives eloquent expression to this situation.

In the case of the eighteen verses that stand at the beginning, the so-called Prologue of the Fourth Gospel, or, more specifically, the hymn generally agreed to lie behind the Prologue, these difficulties are only aggravated, and the quantity of secondary literature swells accordingly! Most of this literature, at least in the post-Bultmannian period, has dealt with the question of the relation of the Prologue to Gnosticism, where opinions vary widely, from gnostic or gnosticizing to anti-gnostic or even completely non-gnostic. This question as to its history-of-religions background has always been important. But since the Nag Hammadi texts have become available, it has again been put into the center of interest.

The East Berlin Nag Hammadi team, the *Arbeitskreis für koptisch-gnostische Schriften*, of which I was a member, published in 1973 the thesis that *Trimorphic Protennoia* from Nag Hammadi Codex XIII, especially the description of Protennoia's third appearance as Logos, might be a genuine parallel to the Prologue of the Fourth Gospel.[2] Since then, the discussion has never ended about the relation between the two texts, or about the possibility of a history-of-religions background being shared by both texts.

The discussion was accelerated by a first translation, which I published on behalf of the Berlin team in 1974, where our earlier thesis was enlarged by our ongoing research on the text. There I argued that one has the impression that the relevant statements of Protennoia stand in their natural context, whereas

---

1 This is a slightly revised version of a paper read at the SBL convention in Boston in December 1987. For the English translation I am indebted to my husband, for whom the present volume has been prepared.
2 Arbeitskreis für die koptisch-gnostische Schriften, "Bedeutung der Texte," 76.

37

their parallels in the Prologue, when seen in terms of the Fourth Gospel, seem to have been artificially made serviceable to a purpose actually alien to them.[3]

At times in the next few years the discussion has unfortunately degenerated into a debate about the dependence of one text on the other. But this early thesis should already have made it clear that a debate as to which text is dependent on the other should have been impossible from the very beginning. For the parallels to our text, which incidentally are found not only to the Prologue, but also, for example, to the hymn of Colossians (1:15–20), do not suggest a relation of *Trimorphic Protennoia* to these New Testament texts themselves, but rather to the sources lying behind them. However for Yvonne Jannsens,[4] in any case, it seemed to be important to suggest a direct dependence of *Trimorphic Protennoia* on the Fourth Gospel. The parallels that she listed led her to the question, "Is it necessary to conclude from this that John borrows these terms from *Trimorphic Protennoia*?" She then went on to assert: "Let us say right away that for us it is rather the reverse that took place." She was followed in this oversimplification of the whole issue, for example, by Jan Helderman[5] and Edwin M. Yamauchi,[6] right down to Peter Hofrichter,[7] for whom the Prologue is even a primitive Christian confession that served as the basis not only for Gnostic theology, but for all New Testament theology as well.

In 1978 the discussion reached its highpoint, at the International Conference on Gnosticism at Yale,[8] which I was not able to attend. The chair of the Yale seminar on Sethianism, George MacRae, later summarized its outcome. I am pleased and honored that he put into focus the issue that I had posed in 1974. He called it "the heart of the argument" and commented:[9]

> In any case, it is easier to envisage the spread of the relevant attributes in the Gnostic work as original than to suppose that the author dismantled the narrowly focused Prologue of the Fourth Gospel to spread the attributes throughout a much broader mythological context. It is important to note here that no one seriously argues that the Fourth Gospel is indebted to the Nag Hammadi tractate as to a literary work. Clearly both are dependent on developments of the wisdom tradition and may simply have had a common ancestor. But whether that ancestor is already a Gnostic modification of the wisdom tradition is the question at stake.

Here MacRae has indeed put his finger on the central issue. How one answers this question depends ultimately on how one assesses the gnostic phenomenon in general and how one understands the origin and development of Gnosticism as a whole.

3 G. Schenke, "Protennoia," 734.
4 "Une source gnostique," 355.
5 "In ihren Zelten," esp. 208–11.
6 "Jewish Gnosticism," esp. 480–84.
7 *Johannesprolog*, esp. 215–21.
8 Layton, *Rediscovery of Gnosticism*, esp. 588–616, 634–85.
9 MacRae, "Gnosticism and the Church," 91.

Regarding *Trimorphic Protennoia*, the Berlin team maintained that, to judge by its mythological material, it is a Sethian document that in its basic substance was not yet influenced by Christianity. But in earlier research it had not been generally agreed that a specifically Sethian variety of Gnosticism ever existed, or that there had ever existed a non-Christian or even pre-Christian kind of Gnosticism.

It is to clarify these preliminary issues that we will investigate, in the first two sections, the relation of our text to Sethianism and Christianity. Only then, in a third section, will we return to the question of the relationship between this non-Christian Sethian variety of Gnosticism, as documented in *Trimorphic Protennoia*, and the Prologue of the Gospel of John.

1. The Relation of *The Trimorphic Protennoia* to Sethianism

The defining of *Trimorphic Protennoia* as a Sethian text may have come at first as a surprise, since the name of Seth does not even occur in the text. Moreover the dominant figure, Protennoia, is, among other designations, also named Barbelo (38,9). Yvonne Janssens[10] used this name to designate the text as Barbelo-Gnostic, a term derived from Irenaeus. John Turner considered the text "a Barbeloite treatise with Sethian influences."[11] But the Berlin group had worked out well-defined criteria for assigning a text to the Sethian corpus.[12] It is in terms of the Sethian system based on these criteria that *Trimorphic Protennoia* has been classified as Sethian. In this system Barbelo is the highest female deity of the Sethian divine triad. Hence the occurrence of the name in the text merely confirms the Sethian classification. As a matter of fact, in the process of identifying the characteristics of Sethianism, it became obvious that Barbelo-Gnosticism and Sethianism are not alternatives to each other but rather refer to the same mythological conceptualization.

The debates about Sethianism have already been settled to a considerable extent by the Yale conference. At least a certain consensus seems to have been reached, namely that in fact there is a group of writings in the Nag Hammadi library that is held together by a specific "system" that they share. Of course the word "system" is not to be pressed, as if one meant a rigorous and rational systematization, but "rather serves as a shorthand for something like a 'complex of interconnected basic beliefs and basic concepts.'"[13] To be sure, these Sethian texts also stand in more or less close relation to other gnostic texts as well.

Remaining divergences among scholars are: How narrow or wide is the

10 "Le codex XIII," 342.
11 "Trimorphic Protennoia," 461.
12 H.-M. Schenke, "Das sethianische System," esp. 166–69.
13 H.-M. Schenke in Layton, *Rediscovery of Gnosticism,* 685 (discussion).

Sethian "net" to be cast, to use a metaphor of George MacRae,[14] so as to include under Sethianism more or fewer texts than the ones that have been identified thus far? Further, should one imagine Sethianism to be more like a sect, a school in the sense of philosophical schools, or a broad movement with a variety of branches within the total gnostic phenomenon? Or should one go with Frederik Wisse,[15] who wishes to deny the existence of Sethianism as such, and to derive Sethian texts not from what he calls a situation of "social control," apparently his euphemism for sect, but rather from "a setting in which individuals were able to present their visionary interests to broad sections of the church." But the extent to which it is inescapable that we postulate a distinct community or movement as the bearers of the Sethian texts is yet to be shown in what follows.

First let us sketch the affinities of *Trimorphic Protennoia* to other Sethian texts and concepts. *Trimorphic Protennoia*, a revelation discourse, corresponds in its mythological material (cosmology, eschatology, soteriology) most closely to the variant of the system found in *Gospel of the Egyptians*. Further, *Trimorphic Protennoia* shares its formal structure, the division into three parts, with the *Three Steles of Seth*. Regarding the characteristic threefold descent of Protennoia, it is especially closely kin to the Pronoia hymn at the end of the long version of the *Apocryphon of John*. Furthermore, in the course of *Trimorphic Protennoia* it becomes increasingly clear that Protennoia, in whom so many functions of the divine have been absorbed, has also assumed the role of the heavenly Seth as the Redeemer figure. Thus, in the course of her revelation Protennoia speaks repeatedly of her children, who are also designated her "seed." In this way the whole text is permeated with the basic Sethian concept of Gnostics as the seed or offspring of Seth.

It is for the purpose of the redemption of her seed that the threefold descent of Protennoia takes place. She instructs her children about their true origin, about the coming into being and the passing away of the present aeon, and about the secrets needed for the successful ascent of the soul when the time comes. Although the text is dominated by I-am predications, a real group of users and transmitters is envisaged not only when, now and then, Protennoia addresses her children *directly*, in the second person plural, but also when the Gnostics themselves even have a chance to speak (36,33–37), in a sort of confession that may well reflect liturgical practice. The mysteries that Protennoia reveals to her children are primarily *gnosis* itself but may also involve the practice that belongs with *gnosis*. Knowing about the secrets effects salvation. But this knowledge is attained in concrete practice. Secret teaching and secret practice in any case belong together and correspond to each other.

In this regard our text makes an important contribution to the question of gnostic cult practice. This in turn helps to answer our question as to whether a real community lies behind the Sethian texts and their world of thought.

---

14 MacRae in Layton, *Rediscovery of Gnosticism*, 677 (discussion).
15 Wisse in Layton, *Rediscovery of Gnosticism*, 677 (discussion).

The decisive coming, the Revealer's third entering of the human sphere, is described with the common topic of the secret and unrecognized descent of the Redeemer, who at each stage of the descent puts on the form of the inhabitants of the region through which he, at the moment, is passing. In a certain sense there corresponds to this descent not only the later reascent of the Redeemer, after having successfully carried through the mission (50,15–18), but also the ascent of the redeemed, each individual Gnostic after death. The Gnostics can enter the higher heavenly sphere only if they, like the Redeemer, have gotten through the hostile archontic spheres unharmed. The mission of the Redeemer consists precisely in communicating to the Gnostics how they can achieve that unimpeded ascent. They achieve it by first undergoing baptism in the "living water" in order to put off chaos, the body of flesh, and put on light (48,7–14), so as to become invisible and out of reach of the Archons (49,32–34).

The actual execution of baptism takes place in five stages, in the course of which three mythological beings in each realm bestow upon the Gnostic one of four heavenly gifts: a heavenly garment of light, heavenly purity through celestial water, a heavenly throne, and a heavenly crown of glory, followed by admission into the realm of eternal light (48,15–30).

This description of the eschatological ascent of the Gnostic through the heavenly spheres is stated in the past tense, because an already redeemed Gnostic is presented as a prototype. But the detailed presentation of the celestial rite is ultimately intended to portray Protennoia as the initiator and guarantor of this rite as a gnostic sacrament, which the community is henceforth to repeat. The idea that she actually came down to establish a gnostic baptismal sacrament had already been expressed as the goal of her first descent, namely to save the divine spirit imprisoned in the human soul by means of rebirth through baptism in the water of life (41,20–24). What occurs here on the tongue of Protennoia is, in terms of the history of tradition, best understood against the background of gnostic baptismal liturgy. There may well have been a prayer with the petition to anticipate mystically the ascent in the cult: Do not let this abandoned part in me be lost, but let it be born anew through the water of life, the incomprehensible miracle of baptism.[16] Thereby the soteriological significance of water in gnostic baptism is also brought to expression. In any case, *Trimorphic Protennoia* provides no basis for assuming with John Turner[17] that the Sethians had completely sublimated and spiritualized their baptismal sacrament and would most likely have rejected water baptism. Rather the Sethians understood heavenly and earthly baptism as cultically identical. What takes place in the heavenly spheres has its equivalent in the earthly sphere, and vice versa. The three mythological beings Micheus, Michar, and Mnesinous, who are in charge of the celestial spring, vouch for the heavenly quality of the water (48,19–20) used in earthly baptism.

---

16 For my detailed exegesis of these passages see G. Schenke, *Dreigestaltige Protennoia*, 124–26.
17 "Sethian Gnosticism," 58, 66–71.

In relation to the ascent there seems also to be a bestowing of the so-called "five seals," no doubt five mysterious names (49,26–29), which are apparently the greatest secret of Sethian Gnosticism. A comparison with other Sethian texts also makes clear that an act of sealing belongs within the baptismal rite. The person being baptized is baptized into a holy five-in-one-ness, where, as each name is called out, there is bestowed a seal, probably a *sphragis* (on the forehead), in the form of a gesture of the hand. (This may have been similar to our making the sign of the cross three times while calling out the names of the persons of the trinity.) Only then does the person being baptized come to know the five secret names, which he can invoke, using them as passwords, during his ascent through the archontic spheres, in order to pass through without hindrance.[18] In this way one can understand why with the statement "he received the five seals" both saving baptism and saving knowledge can come to expression (48,30–34), and why immediately after communicating knowledge of the names of the seals the text speaks of life in eternal blessedness (48,34–35). The person who is born again in baptism and comes to know the names of the five seals has already put off ignorance and put on radiant light (49,28–32). Therefore total salvation is already anticipated in baptism.

The importance that baptism had for the Sethians is also shown by the *Gospel of the Egyptians*, which is a long aetiology of the baptismal mystery. Hans-Martin Schenke,[19] on the basis of his investigations of the Sethian texts, had already drawn attention to the "strong, deep-rooted and obviously already traditional practice of water baptism" of the Sethian community, and has extended this line of thought one step further in concluding that "one could draw a parallel between the Sethians and the Mandaeans, both being gnosticized baptist sects, and accordingly look for the ultimate origin of gnostic Sethianism in the baptist circles of Palestine."

2. The Relation of *The Trimorphic Protennoia* to Christianity

In *Trimorphic Protennoia* there are a number of parallels to New Testament texts. R. McL. Wilson inferred from the parallels collected by Yvonne Janssens "that the Christian element in the text as it now stands is rather stronger than the Berlin group have recognized."[20] Wilson was unaware that my edition,[21] at that time still unpublished but accessible as dissertation, listed even more parallels to the New Testament than did Janssens. But what is decisive for assessing whether a gnostic text is influenced by Christianity is not the number of parallels to the New Testament, for neither the New Testament nor the Sethian texts were created in a vacuum. Rather both presuppose many

18 See G. Schenke, *Dreigestaltige Protennoia*, 153–55.
19 "Gnostic Sethianism," 606–7.
20 "Trimorphic Protennoia," 54.
21 See the index to my commentary, G. Schenke, *Dreigestaltige Protennoia*, 167.

non-Christian traditions on which each built. Hence they can readily be parallel to each other without one being dependent on the other. A dependence on the New Testament would only be obvious if shared traditions were used by the gnostic text in a distinctively Christian way. But *Trimorphic Protennoia* is by and large not to be explained as derived from Christian concepts or as dependent on Christian texts. The few distinctively Christian traits are the result of secondary Christianization that took place in a rather superficial way.

The very fact that originally non-Christian gnostic texts underwent a process of various kinds and degrees of Christianization is something that I may presuppose as uncontested, at least now that this procedure is documented in one and the same codex of the Nag Hammadi library itself, where one may observe that the non-Christian gnostic text *Eugnostos* becomes the Christian gnostic text *Sophia of Jesus Christ*.[22] Sethian texts shared this fate, though among them the proportion of uncontaminated non-Christian gnostic texts is especially high: *Three Steles of Seth, Thought of Norea, Marsanes, Allogenes,* and, with but trivial exceptions, *Apocalypse of Adam* and *Zostrianos*. (Other Sethian texts were given a Christian framework, such as *Apocryphon of John* and *Hypostasis of the Archons*; or Christian elements and motifs were interpolated.) Christianity apparently affected largely non-Christian Sethian texts that were already extant. Hence we may speak of secondary Christianization.

Of course Sethianism reacted to Christianity, as well as it did to philosophy. Where in general Christianity and Gnosticism met, it usually had to do with the shared understanding of existence and with the Redeemer myth that each had. But in the case of Sethianism there never took place a genuine penetration of Christian thought, in the sense of a fusion, such as one finds for example in Valentinianism. This may be due to the fact that Sethian Gnosticism encountered its environment with such a closed and profiled mythological concept that it largely blocked Christianizing tendencies.

With regard to the question of Christianizing in *Trimorphic Protennoia*, an answer is easiest at the two places where the bare *nomen sacrum* XR, Christos, is appended to two of the several references to the divine Son of the Sethian triad (38,22; 39,7). This addition does not serve any apparent purpose other than to identify him with the pre-existent Christ. Christ has no function of his own in the text. It may also be noted from other Sethian texts that this seems to have been the simplest way to "Christianize" a gnostic text externally.

Further redactional manipulations of our text, however, apparently attest that debates were already taking place within the various religious streams of early Christianity. A passage obviously interpolated into the third discourse (49,6–22) portrays for a second time the final incognito descent of the Redeemer, for this common gnostic topic of a deceptive maneuver had already been narrated (47,13–28). There Protennoia as Logos descended, wearing

22 Krause, "Literarisches Verhältnis," 215–23.

successively the garment of the inhabitants of each archontic sphere. Then she put on the chaos, the body of flesh, and began her saving work (47,31–48,35). This procedure comes to its end with her granting the five seals to the redeemed spirit and his entering the eternal light. Then at 49,22 Protennoia goes on to teach her children about the significance of the five seals, so that they too may put off their garment of ignorance and enter the light.

Yet, between 48,35 (or 49,6, since 49,1–5 is missing) and 49,22 there occurs the repetition of the camouflaged descent, which interrupts the ongoing train of thought. Moreover, the topic is here developed in a quite different way. The purpose of this interpolation seems to be to provide an aetiological explanation of certain common designations usually applied to Jesus by early Christianity. The point being scored is that such titles as Christ, Beloved, Son of God, Angel, and Son of man do not really belong to Jesus. They are conferred upon Jesus only because of a failure to recognize the true Redeemer. During his incognito descent, the Redeemer only clothed himself in such a way that the Archigenetor could see in him his son, but the angels could take him for an angel and the powers consider him one of their own. (He is the Beloved only for his brethren.) Humans too mistook him for a human because he wore a body of flesh.

It is at this point that the interpolation is resumed just before the end of the document. It reads: "I put on Jesus. I carried him away from the accursed wood and transplanted him into the dwelling places of his father" (50,12–15). This concluding interpolation obviously still belongs to the motif of descent. The deceptive maneuver worked. The Redeemer retained his camouflaged role right down to the cross. Only when he lets his true nature be known will the error be exposed, and the Archons as well as the ignorant humans, the non-Gnostics, will be put to shame. And that happens first at Easter! The Redeemer keeps his true nature secret until the ascension. The communication of *gnosis* takes place only after the resurrection and only by means of the Resurrected. Only then is ignorance removed and access to knowledge provided. This whole concept is common in Christian Gnosticism but is completely foreign to our text elsewhere.

At the same time, the orthodox concept of Jesus "sitting at the right hand of God" seems to have been corrected in terms of the Sethian view, namely: After the resurrection Jesus neither sits at the right hand of the biblical God, Yaldabaoth, nor at the right hand of the highest unknown God, but rather at the right hand of his own father Seth in his light Oroiael where he belongs! Incidentally, to explain the plural form "dwelling places" one does not need to appeal to John 14:2. Rather it can be explained quite naturally on the basis of the plurality of the aeons of light.

Actually, neither part of this interpolation seems to be developed in view of a specific New Testament text. Rather, the imprecise allusions to titles indicate that one has to do with orally circulating tradition. In any case, it is not possible to assume with John Turner[23] that "these polemical Sethian reinterpretations of 'orthodox' Christology seemed to depend on key texts from the Gospel of John." This is especially obvious when one notes that "in their tents" and "the likeness of their shape," Turner's points of comparison to John 1:14 as his main "key text," are as a matter of fact not in the interpolation at all! There is much the same problem with the supposed reference to the other "key text," John 14:2–3: "Dwelling places" does occur in the interpolation, but also outside of it, as the catchword leading to the interpolation at this point.

Incidentally, Turner's whole assessment is based, furthermore, on a serious misunderstanding of the text. He takes the expression "in their tents" (47,15) to be a "gloss" on "likeness of their shape" (47,16). Yet one reference ends one paragraph summarizing the goals of each of the Redeemer's three descents; the other reference begins another paragraph describing the unrecognized descent through the archontic spheres. And the word "their" refers in the first case to humans ("in their tents") but in the second case to powers ("likeness of their shape"). Therefore obviously "likeness of their shape" has nothing to do with John 1:14, whereas "in their tents" may well be parallel to, but is not dependent on, John 1:14; and in any case neither is part of the interpolation.

Regarding the whole double interpolation, one may conclude that it might have originally been an independent fragment of tradition, which in the process of the Christianizing of Gnosticism found its way into our text and thus effected an overlaying of diverging strands of tradition.

3. The Relation of *The Trimorphic Protennoia* to the Johannine Prologue

The most frequently debated and most sharply contested of the Berlin theses has to do with the scholarly value of *Trimorphic Protennoia* for critical New Testament scholarship, especially with regard to the Fourth Gospel. For even if *Trimorphic Protennoia*, in the form in which we have it, is no doubt younger than the Fourth Gospel, it nonetheless provides the natural context for the Fourth Gospel's Prologue. For it is not the last, extant copy of *Trimorphic Protennoia* with its redactional interpolations that is important, but rather its basic substance, which is no doubt pre-Christian, if not perhaps in a chronological sense, at least in terms of the history of tradition.

In the meantime other scholars also have seen the striking parallelism of the two documents, and individual parallels to every verse of the hymn quoted in the Prologue have been tabulated. Craig Evans[24] observes, on the basis of his tabulation of parallels, "(1) *Protennoia* opens, proceeds and closes with the same vocabulary and the same world of thought. . . . Virtually all of the vocabulary items of the Prologue are to be found in *Protennoia*, but the reverse

---

23 "Sethian Gnosticism," 65.
24 "Prologue," 398.

cannot be said. (2) The Fourth Gospel does not maintain the same lofty plane as its Prologue. It is as though the evangelist approaches, but never reaches, the sublime level of the Prologue. In view of this . . . it is possible to understand the Prologue as drawing from the [same] milieu which produced *Protennoia* (though not [from] *Protennoia* itself)."

In comparing the many scattered parallels to the Prologue that previous scholarship had found in wisdom literature with those that he located in *Trimorphic Protennoia*, Carsten Colpe[25] affirms, "But what is disparate there [in wisdom literature] is found together here [in *Trimorphic Protennoia*], even though not in the sequence of the Prologue. This may well be unique. . . ." With obvious relief he goes on to ask, "In order to find points of reference for the creation of the theology of the Prologue of John, does one in the future no longer need, as in the past, to sift through the very diffuse sapiential streams of the First Century CE in the Mediterranean area? Rather, are such points of reference now to be expected more precisely in that sapiential speculation that was to become one basis among others for Sethian mythology?"

In order to define more clearly "that sapiential speculation" to which Colpe calls attention as the background of the Prologue, we return to the question that MacRae put before us so inescapably. The statements and thought patterns of the hymn worked into the Prologue are generally agreed to be derived from Jewish-Hellenistic Wisdom speculation. But do we, in the hymn, already have to do with a gnostic modification of Jewish Wisdom speculation? And could one not then after all infer from the uniqueness of the parallelism of our Sethian text to the Logos hymn that this modification owes its specific form to the Sethian variant of Gnosticism?

In order to answer these questions we should look a bit more closely at the two texts themselves. Both times the revealer is not only a "messenger" or "mouth of Wisdom," but rather is the figure Wisdom herself. In both texts the statements about Wisdom have already come into focus as myth. The Logos hymn has to do *first* with the divinity of the Logos, with his pre-existence, and with the creation of everything, which came into being through him. *Second*, it speaks of his entering into the human realm, though practically nobody recognized him. Only individuals perceive his message, and them he makes into children of God. *Third*, in order to bring the revelation finally to all persons, he himself becomes human, though retaining all his glory.

We also find this striking sequence of three phases in *Trimorphic Protennoia*, distributed in three discourses, and again, in compressed form, reflected within the third discourse itself (47,4–15). As gnostically modified Lady Wisdom, and again in her appearance in the Son as Logos, Protennoia, like the Logos in the Prologue, reveals *first* her pre-existence with the Father and her all-encompassing creative activity (e.g., 35,1–32; 46,5–8; 47,9–10). *Second*, she comes to the world to bring knowledge to humans (e.g., 36,10–16; 42,11–17). Persons who perceive her call only then belong, she says, to the "children

25 "Heidnische, jüdische und christliche Überlieferung," 122, 124.

of light whose father I am" (40,36–41,2). Thus she, like the Logos in the Prologue, makes people into children of God, and again precisely only those who "accept" this gift (e.g., 47,12–13). Then, *third*, she undertakes the decisive descent to redeem all her "brethren" (e.g., 47,13–32).

This three-layeredness, shared by *Trimorphic Protennoia* and the Prologue, seems to be natural in Sethian texts but not in the New Testament. James Robinson[26] inferred from this that "the traces in the Prologue of John of periodizing, namely the Logos being in the primordial period, in the pre-Christian 'spermatic' period, and in the incarnate period, would then become intelligible as the way in which that non-Christian tradition was adapted and unified in Christ."

In the schematism of the revelation there is another remarkable agreement: In both texts the Redeemer is both the primal revealer and also the mediator of the continuous revelation. Furthermore, in both documents he is here described as light. In the Prologue the Logos reveals the creation, and also reveals himself in a primal way by lighting up the darkness. In *Trimorphic Protennoia* the primal revelation also takes place through the Logos. He alone knows the highest God and can make him known; and he alone reveals the creation; luminously shining, he reveals himself (37,3–20). He is the "Logos . . . who was sent to illuminate those who dwell in the darkness" (46,30–33). Thus here as in the Prologue the revealer is the light of the world, the cosmic light (36,4–7; 47,28–29), and the light of spiritual illumination (36,7–14; 47,30–31).

In the Prologue, the continuous revelation that follows the primal revelation is expressed by the well-known topic of Wisdom wandering through the world but initially finding no acceptance and dwelling only in individuals— until the incarnation finally takes place. This schematism of revelation taking place repeatedly in the course of history is a common theme of Gnosticism and is especially constitutive for Sethianism with its distinctive speculation about epochs of history (the epoch of Seth, the epoch of the primal Sethians, and the epoch of the contemporary Sethians). The special form of a three-fold descent is merely a particular concretion of this idea of continuous revelation. According to Hans-Martin Schenke[27] this "doubleness of the redemptive activity of the Logos in the primal revelation and the continuous revelation, in connection with the break in the world view marked by the conception of σκοτία ["darkness"] (vs 5)," shows that the Logos hymn of the Prologue is already Gnostic.

A further oddity and gnostic proclivity also seems to shine through vs 14, although it is precisely this verse with its phenomenon of incarnation that has always been regarded as the most orthodoxly Christian of all the formulations. Yet the beholding of the *doxa* of the incarnate has always been sensed as perplexing. For the *doxa* of the Monogenes ("only begotten") is often regarded

---

26 "Sethians and Johannine Thought," 662.
27 "Gnostischer Erlöser," 226.

as referring to his deity, whereas his fleshly body would only be a transparency through which his deity shines. But this implies a dangerous proximity to Gnosticism. In the body of the Fourth Gospel, the Evangelist is concerned to remove the *doxa* from the miracle stories of the public ministry, as he found them in his *semeia* source, and limit the *doxa* to Jesus being lifted up to cross and exaltation, a very different interest from that of the Prologue.

In the case of the Logos in *Trimorphic Protennoia*, the incarnation seems logically to be the last stage in the schematism of the Redeemer's descent, in the course of which he "bore the clothing of all of them," i.e., the archontic powers, until he "revealed himself among them [the humans] in their tents" (47,14–35). Unfortunately the missing first five lines of the following page of the codex deprive us in all probability of the exact description of this last stage. In any case it is certain that the last statement of p. 47, which can be restored on lines 34–35, and the sentence 48,11–12 are the extreme limits of the text expressing the idea of the saving change of clothing within the metaphorical narration of the garment changes. On the basis of these surviving framing statements one may assume that the missing intervening material (except for the extant baptismal intrusion 48,5–11) contained the following gist: "I came and removed my living garment and the divine light. And I put on dark chaos and the transient body of flesh and thus saved mankind caught in darkness." The extant fragments and the context in any case suggest this train of thought,[28] for obviously Protennoia put on a garment of chaos precisely like the one that she had stripped off the prototypical Gnostic during baptism. Then she gave him her garment of light (48,5–14). Thus the text shows clearly enough that this equivalent to incarnation is not necessarily "orthodox" but, as part of the whole topic of the change of garments, was naturally integrated into the gnostic mythology. On the other hand, it is quite conceivable that the Logos hymn, in its condensed linguistic form, had summarized this last stage into "the Logos became flesh." From the allegorical interpretation of the Logos hymn as referring to Jesus there must have resulted of necessity a kind of docetism, an outcome that incidentally we can observe elsewhere in the New Testament, where the gnostic redeemer concept was applied to Jesus.[29]

There is to be found in connection with the camouflaged-descent schematism a further, surprising correspondence to the Prologue. In vs 10 it is said that the Logos has been in the "cosmos" that came into being through him but did not recognize him—until he came to "his own." Usually one translates "cosmos" merely "world," but the parallel in *Trimorphic Protennoia* shows that what is here intended is perhaps not yet the world of humans. (The same may also be true of the ambivalent conception of "darkness" in vs 5.) For 47,15–28 reads: "I [the Logos] showed myself [to the archontic powers] in the likeness of their shape. . . . And none of them recognized me, although it is I

28 For the philological analysis, see G. Schenke, *Dreigestaltige Protennoia*, 46–47, 151–53. The interpretation of *Trimorphic Protennoia* in this essay of course presupposes in each instance my own reconstruction of the text in that edition.
29 See H.-M. Schenke, "Gnostischer Erlöser," 205–29.

who work in them; for they thought that the All had been created by them, because they are ignorant . . . I concealed myself among them until I revealed myself to my brethren."[30] This may illustrate what is meant by the Berlin thesis that "the two texts interpret each other mutually, whereby however . . . the light falls more from Protennoia upon the Prologue of John than the reverse."[31]

Vs 18 of the Prologue is also interesting for our comparison. The formulation $\mu o \nu o \gamma \epsilon \nu \dot{\eta} s$ $\theta \epsilon \dot{o} s$ ("only begotten god") has been sensed as difficult by textual critics all along. Finally Bodmer Papyri P 66 and P 75 have forced its acceptance into the Greek text, though it still has not made its way into the RSV and many other translations. But in *Trimorphic Protennoia* the odd expression seems to be at home; for in the description of the divine Son of the Sethian triad, Autogenes, there is a Coptic expression that almost seems to translate $\mu o \nu o \gamma \epsilon \nu \dot{\eta} s$, which is then followed by a relative clause for God, thus producing the exact Coptic equivalent to $\mu o \nu o \gamma \epsilon \nu \dot{\eta} s$ $\theta \epsilon \dot{o} s$. Bentley Layton[32] translates the passage: "the deity, the only begotten," and at two other places he translates an abbreviated formulation "the begotten deity." Since Autogenes and Monogenes are names readily used for a deity in Sethian texts, it seems not at all surprising that one or both apparently modified $\theta \epsilon \dot{o} s$ in the Greek original. But in the New Testament $\mu o \nu o \gamma \epsilon \nu \dot{\eta} s$ $\theta \epsilon \dot{o} s$ occurs only here and does not fit when applied to Jesus nearly so well as the common combination with $\upsilon \dot{i} \dot{o} s$ ("Son"). This could suggest that the expression in the Prologue is also to be explained as due to the material found in the gnostic source.

Another parallel suggests still further inferences. The attempt is not new to understand at least the third part of the Prologue (beginning with vs 14), with its transition from "he" to "we," as the confession-like praise of those being baptized. They would be bringing to expression their baptismal experience in the phrases "we have seen" the glory and "we have received" grace. Now we find the same situation in *Trimorphic Protennoia*. First there is an acclamation of the Gnostics in the third person, which corresponds to seeing the *doxa*: "An incomprehensible mystery is he. . . . He is light that dwells in the light" (36,28–33). Thereupon there follows in the first-person plural the confession: "We alone are those whom thou hast redeemed from the visible world, in that we have been saved" (36,33–37,1). This emphatic statement of redemption is just about what one should most probably understand under the expression to receive "grace for grace" in the Prologue (vs 16). Such a liturgical reflection does indeed have its *Sitz im Leben* in the baptismal mystery of Sethians. This is shown by the statement that immediately follows: "And the [man] hidden in us pays taxes with his fruit to the water of life" (37,1–3). Here there comes to expression ultimately a version of gnostic ethics, according to which, as a result of baptism, good works must follow.

30 Janssens also saw this parallel to vs 10, without however drawing any inference from it. See "Une source gnostique," 356.
31 G. Schenke, "Protennoia," 733.
32 *The Gnostic Scriptures*, 92.

Seen in this light, it may after all not have been completely erroneous to seek the *Sitz im Leben* of the Logos hymn in the baptismal sacrament, even if the path via the Mandaean baptismal sect turned out to be a dead-end street. For the intention and the insight lying behind that conjecture apparently pointed in the right direction, as has become increasingly clear on the basis of texts that are accessible to us but were not at that time accessible to those who drew attention to the Mandaean texts. Thus the question as to the *Sitz im Leben* of the Prologue is to be posed anew and is to be answered somewhat differently, in view of the parallelism with *Trimorphic Protennoia*. For it cannot be irrelevant that all the parallels are to be found in a Sethian text. We have already mentioned what a significant roll precisely baptism plays in Sethianism; so is it appropriate to locate the history-of-religions background of the Prologue in this Sethian baptismal movement? The whole congregational hymn, which is what the Prologue is usually taken to be, could quite well have been at home originally in the baptismal cult, borne by a community to whose spiritual superstructure belonged the gnostic Wisdom myth. The interpolations relative to John the Baptist could indeed suggest a corrective aimed at just such circles: Wisdom has now finally found her true believing community. Not just any baptism, but that in the name of Christ, is what grants grace for grace. It is on this soteriological relevance that a Gospel could be built!

Let us then in conclusion seek to assess the situation in which we find ourselves, once we have recognized that the most striking parallels to the Prologue are clustered in a Sethian gnostic text. Regarding the history-of-religions background, it has of course been uncontested that the Prologue, in its cosmological and salvation-historical speculations, is dependent on pre-Christian traditions that ultimately go back to Genesis. Most would also insist that this was mediated through Hellenistic-Jewish Wisdom or Logos speculation. But it should be also clear, especially in view of the Nag Hammadi texts, that neither of these roots precludes a gnostic orientation, in that Gnosticism itself appealed to Genesis and built on Wisdom speculation. On the fast-moving field of late antiquity, Wisdom speculation and gnostic myth influenced and accelerated each other mutually. The particular form of this speculation that is closest to the Prologue is the Sethian *Trimorphic Protennoia*, which has soaked up the Wisdom speculations of its environment and integrated them into its gnostic myth. As we have seen in the case of a few examples, all the statements of *Trimorphic Protennoia* are integrated so organically into the Sethian myth that it would hardly be possible to interpret them in a Christian way and derive them from the Fourth Gospel. The Prologue, on the other hand, is not explicable on the basis of the rest of the Fourth Gospel. Thus since *Trimorphic Protennoia* is the best-attested matrix for the Logos hymn, the most obvious conclusion would seem to be that the Prologue derives from a Wisdom tradition that has already passed through this gnostic filter.

Nag Hammadi,
Odes of Solomon, and
NT Christological Hymns

Jack T. Sanders

0. Introduction

Scholars have discussed the origin of Gnosticism (*Gnosis*) and its relation to Christianity for so long and so intensively that one would expect that the issue would have been decided before now, but that is hardly the case. While James Robinson is convinced that the *Trimorphic Protennoia* proves the existence of a pre-Christian gnostic redeemer myth,[1] and that he can trace various trajectories from pre-Christian and from Christian motifs through the New Testament into Gnosticism and into orthodoxy,[2] and while he emphasizes agreement with Carsten Colpe on the matter of the pre-Christian redeemer myth,[3] others (Pheme Perkins,[4] Bentley Layton[5]) continue to regard Gnosticism as a Christian heresy. Perkins even speaks of adoption of language from the Johannine prologue in the *Trimorphic Protennoia*. Hans-Martin Schenke, who also considers Gnosticism to have been originally pre-Christian, prefers to speak of multiple manifestations, of a tree-like development of different branches from a common trunk, rather than of a trajectory.[6] At the same time, however, he now even refers to *multiple origins* for Gnosticism.[7] Schenke also appeals to Colpe for this latter view, although Colpe's point seems to have been rather a different one, namely that different elements of Gnosticism came from different sources.[8] The theory of a variety of sources is, further, emphat-

---

1 J. M. Robinson, "Gnosticism and the New Testament," 128–31; "Sethians and Johannine Thought."
2 J. M. Robinson, "Jesus—From Easter to Valentinus."
3 Cf. n. 1, above.
4 Perkins, "Logos Christologies," 382; but she accepts Judaism as the ultimate origin.
5 Layton, *The Gnostic Scriptures*, 5–21, esp. 8; cf. his commentary on *Trimorphic Protennoia* 36 (*The Gnostic Scriptures*, 90), where he finds the author working with a Platonic model, an earlier form of which can be found in the Johannine prologue.
6 H.-M. Schenke, "Problem of Gnosis," 85.
7 H.-M. Schenke, "Problem of Gnosis," 80.
8 Colpe, "Gnosis, I: Religionsgeschichtlich," 1651. In Colpe's more recent discussion of the *Trimorphic Protennoia* and its relation to the Johannine prologue, he has suggested that the background of the prologue should be narrowed from "very diffuse wisdom

ically that of Kurt Rudolph.[9] Perhaps that is what Schenke also means, but if so his tree metaphor is not accurate. The position of Bentley Layton, who finds a variety of origins for Valentinianism (Sethian Gnosticism, Syrian Thomas mysticism, and other traditions as well) may be compared to Colpe's understanding of gnostic origins.[10] Still others insist on the Jewish origin of Gnosticism (George MacRae,[11] Birger Pearson;[12] to a great degree also Rudolph[13]), although such a view also considers Gnosticism to have been originally pre-Christian.

What separates all these positions is not evidence but theory. We are all working with the same evidence—New Testament, Coptic gnostic library, Dead Sea Scrolls, Jewish wisdom literature, Hermetic corpus, etc.—so that it is not different evidence that separates these several explanations of the relation of Gnosticism to Christianity, but rather the way of understanding the relationships of one body of literature to another. Since the issue is one of development, we may say that we are dealing with different evolutionary theories—that is to say, with different *models* of the evolution of early Gnosticism and Christianity. James Robinson's model is that of the trajectory, along the path of which different moments may be plotted in the evolutionary progression; and those who emphasize the Jewish origin more or less follow this model, as well. Colpe's model of gnostic evolution and Layton's of Valentinian is that of a river system: a variety of tributaries that flow together finally, not necessarily all at once, into the main stream. Schenke thinks of a tree with different branches (the opposite, therefore, of the river system).

What I propose to do in this essay is to examine somewhat in detail one aspect of the issue of the relation of early Gnosticism to early Christianity, namely the myth of the redeemer that appears in the New Testament christological hymns, in order to bring the most relevant evidence on that subject into view. Then I should like to turn to a brief discussion of current evolutionary theory, because I believe that it can show those of us who try to analyze the development of ideas and societies a few things about the nature of evolution that may be of help. This discussion will show that one of the models already mentioned as a way of explaining the relation of early Gnosticism to early Christianity, while it may be rather less than apt for that function, is in fact highly appropriate as a way of understanding how the myth of the redeemer/revealer developed.

currents of the first century BCE in the eastern Mediterranean region" to "that wisdom speculation . . . that was to become one of the numerous bases for Sethian mythology" ("Heidnische, jüdische und christliche Überlieferung," 124).

9 *Gnosis*, 275–91.
10 Layton, *The Gnostic Scriptures*, xvi.
11 MacRae, "Jewish Background."
12 Pearson, "Jewish Sources in Gnostic Literature."
13 Cf. n. 9.

1. The Evidence

Elsewhere in this volume appears an essay by Gesine Robinson that reviews her earlier study of the *Trimorphic Protennoia* and discusses recent developments in the analysis of that document. That essay makes it clear that the Nag Hammadi literature, and the *Trimorphic Protennoia* in particular, is of prime importance for an adequate understanding of the christological expressions in the Johannine prologue, whichever way one thinks the development went. Yet, under no circumstances can the *Trimorphic Protennoia* have been influenced directly by the Johannine prologue. The analyses of the *Berliner Arbeitskreis,* especially of Gesine Robinson, and of Carsten Colpe leave no doubt that there is no direct influence in that direction. Their evidence will not be repeated here.[14] The statement of James Robinson on this subject is pure reason. Robinson said in the discussion following his paper at the Sethian conference in 1978, regarding the relation of the *Trimorphic Protennoia* to the Johannine prologue,

> I cannot conceive of someone distributing a hymnic description of a single personage, the Logos, among the three personages of a triad, the last of which is called "Logos." To hold such a position is to imply the pre-Jonas view of Gnostics as senseless people who would do anything. But it is historically intelligible to see the author of the prologue focusing the different concepts of a mythological thought world into the one Christ, just as the evangelist has ascribed "way," "light," "door," etc., solely to Jesus.[15]

I do not see how anyone can compare the two documents under question and come to any other conclusion. But then I do not see how anyone can see that the Kaibab Limestone (at the Grand Canyon, in Arizona), with all its fossilized clam shells, lies above the Coconino Sandstone and come to any other conclusion than that an ancient ocean once covered a still more ancient sand desert, all of which has turned to rock and has now risen to some 4000–8000 feet above sea level. However we are going to understand what came earlier and what came later in this discussion, we have to take account of this: The Johannine prologue is not a direct source of the *Trimorphic Protennoia.*

We cannot, however, have an adequate body of evidence on which to base an evolutionary theory without taking into consideration other closely related documents. Philo remains relevant, and so do the Odes of Solomon. I do not propose to discuss Philo here, since the relation of his Logos, Son of God, and two Kosmoi to the Christian redeemer myth seems to have remained in consideration, albeit somewhat in the background; but the relevance of the Odes of Solomon—the Coptic gnostic library of the early part of this cen-

---

14 See G. Schenke, "Protennoia"; and *Dreigestaltige Protennoia;* Colpe, "Heidnische, jüdische und christliche Überlieferung."
15 "Sethians and Johannine Thought," 665.

tury—to the New Testament redeemer myth has almost dropped out of discussion. How shall we now view the Odes of Solomon, whose striking parallels to not only the prologue, but the rest of the Fourth Gospel as well Bultmann so effectively emphasized in his commentary?[16] Scholars seeking to understand the Fourth Gospel still recognize and note these parallels, but almost no one seems to know what to do with them.[17] Do the Odes of Solomon offer any information that is of significance for our evolutionary question, or does the *Trimorphic Protennoia* tell us everything that we want to know?

We may begin answering that question by recalling the many parallels between lines in the Odes of Solomon and the prologue of John's gospel.

John, RSV (adjusted)		*Odes of Solomon*[18]	
1:1	In the beginning was the Word.	16:18	He was before anything came to be.
1:3	All things were made through him,	12:8, 10	By him (i.e., ptgm' ["Word"], vs 5) the generations spoke to one another, and those that were silent acquired speech. . . . And they were stimulated by the *Word* (ptgm').
		16:19	The worlds are by his *Word* (bmlt').
	and without him was not anything made.	16:18	There is nothing outside of the Lord (because he was before anything came to be).
		32:2	. . . the *Word* (ptgm') from the truth who is self-originate . . .
1:3–4	What was made in him was life.	12:8, 10	The generations . . . were stimulated by the *Word* (ptgm').
1:4–5	The life was the light of people,[19] (and) the light shines in the darkness,	10:1–2	The Lord directed my mouth by his *Word* (bmlt'), and has opened my heart by his Light. And he has caused to dwell in me his immortal life.

16 Bultmann, *Das Evangelium des Johannes.*
17 H.-M. Schenke and Rudolph are notable exceptions to this generalization. Cf. Schenke, *Die Herkunft des sogenannten Evangelium Veritatis,* esp. 25–29; and, more recently, "Gnostische Erlöser," 226–27. Rudolph, *Gnosis,* routinely includes the Odes among gnostic literature; see his index. One may note esp. p. 122, where Rudolph sees the redeemed redeemer in the Odes. Cf. further Schenke and Fischer, *Einleitung,* 191. Cullmann, *Johannine Circle,* 36, makes a brief correct statement.
18 Charlesworth, "Odes of Solomon."
19 Ἄνθρωποι.

		41:14	Light dawned from the *Word* (mlt').
		12:3	The mouth of the Lord is the true *Word* (ptgm'), and the door of his light.
	and the darkness has not overcome it.	18:6	Let not light be conquered by darkness.
		21:3	I stripped off darkness and put on light.
1:9	He was the true light	36:3	She brought me forth before the Lord's face, and because I was the Son of Man,[20] I was named the Light, the Son of God.
	that enlightens every person.[21]	12:12	The dwelling place of the *Word* (ptgm') is *human kind* (br 'nš').
1:10	The world knew him not.	24:12	They were rejected, because the truth was not with them.
1:11	He came to his own,	7:12	He has allowed him to appear to them that are his own; in order that they may recognize him that made them.
		41:11	His *word* (mlt') is with us in all our way.
	and his own received him not.	8:12	I turn not my face from my own, because I know them.
1:12	He gave them power to become children of God.	12:13	Blessed are they who by means of him (ptgm', vs 12) have recognized everything.
		42:4	I will be with those who love me.

Clearly the evidence of all these parallels between statements in the Odes of Solomon and the prologue of the Fourth Gospel is that there is some relation between the two, but what relation? We may note the conclusion of a scholar who has given a major portion of his career to the understanding of this puzzling little collection: "The Odes share with the Gospel of John many striking and significant parallels, but specialists on the Odes have cautioned against assuming that the Odes are dependent on John and have urged con-

20 Or: Because I was a human (brnš').
21 Ἄνθρωπος.

56 • Jack T. Sanders

sideration of a shared community."[22] Thus James Charlesworth, while considering the Odes of Solomon to be of Christian provenance, judges that they and the Gospel of John represent parallel developments, and that one is not dependent on the other. The Odes of Solomon might in fact readily be taken to be no more Christian than the *Trimorphic Protennoia*. One might recall, for example, that the name "Jesus" does not occur in the Odes of Solomon, whereas it does in the *Trimorphic Protennoia* (NHC XIII, *1:* 50, 12). Both could be equally pre-Christian complexes that have been Christianized; but it is not necessary to debate that point for our purposes here. As far as the present discussion is concerned, we need only agree with Charlesworth that the Odes of Solomon, while Christian in their present form and containing many and striking parallels with the Johannine prologue, give evidence of parallel development and are not dependent on the Gospel of John. The discussion that follows will also illustrate one aspect of the evidence leading to that conclusion.

Here we need to recall an unusual feature of the parallels between the Odes and the prologue that Charlesworth and I both noted—independently—in the 1960's (although Charlesworth, who continues to note this unusual feature, has never attempted an explanation of it),[23] and that is that, while there are many things said about the Word in the Odes of Solomon that are like or highly similar to what is said about the Word in the prologue of John's Gospel, there is no direct analogy, because the Odes of Solomon use two words for the divine Word, *ml'*,[24] emphatic *mlt'*, a feminine noun, and *ptgm*, emphatic *ptgm'*, a masculine. The occurrences of the two words are as follows.

Mlt'

10:1 The Lord has directed my mouth *by his Word* (bmlth).
12:8 By him (ptgm') the generations spoke to one another, and *those* that were silent *acquired speech* (hww bmlt' hnwn).
15:9 Sheol has been vanquished *by my word* (bmlty).
16:7 For . . . the strength of his word.
16:8 The Word of the Lord investigates that which is invisible, and perceives his thought.
16:14 The hosts are subject to his Word.
16:19 The worlds are *by his Word* (bmlth).
29:9 To make war *by his Word* (bmlth).
29:10 The Lord overthrew my enemy *by his Word* (bmlth).
39:9 The Lord has bridged them *by his Word* (bmlth).
41:11 His Word is with us in all our way.
41:14 Light dawned from the Word.

22 Charlesworth, "Odes of Solomon," 732.
23 Cf. Charlesworth, "Qumran, John and Odes of Solomon," 124–25: The presence of the two words for Word in the Odes "has not received the attention it deserves; it reduces the possibility that the Odes are dependent on John."
24 I am employing Lattke's consonantal transliteration system. Cf. *Die Oden Salomos.*

Ptgm'

7:7   The Father of knowledge is the Word of knowledge.

8:8   Hear the word of truth.

9:3   The word of the Lord and his desires.

12:3   He has caused his knowledge to abound in me, because the mouth of the Lord is the true word, and the door of his light.

12:5   The subtlety of the Word is inexpressible, and like his expression so also is his swiftness and his acuteness.

12:10 They [the generations, vs 8] were stimulated by the Word.

12:12 The dwelling place of the Word is man.

12:13 Blessed are they who by means of him [ptgm', vs 12] have recognized everything.

18:4   O Lord, . . . do not expel your word from me.

24:9   All of them who were lacking perished, because they were not able to express the word so that they might remain.

32:2   The Word from the truth, who is self-originate.[25]

37:3   His Word came toward me.

42:14 I spoke with them by living lips, in order that my word may not fail.

We have here two distinct entities. The *mlt'* is usually an instrument of God's action (note the frequency of the phrase *bmlth*) and thus falls into the line of feminine hypostases in Judaism, headed by Wisdom, who are preexistent with God and who assist him at creation and in the further carrying out of his will. The *mlt'* is demiurge (OdesSol 16:19), revealer (OdesSol 41:14), and savior (OdesSol 15:9; 29:10).

The *ptgm'*, however, the masculine word for Word, is a rather different character. Whereas *mlt'*, for example, is never associated with truth and knowledge, *ptgm'* regularly is and seems indeed to be equated with Truth. When the *ptgm'* emanates from Truth, it emanates from itself (OdesSol 32:2), and OdesSol 12:3 refers to the "true *ptgm'*." OdesSol 7:7, furthermore, equates the Father with the *ptgm'*. Such lofty statements are never made in the Odes of Solomon regarding the *mlt'*. OdesSol 12:5 refers to the swiftness of the *ptgm'*, and when 37:3 says that the *ptgm'* "came toward me," i.e., toward the odist, we see that there seems to exist for the writer or writers of the Odes of Solomon an understanding of the *ptgm'* as an entity capable of having a more direct or personal relation with the individual worshipper than is the case with the *mlt'*. It appears that the *ptgm'* bridges the gap between divine and human in a way that the *mlt'* does not, being equated with the divine, on the one hand (OdesSol 7:7), and coming to and dwelling within human beings on the other (OdesSol 12:12). Such spiritual osmosis is, one will of course recall, one of the more marked features of the spirituality of the Odes of Solomon, inasmuch as the dividing line between odist and redeemer or lord regularly becomes permeable, leading editors frequently to insert "Christ speaks" or "The Odist

25 Literally: "And the Word is from the Truth, which (masc., therefore *ptgm'*, not *šrr'*) is from itself."

speaks" or something like that into an ode in order to alert the reader to a change in the identity of the singer.[26] In this connection we should note OdesSol 12:10, where we read that the worlds "were stimulated by the *ptgm'*, and knew him who made them." Thus here again, if we may think of the "worlds" as in some sense "persons"—using the term here not as a synonym for human but in the sense in which we may refer to the gnostic aeons as persons (and the word translated "worlds" here is *'lm'*, which might very well be translated "aeons")—we see the kind of personal contact with sentient created beings that the *ptgm'* is capable of having. This somewhat over-shadowing of the *mlt'* by the *ptgm'* is underscored by the one occasion in the Odes of Solomon on which the two words appear together (12:8). This occasion is the only occurrence of *mlt'* in the Odes where it is not an entity, a hypostasis; rather, the clause here means that "those who were silent acquired speech."

It is quite clear, then, that *ml'* and *ptgm* in the Odes of Solomon are discrete entities. While they overlap to a certain degree, they are not the same. One is a feminine hypostasis highly reminiscent of Wisdom in, say, the Wisdom of Solomon; the other, masculine, seems to possess a somewhat broader range of powers and to be rather more independent.

Thus one sees that the situation regarding the parallels between the Odes of Solomon and John's prologue is exactly analogous to that between the *Trimorphic Protennoia* and the prologue. In both comparator documents the parallels to the Johannine prologue are scattered throughout and occur in different contexts—that is, nowhere in the *Trimorphic Protennoia* or in the Odes of Solomon do we find the Johannine prologue more or less repeated; what we rather find is very close parallels to individual statements in the prologue, but in different contexts, in which contexts these statements occur in a way that reveals that their meaning and significance are at home. They are not foreign bodies in the Odes of Solomon—obvious quotations from the Gospel of John—but rather cohere in their contexts. Furthermore, in none of the three texts are *all* the statements that we are considering made about a or the word. (One may sometimes forget that the *Logos* is not the subject of every statement in the Johannine prologue.) Rather, sometimes a or the word is subject or agent, but sometimes the subject or agent is some other divine or cosmic being, such as light, or mother, or lord.

In their relation to the Johannine prologue, then, the *Trimorphic Protennoia* and the Odes of Solomon present us with a completely analogous situation. They are both—in their present forms—later than the Fourth Gospel (although the Odes of Solomon are not nearly as late as the *Trimorphic Protennoia*), and they are both either Christian or Christianized. Both also contain statements remarkably similar to statements made in the Johannine

26 Cf. Rudolph, *Gnosis,* 122.

prologue, but scattered around in different contexts. Thus with James Robinson's statement quoted above on the relevance of the *Trimorphic Protennoia* for understanding the Johannine prologue may be compared my earlier summary about the relation between the words of the Odes of Solomon and the word of the Johannine prologue:

> It would seem to be quite difficult to explain these separate hypostases [i.e., mlt' and ptgm'] as *outgrowths* of the Johannine *Logos*. Certainly no reason can be advanced why the *Logos* of John 1 would have been translated into two Words. Rather it would make more sense to suppose that both these traditions developed independently of the *Vorlage* of the prologue of John, and that the *Logos* of John 1 represents a more advanced stage of hypostatization, or perhaps rather an independent tradition.[27]

We are thus forced to recognize two facts: (1) that the Odes of Solomon belong, together with the *Trimorphic Protennoia*, in the context of the Johannine prologue but not dependent on it, and (2) that the provenance of all three has to be explained together. The Odes of Solomon and the *Trimorphic Protennoia* are kindred documents in that they help to show what sort of speculative thinking existed in the intellectual milieu out of which the prologue arose.[28] All three documents imply non-rabbinic speculative Judaism of the Roman period—probably of the Diaspora (I would say of the near Diaspora) as their common matrix. For the *Trimorphic Protennoia*, the evidence for that matrix is given by Gesine Robinson in her book, where she repeatedly shows that the *Protennoia* is "a modified form of the Jewish *Sophia*."[29] She

27 *New Testament Christological Hymns*, 118. Of this work Charlesworth writes ("Prolegomenon to a New Study of the Jewish Background," 278), "He appears uninformed about much of the Jewish data, is preoccupied with trying to prove the pre-Christian date of the so-called redeemer myth, and focuses upon only three works, the Odes of Solomon, the Gospel of Truth, and the Apocalypse of Adam." The first charge lacks sufficient precision, and the second is disproved by the quotation above. The third charge is meaningless, since, for anyone writing in 1963–65, when the manuscript was being prepared, those were the obvious works to focus on. Charlesworth elsewhere ("Odes of Solomon and Gospel of John," 318) quotes my statement that, with regard to the hypostatization of the divine Word, the Odes of Solomon are "logically prior" to the Gospel of John and concludes that I meant that the Odes were "earlier than John"; (cf. my *New Testament Christological Hymns*, 119). The reason for writing "logically prior," of course, was to contrast *logically* prior to *temporally* prior.

28 Here lies the mistake of Fiorenza, who thought that my earlier attempt to uncover the background of the New Testament christological hymns was a doomed quest for "essence." Of such folly, she wrote ("Wisdom Mythology," 26), "Linguistic philosophy has uncovered as mistaken such a craving for unity. Wittgenstein has shown that this desire for unity, the craving for essences, leads us into confusion." Having misrepresented my position, Fiorenza then declared that the New Testament christological hymns were the product of "a trajectory of 'reflective mythology'" that "borrowed primarily from the myth of Isis-Osiris though it could have also taken over elements from the myth of Tammuz-Adonis" ("Wisdom Mythology," 34). Was Wittgenstein forgotten in eight pages?

29 G. Schenke, *Dreigestaltige Protennoia*, 89; see also her essay elsewhere in this volume.

mentions such things as the *Protennoia's* dwelling in the Father and the manner in which the *Protennoia* is creatrix. For the Odes of Solomon, the most obvious line of connection with Judaism is the heavy reliance on the Psalms of the Jewish scripture. Charlesworth refers to numerous cases of such dependence; we might note as an example that the expression of the odist's endurance in the face of condemnation and defeat at the hands of enemies in OdesSol 31:8–13 draws on Psalm 22.[30] Further, of course, there is the sort of hypostatization that we have already noted that is so much like Wisdom speculation in the *Sophia* tradition. Interestingly, the word, "wisdom," appears in the Odes of Solomon only four times, and in only one of those instances do we possibly have to do with Lady Wisdom. That is OdesSol 7:8, "He who created Wisdom is wiser than his works." Other hypostases—*mlt', ptgm',* and *šrr'* ("truth")—have tended to displace Wisdom in this particular branch of the wisdom tradition. In the *Trimorphic Protennoia,* of course, Wisdom has completely disappeared into the *Protennoia.*

Very well, then; we have Jewish wisdom speculation behind our three documents.[31] Can that background be more narrowly defined, and can we say anything about evolutionary development that will make sense of all the evidence?

The Johannine prologue is now widely recognized as having been originally some kind of hymn, and the Odes of Solomon are certainly hymns of some sort—odes.[32] Does this not strongly imply that both arose out of some kind of wisdom movement in Judaism in which such original hymnic compositions played an important role in preserving and promoting the ideas of the movement—an ancient *Sophia Ṣufi* group, so to speak? I earlier proposed that wisdom groups using the thanksgiving psalm as a didactic device were to be seen as the matrix for both, but the thanksgiving-psalm hypothesis works much better for some other documents than it does for the Johannine prologue and the Odes of Solomon; nevertheless, we seem to have a hymnic background of some kind for the Johannine prologue and for the Odes of Solomon, located within Jewish Wisdom speculation. Yet the *Trimorphic Protennoia* is not hymnic ... except in one place. In *Trim. Prot.* 38, 22–29 we have this said of the Aeons: "They blessed the Perfect Son, the Christ, the God who came into being by himself. And they gave glory, saying, 'He is! He is! The Son of God! The Son of God! It is he who is! The Aeon of Aeons! He beholds the Aeons which he begot. For (it is) thou (who) hast begotten by

30 Charlesworth, "Odes of Solomon," 731.
31 Cf. Pearson, "Philo, Gnosis and the New Testament," 84, who prefers "speculative wisdom" to "Gnosis" for the stage of the development that we are discussing.
32 Cf. further to this point Blaszczak, *Formcritical Study of Selected Odes of Solomon,* 25. Further to the point are the numerous parallels, both material and stylistic, between the Odes and 1QH detailed by Charlesworth, "Les Odes de Salomon et les manuscrits de la Mer Morte," 540–48.

thine own desire! Therefore [we] glorify thee: ma mo o o o eia ei on ei![33] The [Aeon] of [Aeons! The] Aeon which he gave!'"[34]

Now, one may affirm not only that blessing and giving glory are likely synonyms for singing a hymn, but that the subsequent set of ascriptions of praise is in fact hymnic, that we therefore have here a gnostic hymn imbedded within the *Trimorphic Protennoia.* Gesine Robinson refers, in her discussion of this passage, to "heavenly acclamation" and asks "whether this laudation is not perhaps a mythological aetiology of a definite congregational prayer that the Gnostics themselves were accustomed to recite."[35] This reasonable proposal may perhaps be modified by changing "prayer" to "hymn" and "recite" to "chant." In support of that alteration I mention again the terms "bless" (cмоγ) and "give glory" († ñoγεooγ or † εooγ), as well as the presence of acclamations and the recitations of divine deeds. All these elements are recognized characteristics of hymns and point to the kind of prayer that is chanted— that is, to what we call a hymn. And do we not see in those nonsense syllables a further attestation of a hymnic origin for our selection, a sort of Coptic ee-i-ee-i-o, that reveals at one and the same time the necessity to retain a certain rhythm and melody *and* a foreign-language origin for at least part of our hymn—a foreign language likely not Greek, since our Nag Hammadi folk seem to have kept up with that language fairly well, but some other foreign language, perhaps Syriac? To come down from the heights of educated guessing to the common denominator, we may affirm this: When we find, in the ancient Mediterranean world, a text that presents itself as a strong candidate to be a close relative of the Johannine prologue, there we find hymn singing.

The Fourth Gospel is the oldest of our three works, and the prologue is surely older. It may have been sung with John the Baptist in mind before it was applied to Jesus. Yet neither the Odes of Solomon nor the *Trimorphic Protennoia* can be dependent on the Fourth Gospel, because of the way both break up (looked at from the Johannine perspective) the duties and attributes of the redeemer and distribute them among various figures, some masculine, some feminine. Of these two, the Odes of Solomon are the older, written in the early part of the second century CE[36] and therefore contemporary with or just a little later than the Fourth Gospel itself; but surely, in any case, later than the original of the Johannine prologue. Yet the Christianizing process has not proceeded sufficiently far in the community that produced the Odes of Solomon to destroy the diversity of revealer/redeemer beings. In that sense, we still see the pre-Christian setting in the Odes of Solomon. And here we need to note something quite revealing about early Syrian Christianity that we learn

---

33 ма̄ мω̄ ω̄ω̄ω̄ ε̄ῑа ε̄ῑ о̄ν ε̄ῑ. Layton, *The Gnostic Scriptures, ad loc.,* translates everything after ма̄ мω̄ as "You are omega, omega, omega! You are alpha! You are being!" This is not impossible, although I should have looked for ωn in place of on, and the problem of what to do with ма̄ мω̄ remains then unsolved.

34 ET by Turner, "Trimorphic Protennoia."

35 *Dreigestaltige Protennoia,* 115.

36 Cf. Charlesworth, "Odes of Solomon," 726–27.

from the later Syrian church; for the Peshitta translation of Λόγος ("Word") is *mlt'*, the feminine Word. That can only be explained if those early Syrians who became Christians already knew of a divine Word, the *mlt'*, who was feminine. The Odes of Solomon explain why Syrian Christians translated Λόγος as *mlt'*. Why the Peshitta does not use *ptgm'* I am unable to say, but *mlt'* obviously appeared the right choice to the translators—on conceptual, not gender grounds. Charlesworth, it is worth pausing to note, fails entirely to grasp this connection and so thinks that the Christian author of the Odes of Solomon sometimes used the "appropriate" word mlt' and sometimes the "inappropriate" word *ptgm'* for Λόγος.[37]

A century and a half or so later the *Trimorphic Protennoia* was written. Not at first under Christian influence, it gives evidence of influence from several traditions. Gnosticism was by nature eclectic, embracing truth where it found it. Thus, for example, whereas the *ptgm'* emanates out of itself in OdesSol 32:2, this motif looks rather more Egyptian in the *Trimorphic Protennoia*, where we read in 45,2–4 that the revealer is "androgynous" and that she/he "[copulate(s)] with [her/him]self," thereby apparently drawing on the old Atum myth. Furthermore, the hymnic setting of the concepts expressed has all but disappeared, remaining only as a relic. But the ideas and forms that we find in the Johannine prologue and in the Odes of Solomon are still present here. The ideas are not expressed in quite the same way, and the forms are all but gone, but we can still see that there is a relationship.

Now I should like briefly to extend the discussion from the Johannine prologue to the other New Testament christological hymns. The degree to which the *Trimorphic Protennoia* and the Odes of Solomon both attest parallels not only for the Johannine prologue, but for the other New Testament christological hymns as well is quite remarkable. We may note first the hymn in Col 1:15–20 as an example. Gesine Robinson points out that the opening of the *Trimorphic Protennoia*, "[I] am the movement that dwells in the [All, she in whom the] All takes its stand, [the first]-born among those who [came to be, she who exists] before the All," recalls Col 1:15–17, where we have the redeemer as first-born and as pantocrator.[38] Further, the dual aspect of being both primal principle/source and active creative force, found in the *Trimorphic Protennoia* in the above text and in the closely following remarks about how the *Protennoia* "shone down [upon the darkness], . . . poured forth the [Water]," and "gradually dawns on the All" (36,6–8), is essentially the same dual aspect that one finds in the Colossians hymn, where the redeemer both creates all things (Col 1:16) and holds them together (vs 17).[39]

Similarly for the Odes of Solomon: That the redeemer was "before all things, and all things cohere in him" (Col 1:17) finds its counterpart in OdesSol 16:18: "There is nothing outside of the Lord, because he was before anything came to be," cf. also OdesSol 41:15: "The Messiah in truth is one,

37 Charlesworth, "Odes of Solomon," 728.
38 *Dreigestaltige Protennoia*, 90–91.
39 *Dreigestaltige Protennoia*, 99.

and he was known *before the foundations of the world*" (*mn qdm trmyth d'lm'*). The redeemer as "head of the body" (Col 1:18) appears in OdesSol 17:16: "They became my members, and I was their head"; and the two concepts— having all cohere in him and being the head of all—come together also in OdesSol 23:18–19, where the image of the letter sent from the Lord is used: "There appeared at its [sc. the letter's] head, the Head which was revealed, . . . and he inherited and possessed everything."

If one will grant that Col 1:12–14 reflects the original thanksgiving introit of the hymn,[40] then a further parallel from the Colossians hymn may be found in the Odes of Solomon, namely the notion of salvation from darkness to light. Thus "The Father," according to Col 1:13, "has rescued us from the power of darkness"; and OdesSol 10:6 affirms that "traces of light were set upon their heart, and they walked according to my life and *were saved*" (*'tprqw*).[41] Such light-darkness imagery is, to be sure, general and widespread; it is only in the context of the other parallels between the Colossians hymn and the Odes of Solomon that it attains some significance.

The New Testament christological hymn, however, that finds the greatest similarity of phrasing and imagery in the Odes of Solomon—aside from the prologue of the Fourth Gospel—is the one in 1 Pet 1:20; 3:18–22. The agreements are extensive enough that they may best be viewed, as with the Johannine prologue, in tables:

1 Peter, RSV		*Odes of Solomon*[42]	
1:20	Christ was destined before the foundation of the world,	41:15	The Messiah . . . was known before the foundations of the world.
		4:14	All . . . was set in order from the beginning before you.
	was made manifest at the end of the times for your sake.	4:12, 14	The end was manifest to you. . . . All was manifest to you as God, and was set in order.
3:18	Made alive in the spirit,	28:8	From that [sc. life, vs 7] is the Spirit which is within me, and it cannot die because it is life.
3:19	[Christ] preached to the spirits in prison.	17:12	I went toward all my bondsmen in order to loose them.
3:22	With angels, authorities, and powers subject to him.	16:14	The hosts are subject to his word.

40 So J. M. Robinson, "Hodajot-Formel," 231–32; Sanders, *New Testament Christological Hymns*, 3–4. I still think that this is correct, but most interpreters of the Colossians hymn have rejected the connection.

41 It is worth noting that the Peshitta translation for ὃς ἐρρύσατο ἡμᾶς ("who rescued us") is prqn.

42 Charlesworth, "Odes of Solomon."

Here, as in the case of the prologue of John's Gospel, we have extensive parallels with concepts and vocabulary in the Odes of Solomon; and again, as there, the statements in the Odes of Solomon that are so close to those of the New Testament hymn appear widely scattered and in different contexts, where they are at home and fit well in their own settings. One could hardly conclude that the author(s) of the Odes had dismantled 1 Pet 3:18–22 and scattered so many of the statements from that fragment around in the Odes of Solomon in often different contexts. One could readily conclude, however, that both the hymn of 1 Pet 1:20; 3:18–22 and the Odes of Solomon go back to a common setting where such language was used when singing of a redeemer.

2. Two Evolutionary Models

We are thus able to affirm two things—that the New Testament christo-logical hymns, the *Trimorphic Protennoia,* and the Odes of Solomon are somehow interrelated *and* that the New Testament christological hymns are not a direct source for the other two. All seem to go back in some way or other to some strain of Jewish wisdom speculation in which hymns were employed didactically. It is at this point of attempting to conceptualize developmental relationships that I think that some aspects of evolutionary theory may be helpful. To be sure, the notion of progress that is often mistakenly associated with evolution is not a part of our consideration; nor should we think that, just because we employ an evolutionary model or two to aid us in our analysis, we are required to view the entire complex of phenomena that we are considering as wholly to be explained by evolutionary theory. Such a notion would lead us into such absurdities as thinking that we could determine the direction of intellectual development, given sufficient details about the intellectual and physical environment. I do not, therefore, wish to propose some new form of "social Darwinism," but rather only that we examine certain models of development that are a part of current evolutionary theory. The models that I have in mind are those of allopatric speciation and of the bush.

Allopatric speciation (which means the production of a new species in a different place—that is, not in the primary habitat) is the theory utilized by Stephen J. Gould and Niles Eldredge to explain punctuated equilibria, i.e., the fact that the fossil record reveals static life forms over a period of time and then apparently sudden and immediate emergence of thriving new life forms.[43] Thus we never see the origin of a species. Such origin, according to the theory of allopatric speciation, takes place in areas peripheral to the

---

43 Allopatric speciation was first explained by Mayr, *Systematics and the Origin of Species.* The original statement of the theory of punctuated equilibria was by Eldredge and Gould, "Punctuated Equilibria"; and the theory was cemented in the succeeding debate in Hecht, Eldredge, and Gould, "Morphological Transformation, the Fossil Record, and the Mechanisms of Evolution." (Hecht argues against Eldredge and Gould.) There is also a very good statement of the position in Eldredge and Cracraft, *Phylogenetic Patterns and the Evolutionary Process;* cf. further a good popular explanation in Gould, *Ever Since Darwin,* 61–62.

primary habitat of the species, where marginal existence forces relatively rapid adaptation among a small minority of the population. The species produced by such adaptation then proliferates and leaves its own fossil record. Most religion scholars understand this principle, and there is no need to belabor it. It is unlikely that we will ever find the "original"—not the original account of the resurrection, not the *ipsissima vox Jesu*, not the original account of the gnostic redeemer myth, not the original early Christian christological hymn. When we encounter these "species" in literature they have already proliferated. It is not *impossible* that someone will someday discover the original version of the gnostic redeemer myth, just as it is not *impossible* that a dig in the Olduvai Gorge will someday produce the first *Australopithecus,* but the odds are against both. We can see that there was an origin somewhere; and perhaps, in the case of the gnostic redeemer myth, we can be pretty sure that it lies in Jewish wisdom speculation. But the precise origin of the movement toward the New Testament christological hymns, toward the *Trimorphic Protennoia,* and toward the Odes of Solomon will most likely remain forever elusive. The first step in the direction of our three corpora of literature was taken in a marginal situation.[44]

The second evolutionary model that we need to consider is that of the bush.[45] What is meant by the bush is that many branches grow in somewhat parallel development from one distant trunk or root. These parallel branches may show many similarities to one another, but one is not the parent of the other. *Australopithecus* is not the direct ancestor to *Homo* but rather a parallel and now extinct branch. The New Testament christological hymns have not directly influenced the *Trimorphic Protennoia* and the Odes of Solomon; we do not have a parental relationship in that direction. That is clear from the clusters of redeemer attributes in the New Testament christological hymns that are then distributed and combined in different ways in the *Trimorphic Protennoia* and in the Odes of Solomon. Yet the parental relationship cannot have proceeded in the other direction either, because the New Testament is much earlier than the other works. What we have is rather different branches on a bush, growing from a root or a trunk that originated in allopatric speciation—parallel developments demonstrating several close similarities. The Odes of Solomon and the *Trimorphic Protennoia* are our *Australopithecines,* so to speak; the New Testament christological hymns are early *Homo.*

This seems to me to be what James Robinson is talking about when he

---

44 In the case of literary developments, of course, we may sometimes see a first. In our literature, for example, we likely see Paul developing the concept of the church as the body of Christ in 1 Corinthians. In the instance under consideration, however, we have been presented with literary collections analogous to fossils. They have been dug up from the ground (Coptic gnostic library), or they have suddenly turned up out of obscurity (Odes of Solomon). Their relationships with other documents and ideologies are not immediately obvious. What relation do they have to the other intellectual movements in antiquity of which we know already? It is in such a situation that evolutionary theory proves helpful.

45 Cf. Gould, *Ever Since Darwin,* 56–62.

speaks of "diverging trajectories" that lead into what later came to be called orthodoxy and heresy.[46] Yet the term trajectory is not entirely apt because it implies velocity and aim. A diverging trajectory would imply a MIRV, a missile containing multiple warheads that would then separate from the original trajectory and take up independent trajectories. But we do not have aim in evolution, either in biological or in social evolution; on this point we may confidently generalize. What we have is adaptation. The religious developments that we are considering grow in different directions as adaptation occurs in response to highly complex situations. Yet we can still map interrelatedness, like that among the New Testament christological hymns, the *Trimorphic Protennoia*, and the Odes of Solomon; and here is where H.-M. Schenke's model of the tree seems to be the more accurate figure, although what Schenke means by the tree is not perfectly clear due to his speaking of "multiple origins." The tree or the bush has one trunk or root but a great many closely related—and less closely related—individual branches. (Schenke was of course discussing the complex of motifs that make up Gnosticism, whereas I am applying his figure to only one motif, that of the redeemer/revealer.)

Evolutionary theory thus seems to provide helpful models for talking about the relationships that we have been discussing. The origin of the gnostic redeemer figure lies in some allopatric environment, likely on the edge of Jewish wisdom speculation. This figure then evolves in related but different directions into the New Testament christological hymns, into the Odes of Solomon, and into the *Trimorphic Protennoia*, adapting to different intellectual and spiritual environments in the process. We now see the bush and, from it, infer the trunk.

---

46 "Jesus—From Easter to Valentinus," 7.

| V |

The Apocalypse of Peter
and Canonical 2 Peter

Birger A. Pearson

The jubilarian to whom this volume is dedicated has challenged our generation of scholarship with the task of "dismantling and reassembling categories
of New Testament scholarship."[1] As one of his own contributions to that effort
he has given to us a new category with which to work, that of "trajectories,"[2]
dynamic movements and streams through the Hellenistic world in which the
New Testament, and Christianity in general, originated and developed. His
own work with various "trajectories" has provided us not only with challenges
to our presuppositions but also with refreshing (or disturbing) surprises.

As one example of what I mean, I cite the Presidential Address given by
Professor Robinson at the annual meeting of the Society of Biblical Literature
held in San Francisco in December 1981.[3] There he brought up the on-going
debate between the traditional view of Gnosticism as a second-century Christian heresy[4] and the history-of-religions view of Gnosticism as a broader
syncretistic movement appearing not only in early Christianity but in other
religions as well.[5] Instead of doing what might be expected, i.e., coming down
sensibly on the side of the history-of-religions approach,[6] he traced a particular
"trajectory," in this case visions of the resurrected Christ, "from Easter to
Valentinus,"[7] i.e., from the earliest accounts of the resurrection appearances
(Paul) to the full-blown Gnosticism of the second century (Valentinus and
others). The results of his investigation are, of course, well known and require
no further comment from me.

What I want to do here, in a more modest effort, is to take up for discussion
two of the many texts cited by Robinson in his landmark essay on the resurrection appearances, one an "orthodox" text and the other a "heretical" (gnos-

1 Robinson's "Dismantling and Reassembling" in Robinson-Koester, *Trajectories*, 1–19.
2 Robinson-Koester, *Trajectories*, 8–13.
3 Robinson, "Jesus—From Easter to Valentinus."
4 Robinson, "Jesus—From Easter to Valentinus," 5. The view that Gnosticism is an inner-
  Christian heresy is still very much alive; see Pétrement, *Le Dieu séparé*, and my review,
  "Early Christianity and Gnosticism," 4–6.
5 The best modern treatment by a historian of religions is Rudolph, *Gnosis*.
6 Of course, as a student of Rudolf Bultmann, he sympathizes with that approach.
7 "Jesus—From Easter to Valentinus," esp. 7–30.

tic) one. I want to propose a new way of looking at the relationship between them. The two texts in question are canonical 2 Peter and the Apocalypse of Peter preserved in Coptic in Nag Hammadi Codex VII.[8]

That 2 Peter is an "orthodox" writing is taken for granted by everyone. For some, indeed, it is *too* orthodox, if by "orthodox" we mean "early catholic." The views expressed by Ernst Käsemann in a famous article[9] are a case in point: 2 Peter's consistent "early catholicism" makes it "the most dubious writing in the canon."[10] The Protestant slant in this opinion is, of course, obvious.

As for the Apocalypse of Peter, no one can doubt that it is a gnostic work and therefore, from the standpoint of early catholic orthodoxy, thoroughly "heretical." What, then, do these two "Petrine" texts have in common, except a bald attempt on the part of both to capture the legacy of the apostle Peter for their respective, thoroughly opposite, worldviews?

Indeed, one of the reasons that the Apocalypse of Peter is such a fascinating text is that it presents the apostle Peter as the founder of the gnostic community and the chief protagonist in a struggle against orthodox ecclesiastical Christianity.[11] Not Paul, the *haereticorum apostolus* ("apostle of the heretics"),[12] but Peter! What is also of interest, by the way, is that the Gospel of Matthew, which alone of the gospels contains the dominical pronouncement on which the Petrine structure of the Roman papacy is putatively built,[13] is a key authority for the Apocalypse of Peter and is extensively quoted and paraphrased throughout the text in support of its anti-ecclesiastical stance.[14] The Apocalypse of Peter has even been cited as evidence for the persistence of a special "Matthean" community of ascetic and charismatic Christians into the second century and beyond.[15] Be that as it may, the authoritative position of the apostle Peter in the gnostic apocalypse is undeniably tied to an interpretation of the Gospel of Matthew.

Could it not be the case that canonical 2 Peter was also put to good use by the author of the Apocalypse of Peter? That is precisely what I intend to argue

8 For references to these two texts in Robinson's article see pp. 8–9 (2 Peter) and 13, 31–32 (Apocalypse of Peter). For a Coptic transcription of the Apocalypse of Peter, with English translation and notes, see Brashler, "The Coptic 'Apocalypse of Peter,'" 14–69.
9 Käsemann, "Apologia."
10 Käsemann, "Apologia," 169.
11 See esp. Koschorke, *Polemik der Gnostiker,* 11–90; cf. Brashler, "The Coptic 'Apocalypse of Peter,'" 197–238.
12 Tertullian, *Adv. Marc.* 3.5. Tertullian refers to the appropriation of Paul by the Marcionites, but he could equally well have included the Gnostics, especially the Valentinians. Cf. Pagels, *The Gnostic Paul.*
13 Matt 16:17–19 was used, from the third century on but not before, to bolster the authority of the Bishop of Rome. See Cullmann, *Peter,* esp. 234; cf. Brown-Donfried-Reumann, *Peter in the New Testament,* 83–101.
14 See esp. A. Werner, "Apokalypse des Petrus," 575–77, 582–83; Perkins, "Peter in Gnostic Revelation," 5–6; Tuckett, *Nag Hammadi and the Gospel Tradition,* 117–24; Dubois, "L'Apocalypse de Pierre," 118 and n. 15.
15 Schweizer, "'Matthean' Church"; Stanton, "5 Ezra and Matthean Christianity," 80–83.

here.[16] In this there lies an anomaly of supreme irony: 2 Peter consists essentially of an attack on heretical opponents and warnings against heresy, the *gnostic* character of which is widely assumed![17]

Terence V. Smith, in his important study of the use of Peter and Petrine writings in the early church,[18] has devoted considerable attention to the problem of the relationship between 2 Peter and the gnostic Apocalypse of Peter.[19] He presents an impressive list of similarities between the two writings, yet he does not argue for a "literary relationship" between them. Instead, he situates the two documents in the context of a "Petrine controversy" and suggests that "in the Apocalypse of Peter we come face to face with the *type* of gnostic opposition encountered by the writer of 2 Peter." The two documents, according to Smith, reflect a "situation in which two pro-Peter groups were polemicizing against each other as rivals."[20]

Smith's analysis is, *prima facie*, quite plausible. But is it finally correct? I would like to suggest here another way of assessing the evidence. Inasmuch as both the Apocalypse of Peter and 2 Peter are highly polemical, we shall look first at how the opponents are presented in the respective writings[21] and then examine some other points of connection between them before coming to our conclusions.

The core of the polemical material in the Apocalypse of Peter is found in the context of the Savior's interpretation of the first of three visions accorded to Peter in the text.[22] The Savior prophesies apostasy from the truth on the part of many, and sure destruction at the Parousia for those who are enemies of the truth (73,19–80,23). The following points of contact with 2 Peter are especially noticeable:[23]

"Many will accept our teaching in the beginning. And they will turn from them again by the will of the Father of their error," 73,23–28 (cf. 74,15–17; 77,25–26). Cf. πλάνη ("error") in 2 Pet 2:18; 3:17; and on apostasy especially 2:2, 21.

"propagation of falsehood," 74,11. Cf. "false teachers," 2 Pet 2:1.

"defiled," 74,15–16. Cf. "blemishes," 2 Pet 2:13; "licentiousness," 2:2.

---

16 Use of 2 Peter on the part of the author of the Apocalypse of Peter, has been suggested before. See Perkins, *Gnostic Dialogue,* 117, and "Peter in Gnostic Revelation," 6 (crediting George MacRae); see now also Dubois, "L'Apocalypse de Pierre," 119.

17 See, e.g., Käsemann, "Apologia," passim. For a good, more recent, statement of the problem see Caulley, "The Idea of 'Inspiration,'" 50–82.

18 T. V. Smith, *Petrine Controversies.*

19 Smith, *Petrine Controversies,* 137–41.

20 Smith, *Petrine Controversies,* 141.

21 Some of the following items are noted by T. V. Smith, *Petrine Controversies,"* 138–39; and Dubois, "L'Apocalypse de Pierre," 119. Surprisingly, neither Koschorke nor Brashler (cf. n. 11) make anything of the connection between the Apocalypse of Peter and 2 Peter.

22 See Brashler's structural analysis, "The Coptic 'Apocalypse of Peter,'" 144–47.

23 Quotations from the Apocalypse of Peter in what follows are from the Bullard-Wisse translation in J. M. Robinson, *The Nag Hammadi Library in English,* 3d ed., 373–78

"For some of them will blaspheme the truth," 74,22–24. Cf. 2 Pet 2:2: "and because of them the way of truth will be blasphemed."

"they will be ruled heretically" (ϩⲛ̄ ⲟⲩⲙⲛ̄ⲧϩⲉⲣⲉⲥⲓⲥ, 74,20–22). Cf. αἱρέσεις, 2 Pet 2:1.

"they shall be given perdition," (ⲡⲓⲧⲁⲕⲟ, 75,6). Cf. ἀπώλεια, 2 Pet 2:1, 3; 3:7, 16.

"not every soul is of the truth," 75,12–13. Cf. 2 Pet 2:14: "unsteady souls."

"For every soul of these ages has death assigned to it . . . since it is created for its desires (ⲉⲡⲓⲑⲩⲙⲓⲁ) and their eternal destruction" (ⲧⲁⲕⲟ, 75,15–20). Cf. 2 Pet 1:4: "that you may escape from the corruption that is in the world because of passion." Cf. ἐπιθυμία, 2:10, 18; 3:3; and ἀπώλεια, 2:1, 3; 3:7, 16.

"creatures of (the) matter," 75,24–25. Cf. "irrational animals, creatures of instinct," 2 Pet 2:12.

"that which exists not will dissolve (ⲃⲱⲗ ⲉⲃⲟⲗ) into what exists not," 76,18–20. Cf. 2 Pet 3:10: "the elements will be dissolved" (λυθήσεται).

"deaf and blind ones," 76,21–22 (cf. 72,12,14; 73,12–13; 81,30). Cf. "blind and short-sighted," 2 Pet 1:9.

"evil words and misleading mysteries," 76,25–27. Cf. "cleverly contrived myths," 2 Pet 1:16; "false words," 2 Pet 2:3.

"speak of things which they do not understand," 76,29–30. Cf. 2 Pet 2:12: "blaspheming in things of which they are ignorant."

"the Way," 77,13. Cf. 2 Pet 2:2, 15, 21.

"messengers (ⲁⲅⲅⲉⲗⲟⲥ) of error," 77,24. Cf. 2 Pet 2:4: "the angels when they sinned."[24]

"They do business in my word," 77,33–78,1. Cf. 2 Pet 2:3: "in their greed they exploit you with false words."

"until my Parousia," 78,6. Cf. παρουσία, 2 Pet 1:16; 3:4, 12.

"slavery . . . freedom," 78,13–15. Cf. 2 Pet 2:19.

ⲁⲇⲓⲕⲓⲁ ("unrighteousness"), 78,19. Cf. ἀδικία, 2 Pet 2:13,15.

"will be cast into the outer darkness," 78,24–25. Cf. 2 Pet 2:17: "for them the nether gloom of darkness has been reserved."

ⲕⲟⲗⲁⲥⲓⲥ ("punishment"), 79,17. Cf. κολάζειν, 2 Pet 2:19.

"Those people are dry canals," 79,30–31. Cf. 2 Pet 2:17: "these are waterless springs."

The last item listed—"dry canals"//"waterless springs"—is the key to the supposition that the Apocalypse of Peter may have used 2 Peter.[25] The author

24 Good angels occur in both texts: ApocPet 82,12 and 2 Pet 2:11.
25 Cf. n. 16, above.

of the gnostic apocalypse has, however, adapted the expression "waterless springs" (πηγαὶ ἄνυδροι)[26] to fit an Egyptian geographical environment, with the substitution of "waterless canals" (ⲚⲒⲞⲞⲢ Ⲛ̄ⲀⲦⲘⲞⲞⲨ). In the process he has picked up a motif from native Egyptian apocalyptic tradition.[27]

What is most striking, however, is the strong eschatological expectation found in the Apocalypse of Peter. Its pronouncement of the judgment that is to come upon false teachers at the Parousia of Christ is very similar, at least on the surface, to the message of 2 Peter. It used to be thought that the eschatological teaching of 2 Peter marks it off as an anti-gnostic text, in that a denial of the Parousia (cf. 2 Pet 3:3–7) is supposedly a characteristic of gnostic doctrine.[28] But now we have a gnostic text that not only contains a vigorous eschatological expectation but even uses 2 Peter itself in giving expression to it! The gnostic author of the Apocalypse of Peter has evidently found 2 Peter to be a very congenial piece of Petrine teaching, one that can freely be used in his own presentation of Petrine *gnosis*.

There are numerous other points of contact between the Apocalypse of Peter and 2 Peter, in addition to those already noted as part of the polemical features of the two writings. The most important feature of the Apocalypse of Peter is, after all, its christology, expressed in terms of a docetic interpretation of the crucifixion of Christ. Indeed, the entire document consists of a series of visions and revelations whose setting is the temple in Jerusalem on Good Friday.[29] The crucifixion that takes place on that day, however, is of a fleshly substitute for the real Jesus who stands apart laughing at the ignorance of those who think that they are destroying him. The "living Savior" is really immune from suffering.[30]

Now it can hardly be argued that this docetic doctrine is derived from 2 Peter. Even so, there are some interesting points of contact between the two documents precisely in their descriptions of Christ.

The key text in 2 Peter, both in terms of its christology and its doctrine of the Parousia, is 1:16–18, describing the transfiguration of Christ:

> For it was not by following cleverly contrived myths that we made known to you the *power and Parousia* (δύναμιν καὶ παρουσίαν) of our Lord Jesus Christ, but it was by becoming eyewitnesses (or "initiates," ἐπόπται) of his *majesty* (μεγα-λειότητος). For when he received honor and glory from God the Father, and such

26 2 Peter makes an analogous adjustment in the use of its source. Cf. Jude 12, νεφέλαι ἄνυδροι, "waterless clouds."

27 The drying-up of the Nile and its canals is a standard feature in the description of apocalyptic woes on Egypt in such Hellenistic texts as the *Oracle of the Potter* (see POxy 2332, lines 73–74; cf. also NHC VI,8: *Asclepius* 71,16–19); but it is a very ancient motif; see e.g., the *Prophecies of Neferti* (Lichtheim, *Ancient Egyptian Literature* 1:139): "Dry is the river of Egypt." For a good discussion of the Hellenistic material see Griffiths, "Apocalyptic in the Hellenistic Era," esp. 287–91.

28 Cf. Käsemann, "Apologia," 171–72.

29 On the difficult opening passage of the Apocalypse of Peter see Dubois, "Le Préambule."

30 On the christology of the Apocalypse of Peter and its relation to that of the *Second Treatise of the Great Seth* (NHC VII,2) see Brashler, "The Coptic 'Apocalypse of Peter,'" 158–96.

a voice as this was borne down upon him from the majestic Glory: "This is my beloved son, with whom I have been well pleased"—even we heard this voice borne from heaven when we were with him on the holy mountain.[31]

In the Apocalypse of Peter, Peter is with the Savior in the temple (70,13–15), i.e., on the temple mount, a "holy mountain"; there he receives visions and revelations. The first vision is described thus: "I saw a new light greater than the light of day. Then it came down upon the Savior" (72,23–27). The Savior tells Peter that he has been chosen to "know him" (71,26), including the "body of his radiance" (71,32–33), and his "reward of honor" (72,1–2). The experience here recounted has to do with divine "majesty" (†MN̄TNO6 = μεγαλαιότης, 70,19).[32]

The language employed here is certainly "resurrection appearance" language, as Robinson has noted.[33] The gnostic apocalypse uses this resurrection language as part of a narrative of the (apparent) crucifixion of Christ, replacing the (orthodox) doctrine of Christ's crucifixion and resurrection with what Robinson refers to as "the idea of his bifurcation at the time of the passion into 'the living Jesus' (81,19) that did not suffer and 'his fleshly part' (81,20), 'the body' (83,5) that was crucified."[34] What is of special interest to us in this case is the apparent use, on the part of the gnostic author, of the transfiguration passage in 2 Peter. This gnostic writer has found the language of 2 Peter in describing the transfiguration quite compatible with his own understanding of Christ's true nature.

It might also be observed here that the rest of 2 Peter presents no obstacle to the use of the transfiguration passage in an explication of the (only apparent) crucifixion of Christ, for in fact the Pauline doctrine of "Christ crucified" is not a feature of 2 Peter's teaching.[35]

But what of the gnostic views in the Apocalypse of Peter concerning the true nature of the elect? Could we not expect to see here a basic incompatibility with what is taught in an "orthodox" writing like 2 Peter? Let us look at the evidence.

For the author of the Apocalypse of Peter—this is typical of Gnosticism in general—the elect, i.e., those who have received *gnosis*, share the divine nature of the Savior, being "consubstantial" (N̄ϢBHP N̄OYCIA = ὁμοούσιος, 71,14–15) with him.[36] The true "nature" (φύσις) of the elect soul is "immor-

---

31 My translation. J. M. Robinson ties this account to the original resurrection appearance of Jesus to Peter mentioned in 1 Cor 15:5 and Luke 24:34. See "Jesus—From Easter to Valentinus," 8–9.

32 In the Sahidic version of 2 Pet 1:16 MN̄TNO6 is used to translate μεγαλαιότης.

33 Robinson, "Jesus—From Easter to Valentinus," 13.

34 Robinson, "Jesus—From Easter to Valentinus."

35 The closest that 2 Peter comes to such a doctrine is at 2:1, "denying the Master who bought them," but even this passage is not explicitly related to the crucifixion. As for Paul, his letters are considered by the author of 2 Peter to contain "some things hard to understand" (3:16).

36 The term *homoousios* is probably a gnostic coinage; see Stead, *Divine Substance*, 190–222.

tal" (75,26–76,4), though it must "receive power in an intellectual spirit" (77,18–19). Those so constituted live in a "brotherhood" (79,1) "united in communion" (κοινωνία, 79,4). What holds the brotherhood together is not only *gnosis* (73,22–23 et passim) but "faith" (76,2) and "renunciation" (76,3) of the world. This community of faith and knowledge has its grounding in the apostle Peter, whom the Savior has "chosen" and from whom he has "established a *base* (ⲁⲣⲭⲏ) for the remnant whom (he has) summoned to knowledge" (71,19–21).

Virtually all of this the author of the Apocalypse of Peter could have read out of 2 Peter—and apparently did.[37] 2 Peter is addressed by its author to those who have "faith" equal to his own, as well as "knowledge" (ἐπίγνωσις, 1:1–2). It is indeed the divine *power* (δύναμις) that has granted the elect the things that pertain to life (1:3), by means of "knowledge" (ἐπίγνωσις, 1:3),[38] thus enabling them to become "partakers of divine nature" (θείας κοινωνοὶ φύσεως) and "escape the corruption that is in the world due to passion" (ἀποφυγόντες τῆς ἐν τῷ κόσμῳ ἐν ἐπιθυμίᾳ φθορᾶς, 1:4). The "brethren" (1:10), united in "knowledge" (1:9), are exhorted by the apostle to "confirm (their) call and election" (1:10).

There is yet more in 2 Peter that can, at least on the surface, be taken as quite compatible with the views reflected in the Apocalypse of Peter. "Peter's" statement that he will soon be "shedding his tent," i.e., his earthly body (1:14), is not on the face of it incompatible with the gnostic anthropology (and christology) found in the gnostic apocalypse. Terminology employed in referring to God ("Father," 1:17) and Christ ("Savior," 1:1,11; 2:20; 3:2,18) is that commonly used by Gnostics and is found also in the Apocalypse of Peter (passim). Even material in 2 Peter that is evidently inimical to the views of the author of the Apocalypse of Peter—the Old Testament prophets are valued in 2 Peter (1:19–21) and devalued in the Apocalypse of Peter (71,6–9)—could easily be resolved with mental recourse to the mention of "false prophets" in 2 Peter 2:1.

In short, what I am arguing here is that 2 Peter could have been, and was, freely used by the gnostic author of the Apocalypse of Peter. That is not, of course, to say that 2 Peter is really a gnostic text! In fact, it probably was an anti-gnostic text, so far as the original intention of its author is concerned.[39] But it can be read "gnostically," and so it was in the case of its use by the author of the Apocalypse of Peter. Just as that writer was able to read the Gospel of Matthew in a gnostic fashion, so also could he do the same with 2 Peter. This would also indicate that the two books would have occupied a prominent place among the "New Testament" writings treasured by the gnostic community to

37 In the last-cited passage there are also echoes of Matt 16:13–20. See esp. Koschorke, *Polemik der Gnostiker*, 27–29.
38 ἐπίγνωσις occurs in 2 Pet at 1:2, 3, 8; 2:20. γνῶσις occurs at 1:5, 6; 3:18.
39 Cf. n. 17, above.

which the apocalypse was addressed. That community honored the apostle Peter as its founder.[40]

I referred earlier to Terence Smith's views on the relationship between the Apocalypse of Peter and 2 Peter, and now I want to specify more clearly my points of agreement and disagreement with him. I disagree with him on the basic nature of the relationship; i.e., I think that there is a literary dependence of the Apocalypse of Peter on 2 Peter. I do agree with his view that the two texts reflect "a situation in which two pro-Peter groups were polemicizing against each other as rivals."[41] His elaboration of that situation, however, pits 2 Peter against the Apocalypse of Peter as representing the two opposing stances. While it may be true that certain features of the gnostic writing, such as its strong anti-clericalism—note especially its attack on the use of the titles "bishop" and "deacon" (79,25–26)—are typical of the gnostic opponents of 2 Peter (e.g., 2:10), it is also the case that 2 Peter itself could easily have been appropriated by the author of the Apocalypse of Peter and given a gnostic reading, as I think I have shown here. There is some indication, too, that the gnostic author was aware of the use of 2 Peter (and/or other Petrine literature) on the part of his ecclesiastical opponents. In the Apocalypse of Peter the Savior tells Peter that "the sons of this age" will "blaspheme (him) in these ages since they are ignorant of (him)" (73,18–21). In other words, the (ecclesiastical) opponents also appeal to the authority of Peter in their propagation of error.

There is considerable indication in the text of the Apocalypse of Peter that its Petrine-gnostic community, probably located somewhere in Egypt, is an embattled one, facing a mounting ecclesiastical opposition. The gnostic author is not able to provide any hope for his co-religionists in this age of "harsh fate." Instead he holds out the hope of vindication for the gnostic elect at the future Parousia of the Savior (78,1–14), when the opponents will get their "just deserts." And, as we have seen, it is just 2 Peter's teaching on the Parousia that provides the ground for this delicious hope!

The results of this investigation offer no help to those who like to keep their "categories" neat and tidy. But, as our jubilarian has himself taught us, study of the real data of Christian history, and history in general, always produces its surprises. This is especially the case when we are confronted with new data, such as the Apocalypse of Peter and the other writings from the Nag Hammadi collection, writings that Professor Robinson himself has labored so hard to make available to scholarship and to the public at large. For that, as well as for his own scholarly contributions, we are all in his debt.

40 A number of "pro-Peter" gnostic groups existed in the early centuries. See, e.g., Perkins, *Gnostic Dialogue*, 113–30; T. V. Smith, *Petrine Controversies*, 117–42.
41 *Petrine Controversies*, 141. Cf. also MacRae, "Nag Hammadi and the New Testament," 157.

Proverbs and Social Control

A NEW PARADIGM FOR WISDOM STUDIES

Arland D. Jacobson

A word fitly spoken is like apples of gold in a setting of silver.
Prov 25:11

Like a lame man's legs, which hang useless, is a proverb in the mouth
of a fool.

Prov 26:7

A proverb from a fool's lips will be rejected,
for he does not tell it at its proper time.
Sir 20:20

I know the proverbs, but I don't know how to apply them.
An Ibo student[1]

This is intended as a programmatic essay on proverbial wisdom. It is meant
to be suggestive; it certainly does not claim to be definitive. My thesis is that
many of the assumptions that we make in wisdom studies are erroneous, and
that we need a new paradigm for understanding wisdom, and proverbs in
particular. Such a paradigm needs to be informed by folkloristic studies of
proverbs. This is not the first effort to integrate the insights of anthropologists
and folklorists into biblical studies, but it does represent a particular perspective for doing so.

1. The Current Dominant Paradigm

The dominant paradigm is based on two assumptions. First, proverbs have a
cognitive function; they are a way of knowing and/or they embody a search for
truth. Second, proverbs are based on experience. These are, of course, closely
related assumptions.

Gerhard von Rad's *Wisdom in Israel* discusses the proverb under the heading, "The Forms in Which Knowledge Is Expressed."[2] The same perspective
is found in James Crenshaw's *Old Testament Wisdom;* his chapter on proverbs

---

1 Cited by Arewa and Dundes, "Proverbs and the Ethnography of Speaking Folklore," 70.
2 Von Rad, *Wisdom in Israel,* chap. 3.

is entitled, "The Pursuit of Knowledge."[3] And Roland Murphy asserts, "The PROVERB draws a conclusion from experience and formulates it in a pithy, succinct way."[4]

Those who emphasize the cognitive function of proverbs, or the cognitive content of proverbs, sometimes, however, go beyond the old notion that proverbs are distillations of insight, nuggets of wisdom, preserved in striking forms. Von Rad, for example, wants to argue that proverbs are, in fact, tools for comprehending the world.

> The phenomenon of "gnomic apperception" (Petsch), that is, a quite particular way of acquiring knowledge and giving expression to it in a particular linguistic form, namely that of the "maxim," exists in every culture in the world and must, therefore, be regarded as a rudimentary expression of man's search for knowledge.[5]

In contrast to sheer intuition or to divine inspiration, proverbs, it has often been emphasized, are based on experience, and hence are to that extent secular, worldly, and in principle, if not in fact, international. To quote Crenshaw, "All proverbs . . . were grounded in experience."[6] But, as von Rad points out, "experience alone would not be sufficient,"[7] for experience requires interpretation to yield meaning. "Thus between the events and the proverbs which deal with them there lay a wide-ranging and fairly complex intellectual activity."[8]

What is discerned, it is said, is an order underlying the welter of experience. "The proverb is an elementary quest for order," asserts Crenshaw.[9] William Beardslee put it this way:

> The proverb is a form of folk or popular literature. It is prediscursive. . . . The proverb grasps a particular kind of situation; it expresses a flash of insight which sees the "order" in a certain kind of happening.[10]

> In the ancient setting the proverb represented an ordering of a particular bit of experience. It is a tract of experience which can be repeated. That is the whole point of the proverb, which by its nature cannot deal with a unique situation. And it is an orderly tract of experience; that is the reason for the declarative form. . . .

---

3 Crenshaw, *Old Testament Wisdom*, chap. 3. See also Crenshaw, "Wisdom" and "Acquisition of Knowledge."
4 Murphy, *Wisdom Literature*, 4.
5 Von Rad, *Wisdom in Israel*, 30. Von Rad's views were greatly influenced by André Jolles's *Einfache Formen* (see esp. the chapter on "Spruch," 150–70). Von Rad's undocumented reference to "Petsch" probably refers to R. Petsch, *Spruchdichtung der Volk: Vor- und Frühformen der Volksdichtung* (1939), which was not accessible to me.
6 Crenshaw, *Old Testament Wisdom*, 67.
7 Von Rad, *Wisdom in Israel*, 31.
8 Von Rad, *Wisdom in Israel*, 31–32.
9 Crenshaw, "Wisdom," 233.
10 Beardslee, *Literary Criticism*, 31.

Thus . . . it is correct to regard the proverb historically as a step on the way toward a systematic view of reality.[11]

Recently James Williams, picking up some earlier observations by von Rad, has emphasized that the gnomic quest for order is only part of the picture. Precisely because "gnomic wisdom is an investigative mode that proceeds empirically"[12] it allows for the contradictoriness of particularity. "The proverb . . . is the literary expression of a type of consciousness whose quest for order is modified by acceptance of experience as multifaceted and unsystematizable."[13]

Furthermore, Beardslee in particular sought to combine the more traditional cognitive view of proverbs with an emphasis on how proverbs work, and especially how Jesus used proverbial wisdom.[14] This, however, led to a sharper contrast than is justified between traditional proverb usage and Jesus' "intensification of the proverb";[15] for, as we shall see, it is in the nature of proverb usage to reframe situations, to cause the hearer to see her or his situation from a very different angle. Nevertheless, Beardslee's recognition that one must consider how proverbs work was a helpful shift in emphasis.

This brief summary does not, of course, do justice to all the nuances present in current descriptions of the proverb and its function. Rather, it focuses attention upon the basic assumptions and emphases in this discussion: the cognitive function of proverbs, their experiential basis, and the cognitive content particular to proverbs, namely order within that experience.

2. Problems with the Dominant Paradigm

The cognitive/experiential model for understanding the proverb, which continues to dominate discussion among biblical, especially New Testament, scholars has already been largely abandoned by folklorists, ethnographers, and anthropologists. They have come to see that folklore, and proverbs in particular, need to be studied not as artifacts abstracted from their social context but as communicative items within particular contexts of usage. This shift in folkloristics to performance, context, and function was announced in a special issue of *The Journal of American Folklore*, published separately as *Toward New Perspectives in Folklore* (1972) and edited by Américo Paredes and Richard Bauman. In retrospect, however, it is clear that there were a number of forerunners, including anthropological studies by Raymond Firth (1926),

11 Beardslee, *Literary Criticism*, 32. The notion that proverbs represent an advance toward abstract thinking is also espoused, e.g., by Loeb, "Function of Proverbs."
12 J. G. Williams, *Those Who Ponder Proverbs*, 36.
13 Williams, *Those Who Ponder Proverbs*, 40.
14 Beardslee, "Uses of the Proverb"; *Literary Criticism*, 30–41; "Parable, Proverb, and Koan"; and "Saving One's Life."
15 Beardslee, "Uses of the Proverb," 72.

Melville Herskovits (1930), George Herzog (1936), and Ruth Finnegan (1970). Especially important for proverb studies was an article by E. Ojo Arewa and Alan Dundes on "Proverbs and the Ethnography of Speaking Folklore" (1964). For Old Testament scholars, the import of these developments was reported first by Carole Fontaine (1982) and then by Claudia Camp (1985).[16]

Preoccupation with the intellectualistic cognitive model is a carryover from the old approach of studying folklore as artifacts to be collected, especially from vanishing groups of the "folk." The problem of focusing on the truth content of proverbs is evident simply by noting that proverbs are often so banal that one can hardly account for their currency on the basis of content. Furthermore, there are many contradictory proverbs (e.g., "Haste makes waste" and "Strike while the iron is hot"; cf. Prov 26:4, 5). Even more revealing are sayings about sayings such as those at the beginning of this essay.[17] In these sayings, the focus is on proverb usage, not on content. The wise are wise not because they have memorized many proverbs but because they know how and when to use them with effect.

Just as the knowledge of proverbs does not guarantee their proper use, so knowledge of a foreign tongue does not guarantee linguistic competence, because there are unspoken rules about when one speaks, to whom, under what circumstances, and so on. The study of the constellation of factors that add up to linguistic competence is called the ethnography of communication, a new subdiscipline.[18] Unspoken rules also govern proverb usage, as is implicit in the sayings previously mentioned. The fool is one who knows the proverbs but has not mastered the rules for using them. As can be seen from Prov 25:11, there are also aesthetic considerations related to usage; proverb usage is an art.

Failure to take account of proverb usage is responsible for the frequently observed incongruity between scholarly classification and native or ethnic terminology.[19] It is well known that the Hebrew *mashal* can refer to proverbs, parables, taunts, even prophetic oracles. Ruth Finnegan noted the apparent terminological confusion in various African words that can refer to proverbs as well as to stories, dark sayings, parables, and so on.[20] Lawrence Boadi noted that the Akan (Ghana, Ivory Coast) would not recognize the proverbial status of many biblical and modern proverbs. Indeed, the truth content of the proverb was of little interest to them; they reckoned as proverbs brief sayings peculiar for their concrete and unusual imagery.[21] Gossen's study of Chamula genres (Mexico) argued that they "are organized according to attributes which also organize other aspects of Chamula expressive behavior and values."[22]

16 Fontaine, *Traditional Sayings*, and Camp, *Wisdom and the Feminine*.
17 Dundes speaks of such sayings as "metafolklore" in his essay of the same name.
18 The origin of this discipline may be traced to Dell Hymes's 1962 article, "The Ethnography of Speaking." For an introduction, see Saville-Troike, *Ethnography*.
19 See especially Ben-Amos, "Analytic Categories."
20 Finnegan, *Oral Literature*, 390–92.
21 Boadi, "Language of the Proverb."
22 Gossen, "Chamula Genres," 145.

The problem, as Ben-Amos has noted, is that "ethnic genres are cultural modes of communication, [whereas] analytical categories are models for the organization of texts."[23] Further, "The basic problem inherent in any analytical scheme for folklore classification is that it must synchronize different folklore classification systems, each with its own internal logical consistency, each based upon distinct socio-historical experiences and cognitive categories."[24] Nevertheless, "the distinctive attributes which speakers of folklore recognize in their communication can be analytically confined to three levels: prosodic, thematic, and behavioral. . . . An ethnic definition of a genre may incorporate distinctions made on any or all three levels."[25]

The claim made in this paper is that the primary function of proverbs is as tools for a mild form of social control, and that other features of the proverb are derivative of this function. It will be evident that this analysis does not resolve the incongruity between ethnic and analytical categories but only makes the claim that among a variety of cultural systems that recognize a form of proverbial speech, some basic commonalities seem to exist, and that these are mainly functional.

3. How Proverbs Work

A proverb works by invoking widely shared values and assumptions precisely to gain immediate acquiescence. As Barbara Kirschenblatt-Gimblett put it, "Proverbs sound authoritative. . . . This is an instrumental part of the proverb's strategy. But this does not mean that proverbs state absolute truths. Proverbs are just supposed to sound like they do."[26] This is why proverbs are often actually quite banal. It is also why they are often very conservative. The critical point to observe is that proverbs, in order to work, must say something that is immediately recognizable as true, that indeed compels attention, that cannot be dismissed.

Yet this appeal to what everyone knows to be true is only the presupposition for the effectiveness of the proverb. The real key to how a proverb works is that it reframes the current situation; it creates a new and self-evident frame of reference so that the hearer is gently but firmly confronted with the incongruity between her or his behavior or situation and what she or he knows to be true. The person fretting over some mistake is told by a friend, "Don't cry over spilt milk." The person knows this, of course, but she needs to be reminded of this truth; it puts her situation in perspective. It is this ability to reframe situations and behaviors that is at the heart of how a proverb works. Proverbs do not invite argument. They are meant to clinch the case, to preclude argument, to reframe the situation so persuasively that the hearer is left with

23 Ben-Amos, "Analytic Categories," 275.
24 Ben-Amos, "Analytic Categories," 275.
25 Ben-Amos, "Analytic Categories," 287.
26 Kirschenblatt-Gimblett, "Theory," 821.

no option but to heed it. Or, as Roger Abrahams put it, "The strategy of the proverb . . . is to direct by appearing to clarify; this is engineered by simplifying the problem and resorting to traditional solutions."[27]

Michael Lieber has described this reframing with somewhat greater precision by speaking of "disambiguation."

> Proverbs appear to be used largely (though not wholly) in situations that are reasonably complex, equivocal, and either adversarial or potentially so. Proverbs serve to interpret such situations, resolving their ambiguities by classifying them as being of a certain sort. Proverbs, thus, are used to *disambiguate* complex situations and events. . . . That is, the analogy proposed by a proverb's use not only interprets a situation, but also implies that it is *this* kind of situation and not *that* or some other kind of situation.[28]

Earlier, in a short essay on "Literature as Equipment for Living," Kenneth Burke made some similar observations. "Proverbs," he argued, "are *strategies* for dealing with *situations*."[29] Burke wished to stress the "active nature" of proverbs.[30] Indeed, it was from this point of view, said Burke, that one could understand how there could be contrary proverbs; the apparent contradictions simply reflect different strategies.[31]

It is worth recalling that Bultmann too had called attention to the situational nature of proverb usage. In an essay on "General Truths and Christian Proclamation," Bultmann noted that much of what is found in Jesus' teachings, and some of Paul's writings as well, can best be characterized as "general truths." He wanted to keep clear the distinction between Christian proclamation, which is not a truth that one can carry around like a possession, and general truths, proverbial truths, which are of universal validity. And yet he observes that "general truths can come to share in the address-character of the Christian proclamation insofar as they lose their character as general truth in a concrete situation by qualifying the now of the person being addressed."[32]

To say, in any case, that proverbs are tools for a mild form of social control is to make the same point. Folklorists and anthropologists, at least those who use a functionalist or a contextualist approach, have examined proverb performance in traditional social settings (and some non-traditional settings) and

---

27 Abrahams, "Rhetorical Theory of Folklore," 150. Cf. the comments of Robert Tannehill: "Imaginative language is important in ethical decisions because it is able to act upon the images which make up this lens [through which we see the world] and thereby change our perception of the situation and our judgment of the action appropriate to it" (*Sword of His Mouth*, 26).

28 Lieber, "Analogic Ambiguity," 424–25. See also Abrahams, "Rhetorical Theory of Folklore" and "Proverbs and Proverbial Expressions"; and cf. Fontaine's concept of "categorization" (*Traditional Sayings*, 41–43).

29 Burke, "Literature as Equipment," 103.

30 Burke, "Literature as Equipment," 102.

31 Burke, "Literature as Equipment," 103.

32 Bultmann, "General Truths," 157.

have come to emphasize the function of the proverb, in particular its use in social control.[33]

4. Proverbs and Social Control

The goal of proverb usage, then, is not insight, or at least not insight only; the point of proverb usage is, through verbal skill, to manipulate the behavior or attitude of other people. Implicit in this definition is the assumption, certainly disputable, that social control is the most fundamental function of proverbs, the one that can account for most other features of the proverb. It should be noted, however, that "social control" is used here rather broadly as the manipulation of the behavior or attitude of others, usually toward the end of preserving the social and cosmic order.

To begin with, focusing on proverbs as tools for social control helps us to see that there is a very close connection between proverbs and admonitions, a connection so close that ancient collectors tended to bunch them all together. Nevertheless, there is a distinction, namely that proverbs are more indirect, more subtle tools for social control. Yet the insight that proverbs have social control as their basic function helps to understand one of the basic characteristics of sayings collections, their preoccupation with right behavior.

The indirectness of proverbs, the fact that their strategy is to influence behavior without resort to direct command, is an essential aspect of the proverb; for, especially when dealing with equals or superiors, a direct approach to manipulating behavior or attitude will not only fail but will result in censure, estrangement, or the creation of social tension. The indirectness of proverbs, thus, can be understood as arising out of their use as tools for social control.

By "indirectness" I refer to a cluster of features: anonymity, impersonality, obliqueness, and a metaphorical quality.

Proverbs, as Abrahams notes, have an "appearance of objectivity."[34] They seem to articulate what is obvious and in that way effectively to depersonalize the effort at manipulating the behavior or attitude of another. This impersonal quality, this anonymity, however, at the same time bestows authority on the proverb, because it seems to give voice to traditional perceptions of reality.[35]

The need to depersonalize speech is especially obvious where one needs to broach a subject that is sensitive or clumsy to deal with, or where one is dealing with a peer or a superior. Proverbs allow people to say what needs to be said without creating additional social tensions. Sometimes, in fact, proverbial

---

33 The functional approach to proverbs, stressing their role in social control, is set forth in the articles and books (cited in this essay) by Abrahams, Arewa and Dundes, Bascom, Ben-Amos, Finnegan, Firth, Fisher and Yoshida, Herskovits, Herzog, Kirschenblatt-Gimblett, Lieber, Messenger (cf. Yankah, "Proverb Rhetoric"), Seitel, and Westermarck.

34 Abrahams, "Proverbs and Proverbial Expressions," 122.

35 Cf. Arewa and Dundes, "Proverbs and the Ethnography of Speaking Folklore," 157, and Abrahams, "Rhetoric," 48–51.

expressions are used as a means of letting off steam and ultimately of helping to keep the social order intact.[36] A further gain from depersonalization is that it allows the speaker to seek to manipulate the behavior or attitude of others without risking loss of honor to either party if the effort is rejected.

The obliqueness of proverbs is achieved not only through the appearance of objectivity but also through the metaphorical quality of proverbs. "Strike while the iron is hot" is, literally, a piece of blacksmith shop advice, but it becomes a metaphor for any situation where action delayed becomes futile. The metaphoric quality helps to give the proverb its well-known out-of-context character, thus signalling its genre, while at the same time depersonalizing the advice and even making it delightful to hear. Further, metaphor gives multivalency to sayings, and thus makes them useful in ever new contexts. These qualities of proverbs go hand in hand with the circumlocutionary quality of so much communication in intimate social groups or in contexts of potential social tension.

The form of proverbs can also be understood in relation to their function as tools for social control.[37] Proverbs consist of a topic and a comment upon it, typically in a binary construction, often adorned with meter, rhyme, assonance and alliteration, striking phraseology, and so on. Not only do these features make proverbs memorable, they also contribute to the impression that proverbs make as out-of-context statements. These same features make proverbs delightful to the ear and mind. Indeed, the genius of the proverb may be that it can delight the hearer and manipulate him or her at the same time.[38]

As we noted earlier, proverbs only seem to encapsulate wisdom, and this quality is an important part of how proverbs work. They must compel assent by representing what seems perfectly obvious, what everyone knows to be true. This also bestows authority on the proverb because it seems to give voice to some venerable truth; the proverb bears the weight of common sense. Indeed, the observations of Clifford Geertz about "Common Sense as a Cultural System" are especially apropos. Common sense, says Geertz, is hardly the articulation of the obvious that it seems to be. It is "as much an interpretation of the immediacies of experience, a gloss on them, as are myth, painting, epistemology, or whatever."[39] It is, in short, a "cultural system"; but "it is an inherent characteristic of common-sense thought precisely to deny this and affirm that its tenets are immediate deliverances of experience, not deliberated reflections upon it."[40]

Geertz is certainly correct that there is a cultural system—an intellectual construct of reality, complex and laden with cultural values and assump-

---

36 See, e.g., Evans-Pritchard, "*Sanza.*"
37 On the form of proverbs, see Dundes, "Structure" and Abrahams, "Proverbs."
38 "If lore is to control or guide, it must not only be embodied in forms that direct action, but these forms must do so by being formally cloaked in wit or cast as drama" (Abrahams, "Personal Power and Social Restraint," 18).
39 Geertz, "Common Sense," 76.
40 Geertz, "Common Sense," 75.

tions—that represents itself as common sense. Proverbs, however, are not so much common-sense pontifications, fragments of this larger system, as they are rhetorical devices that trade upon common sense.[41] Geertz, too, operates with a cognitive model for understanding proverbs that ultimately misunderstands their function. To reiterate the point by example, my mother impressed upon me, as a child, that "The truth will out," which I mistakenly assumed was how the cosmos worked, until I learned another truth, that "What she doesn't know doesn't hurt her." Of course, neither truth is true except sometimes, but they both have their uses.

The knowledge of proverbs and the art of knowing when and how to use them, the ability to use language that is indirect yet powerful, the knack for persuasive and colorful speech, the sense of when to speak and when to be silent—all of these add up to verbal skill and constitute the "wisdom" prized especially in traditional societies.[42] The sayings cited at the beginning of this essay show, indeed, that "wisdom" consists not in the content of the proverbs but in their proper use—or, rather, that wisdom is an attribute not of the sayings but of the speaker. Plato provides a nice description of the verbal skill associated specifically with proverb usage (the speaker is Socrates).

> Now philosophy is of more ancient and abundant growth in Crete and Lacedaemon than in any other part of Greece, . . . but the people there deny it and make pretence of ignorance, in order to prevent the discovery that it is by wisdom that they have ascendancy over the rest of the Greeks. . . . In those two states there are not only men but women also who pride themselves on their education; and you can tell that what I say is true and that the Spartans have the best education in philosophy by this: If you choose to consort with the meanest of Spartans, at first you will find him making a poor show in the conversation; but soon, at some point or other in the discussion, he gets home with a notable remark, short and compressed—a deadly shot that makes his interlocutor seem like a helpless child.[43]

It is, of course, from this Spartan adeptness at verbal skill that we get the word "laconic."

Plato's comments call attention to another feature that is frequently noted in connection with proverb usage, and that is that it is a popular phenomenon ("the meanest of the Spartans"), which, nevertheless, could be admired by the intelligentsia. Further, proverb usage is associated not only with men with but women as well.

---

41 Cf. Camp (*Wisdom and the Feminine*, 160–64) who makes use of Geertz's notion and seems to accept its implicit cognitive model.

42 In the ethnography of speaking, this would be excellence in "communicative competence"; cf. Saville-Troike, *Ethnography*, 22–27. Folklorists speak more specifically of "proverb performance" or more generally of "verbal art as performance," to cite an influential article by Richard Bauman, later expanded into the lead essay of a book of that title.

43 Plato, *Protagoras* 342.

5. Implications for the Study of Wisdom

It may not be immediately obvious that a different paradigm for understanding folk proverbs would be of relevance for an understanding of other forms of wisdom. It is hoped, however, that the ensuing discussion will demonstrate that this approach to proverbs helps to put other aspects of wisdom into sharper focus. We will confine our attention largely to two areas: the distinction between proverbs and aphorisms and some reflections on collections of wisdom.

The model that we have set forth for understanding folk wisdom emphasized the use rather than the content of proverbs. We noted that they are used as tools for a mild form of social control in relatively intimate social settings, especially in situations of potential conflict.[44] Further, we noted their indirectness, the way in which they could influence behavior or attitudes without creating social tensions.

When it is possible to observe important changes in any of the aspects of this model, we may assume that an important change has taken place in the use or function of proverbs. For example, it is certainly the case that many proverbial sayings tend to move away from indirection toward direction. This we would assume, on the basis of our model, to mean that their context of usage has changed. We no longer have the ordinary intimate social life where proverbs are used strategically to exert social control. Rather, someone is undertaking to give instruction to someone else, and the goal is the inculcation of the values embodied in the proverbs. A different authority structure is presupposed; and the very function of proverbs has changed in fundamental ways, as has their form: They are on their way to becoming admonitions. Similarly, when the values expressed are not the traditional values of small-scale social groups, we have probably moved into a different context. Likewise, when the content of proverbs rather than their function has become the organizing principle for their collection and use, the context of usage has changed. Or, again, when proverbial sayings no longer give voice to anonymous traditional values but are attributed sayings expressing the wisdom of a particular person, we have moved into a different situation. The goal of such sayings may remain the same: to exert social control. But the sayings function in a very different way. Personal authority is now at stake. A set of values must be inculcated to support this imposition of authority, such as the importance and legitimacy of the wise, the importance of being willing to submit to instruction and reproof, humility, willingness to learn, and social disapproval of the "fool." All of these,

---

44 "Though proverbs can occur in very many different kinds of contexts, they seem to be particularly important in situations where there is both conflict and, at the same time, some obligation that this conflict should not take on too open and personal a form" (Finnegan, *Oral Literature*, 411–12). Albig ("Proverbs," 534) had already noted this connection to conflict. See further, Abrahams, "Rhetoric," esp. 48: "Proverbs are expressions suggested in the popular mind at those times when a member of the group collides in some way with others, or at least threatens to do so."

of course, can be found in abundance in collections such as Proverbs and the Wisdom of Jesus, son of Sirach.

If, now, we designate attributed proverbial sayings as aphorisms, then it will be clear that we have arrived, though by a different route, at the same point reached by John Dominic Crossan. According to Crossan, proverbs give voice to the common mind, the ancestral tradition, while aphorisms give voice to personal vision. What proverb and aphorism have in common, however, is more important than what distinguishes them, because according to Crossan the aphorism cloaks its personal vision in the guise of ancestral tradition.

> Both [proverbs and aphorisms] are short and pithy formulations. And both resolutely refuse to append any reason, argument, or explanation. But proverb gives no reason since none is necessary; it is the summation of the wisdom of the past. Aphorism, on the other hand, gives no reason because none is possible; it is the formulation of the wisdom of the future. Proverb is the last word, aphorism the first word. And the aphorist is quite content if one gets mixed up and cannot tell aphorism from proverb. But whether in form alone or content alone or in form and content together, the aphorism appears as a voice from Eden, a dictum of dawn.[45]

A distinction should also be made between individual sayings attributed to a particular sage and collections of sayings attributed en masse to a particular sage or king. The latter serves the purpose of legitimating the sayings collected, as Kloppenborg has noted frequently.[46] But individual sayings attributed to a particular sage are not necessarily legitimated by such attribution; instead, the sayings help to establish the authority of the sage and to display her or his wisdom. This attempt to establish the authority of a particular sage may probably be assumed to be related to the development of a group around this sage, i.e., it has to do with social formation.

The second area that we will examine is the phenomenon of sayings collections.

Folk wisdom is an oral phenomenon, so a collection of sayings represents a quite different type of wisdom.[47] Nevertheless, the discontinuity between folk proverbs and collected proverbs is not total. Perhaps the most notable characteristic of many sayings collections is their apparent lack of organization. But, as Max Küchler has noted, this should not be regarded as evidence of carelessness or primitiveness. For "wisdom sayings have a tendency to lead as contextless an existence as possible, so as to prove useful in ever new contexts."[48] Put otherwise, multivalency is an essential part of proverbs. This multivalency derives from the metaphoric character of proverbs and is also

---

45 Crossan, *In Fragments*, 25.
46 Kloppenborg, *Formation of Q,* chap. 7, "Q and Ancient Sayings Collections."
47 The significance of this transition from folk proverb to collection is discussed by both Fontaine, *Traditional Sayings,* and Camp, *Wisdom and the Feminine.*
48 Küchler, *Frühjüdische Weisheitstraditionen,* 167.

related to the fact that wisdom has to do not with the content but rather with the use of proverbs. To preserve multivalency, proverbs are best strung together in such a way that their interpretation does not become fixed but remains open. The use of simple devices such as catchword and thematic association has the effect of preserving the multivalency of the sayings gathered together. In this way, the discontinuity between proverbs in oral circulation and proverbs in written collections can be minimized. Nevertheless, collections are extremely rare in oral contexts, though occasionally bunches of proverbs may be recited in various contexts.[49] This rarity of oral collections has little to do with technological or educational deficiencies but has more to do with the nature of proverb usage as an oral phenomenon, and specifically as an aspect of verbal skill. However, where proverbial speech—or metaphor, circumlocution, and so on—become valued evidence of verbal skill, and verbal skill is taught in some formal way, then collections of proverbs become very useful.

A common feature of sayings collections is the use of a fictional domestic context in which the father is instructing his son. While such occasions no doubt occurred, such usage of proverbs—i.e., as subject matter for instruction—represents a deviation from our model of folk proverb usage, because the proverb's refusal to adopt an overtly authoritarian stance has been replaced by a stance in which a superior is addressing an inferior.[50] Nevertheless, it is important to note that it is just this context of proverb usage that has become prototypical in many collections. Moreover, the patriarchal nature of this fiction may well represent a projection of patriarchalism into the past rather than a reflection of the reality of domestic life. Furthermore, rather than being used strategically as means of intervention in situations that arise in daily life, proverbs are now being used in a process of socialization by means of which the values of the group are inculcated in the youth. This clearly will tend to push and reshape proverbs toward didactic ends. Indirection here gives way to direct admonition and instruction; and the situation is not essentially different for the teacher-pupil relationship, which replicates the familial context by the use of the fictional "father/son" relationship, and perhaps by the creation of an ersatz family, the school. Nevertheless, here too elements of continuity with folk wisdom are evident. For example, the proverbs used in familial and school contexts continue to use reason and verbal skill, i.e., persuasion, rather than command or appeal to authority.

In many sayings collections we can observe types of internal organization that go well beyond simple types of organization mentioned earlier, such as catchword or thematic association. The multivalency of sayings has not been

---

49 See Finnegan, *Oral Literature*, 413–14, 415–16, 488–49.

50 Westermann ("Weisheit," 76–77), making rather cursory reference to anthropological data concerning proverb usage among the Ewe (Ghana, Togo), noted that the declaratory proverb, which Westermann believes is the original form of wisdom saying, assumes that the recipient stands on the same level as the speaker, whereas admonitions presuppose inequality (e.g., father/son, king/prince).

preserved; rather, by means of sayings compositions of various kinds, an interpretation has been imposed on the sayings. An author has shaped the tradition to some preconceived end. Here, too, we have moved well beyond folk wisdom.

The functional model for understanding the proverb also helps to explain why collections of wisdom, which abstract proverbs from their context of oral usage, would fix on the intellectual content of the sayings. This is a process described by Claudia Camp,[51] though her model continues to be a primarily cognitive one. Camp noted that proverbs placed in collections are decontextualized, and that this loss of performance context leads to the appearance of dogmatism. I would prefer to say that the decontextualizing of proverbs by their inclusion in certain kinds of collections (i.e., those that are not organized so as to preserve the multivalency of the proverb) leads to the mistaken assumption that intellectual content is what proverbs are about. Here, in fact, is where the cognitive model for understanding proverbs arose.

It is certainly possible, and desirable, to examine the trajectories of various genres of sayings collections, as Küchler and Kloppenborg have done. Yet it may also be useful to consider another way of categorizing sayings collections, based upon the model we have presented. Here again, the focus will not be on the content of the collection so much as on its use.

We noted earlier that folk wisdom simply takes for granted the dominant assumptions and values of its culture. Folk proverbs do not so much seek to inculcate these assumptions and values as simply to assume and trade upon them. Put otherwise, folk proverbs presuppose a "world" in the sense of an ethos or a socially constructed reality. Proverbs may help to maintain this "world," but this function is subordinate to their function of regulating life in intimate social contexts. Moreover, though folk proverbs are often used primarily by elders, they are not the property of a special or professional class.

Collections of wisdom, however, usually go well beyond merely presupposing a world. Further, they are the products of a special, professional class, the "wise." Often such collections seek actively to inculcate this "world" or ethos; sometimes the collection, in fact, seeks to enforce conformity to the ethos or world. This, of course, assumes some sort of disturbance to the presupposed world or ethos. It is no longer taken for granted; there are alternatives to this cultural scheme. So the function of the collection is to maintain a threatened ethos or world. Admonitions, warnings, and instructions are the dominant types of wisdom in these collections. Proverbs, Sirach, and perhaps the Didache may be taken as examples of this type of collection. The wise who seek to maintain the world are here a special class who have an important stake in a particular set of social arrangements.

In some cases, the world or ethos has become the object of reflection. Here, the goal is not to inculcate the established world or ethos in pupils but to reflect on an ethos or world that is threatened or that has lost its power to

51 Camp, *Wisdom and the Feminine,* 165–78.

interpret or order experienced reality; for the ethos or world is genuinely open to question. Ecclesiastes would be an example of this type. The sociological context is that the wise—or the class that they represent—are no longer secure in their roles, due to profound socio-cultural change. Their world can no longer be taken for granted.[52]

A third type of collection seeks the transformation of an ethos or world. Here, one world is decisively rejected, and a new one is being created to take its place. Unlike the world-maintenance types of collections, this type must seek to undo the dominant world and to inflate the role and authority of the one seeking to dismantle the old world and then to propose a new one. Alternatively, authority may be said to derive from revelations by Wisdom herself (not identified with Torah). The synoptic sayings source, Q, and the Gospel of Thomas belong to this type.

Both Q and the Gospel of Thomas, however, contain an inherent risk. They are collections of sayings; and though an interpretive scheme has been imposed on the sayings, especially in Q, so that they no longer admit of just any interpretation, yet, as collections, they are open to divergent interpretations as well as to the addition and subtraction of sayings. Such a substantial risk could probably be taken only by rather small, well-defined groups. That would be true for Q much more than for the Gospel of Thomas, which explicitly invites reflection and thus risks variant interpretations. The Gospel of Thomas is inherently more portable than Q; but Q is very limited in its power to create a new world. Such power is resident in narrative much more than in sayings or sayings compositions. Q is episodic and polemical; it has only a weak ability to create a new world. Narrative, however, can create a new world and can people it with characters invested with authority. Narrative is, or can be, incipiently authoritarian and hierarchical. Apocalyptic, likewise, has the power to create a counter-vision of the world, a massive construction of an alternative reality. Q contains little of either narrative or apocalyptic and thus was doomed to fade away.

6. Conclusion

It has been the purpose of this essay to present an alternative model for understanding folk proverbs—a model which, it is argued, can help to bring other types of wisdom into sharper focus. We have urged that concentration on the content of wisdom, and upon proverbs as a prediscursive mode of thinking, be replaced with concentration on the function or use of wisdom. Both the model of the folk proverb that is presented and the typology of wisdom collections are intended as heuristic models. If this discussion stimulates some reflection on the function of wisdom and wisdom collections, it will, in its own small way, have done what the honoree of these papers was able to do consistently and brilliantly.

---

52 See Crüsemann, "Unchangeable World."

Sophrosyne

GRECO-ROMAN ORIGINS OF A
TYPE OF ASCETIC BEHAVIOR

Vincent L. Wimbush

1. Tracing Cultural Shifts: The Methodological Challenge

Scholarly efforts to account for the major shifts in socio-political, cultural, and ethical orientations in Greco-Roman antiquity have traditionally focused on the subjects of conflict, anxiety and individualism. The conflicts between Greece and Persia and among the Greek city-states, the hegemony of Macedonia over the Greeks and of Alexander and his successors over a great number of other peoples—these events and others were understood to have provoked a crisis of anxiety and identity. The decline of the familiar and the traditional in the local worlds and the imposition of the more universal, viz., the pan-hellenistic, forced reconsiderations of fundamental values and structures, especially of political values and structures. The failure of the experiment that was the city-state forced some among the ranks of the local elite, especially among the Greeks, to think seriously about alternatives—alternative values, structures, societies, personal orientations.

Many scholars have argued that the rethinking that the new socio-political situations—first the Hellenistic kingdoms, then Rome—inspired was manifested through "the surge of individualism," a renunciation of, or turning inward and away from, the clamor and disappointments of public life.[1] The classic and most dramatic scholarly expression is still to be found in the 1925 publication of Gilbert Murray's lectures on the stages in Greek religion:

> Anyone who turns from the great writers of classical Athens, say Sophocles or Aristotle, to those of the Christian era must be conscious of a great difference in tone. There is a change in the whole relation of the writer to the world about him. The new quality is not specifically Christian: It is just as marked in the Gnostics and Mithras-worshippers as in the Gospels and the Apocalypse, in Julian and Plotinus as in Gregory and Jerome. It is hard to describe. It is a rise of asceticism, of mysticism, in a sense, of pessimism; a loss of confidence, of hope in this life and of faith in normal human effort; a despair of patient inquiry, a cry for infallible

---

1 Sabine, *History*, 143.

revelation; an indifference to the welfare of the state, a conversion of the soul to God . . . an intensifying of certain spiritual emotions; an increase of sensitiveness, a failure of nerve.[2]

E. R. Dodds, in his now classic *Pagan and Christian in an Age of Anxiety,* argued that the whole period and culture was caught up in renunciation, in "contempt for the human condition and hatred for the body."[3] His explanation for this "madness" was in what he discerned as the concomitant relationship between belief in transcendence and renunciation: "The visible cosmos as a whole could only be called evil in contrast with some invisible Good Place or Good Person outside or beyond the cosmos."[4]

Although the last twenty or so years since the publication of Dodds's book have inspired some modifications in the articulations of explanations—socio-historical, psychological, theological—for the shifts and changes in the period, a basic consensus, greatly influenced by the likes of both Murray and Dodd, has emerged: In the Hellenistic-Roman period, across traditional cultural boundaries, a negative view of the social and physical world was popular; the idea of the self and of self-cultivation, of personal salvation, or conversion, was emerging; and almost universally, viz., pan-hellenistically, "salvation," or "happiness" ($\varepsilon\dot{v}\delta\alpha\iota\mu o\nu\acute{\iota}\alpha$) required some form of renunciation.[5]

Some cultural critics have argued that the socio-political conflicts that extended from the late fifth century among the Greeks through Late Antiquity cannot adequately explain the changes of the period. Louis Dumont has argued that the changes to which much scholarship has pointed should be understood as the phenomenon of "the emergence of the individual as a value, as a creation ex nihilo." Such a phenomenon is to be accounted for by reference not to socio-political upheavals, but to "philosophical activity."[6] But Dumont appears to have missed an important point when he argued that the crises and conflicts among the Greeks could not have led to the popularization of individualism, and that individualism in the classical period must have had its origins in "philosophical activity." The latter, defined as "the sustained exercise of rational inquiry," was said to have given birth to individualism, because "reason, universal in principle, is in practice at work through the particular person who exercises it and takes precedence, at least implicitly, over everything else."[7] Plato and Aristotle were seen by Dumont as aberrations against the trend in the direction of a turn inward, away from social engagement and responsibility. Their successors and students in the Hellenistic period established the trend to the point of positing the lone *wise man* ($\sigma o\phi\grave{o}s$

2 *Five Stages,* 155.
3 *Pagan and Christian,* 35.
4 *Pagan and Christian,* 13.
5 See MacMullen, *Enemies,* 49–94; F. E. Peters, *Harvest,* 410–20; 614–46; P. Brown, "Philosopher," 1–17.
6 Dumont, *Essays,* 28.
7 Dumont, *Essays,* 28.

ἀνήρ) as an ideal. Thus the "movement" toward inwardness was "favored" by the socio-political changes of the period, but was not a "consequence" of them.[8]

What is behind Dumont's use of "favored" and "consequence" in the context of discussion about the origins of the emergence of individualism and inwardness is an effort to go beyond positing socio-political changes as simple and direct determinatives of, and explanations for, changes in personal orientation. But the substitution of "philosophical activity" as the explanation for the origins of the movement is no less problematic. "Philosophical activity" itself cannot possibly have begun apart from socio-political inspiration or provocation.

Michel Foucault also attempted to gainsay the popular scholarly-consensus explanation for the rise of individualism and inwardness in the Greco-Roman world. For Foucault as well as for Dumont the break up and/or frustration of the political economies and social worlds along the Mediterranean in the coming first of the Hellenistic kingdoms, then of the Roman empire, cannot of itself explain the popular turn toward inwardness. The latter, according to Foucault, must be accounted for as a part of the discovery and cultivation of the ethical self, "the relation to self by which the individual constitutes and recognizes himself *qua* subject."[9] It is esentially, then, the individual's ethical and moral self-seeking that inspires inwardness and renunciation of the world.

> All moral action involves a relationship with the self. The latter is not simply "self-awareness" but self-formation as an "ethical subject," a process in which the individual delimits that part of himself that will form the object of his moral practice, defines his position relative to the precept he will follow, and decides on a certain mode of being that will serve as his moral goal. And this requires him to act upon himself, to monitor, test, improve, and transform himself. There is no specific moral action that does not refer to a unified moral conduct; no moral conduct that does not call for the forming of oneself as an ethical subject; and no forming of the ethical subject without "modes of subjectivation" and an "ascetics" or "practices of the self" that support them.[10]

2. The Origins of Ethical Self-Cultivation in the Greek Classical Period

The philosophic activity that was the cultivation of the ethical self was embraced by aristocratic males of Greek and Roman antiquity (a period that should be understood to have extended from the Greek classical period through the Hellenistic-Roman era). In the classical period such activity was exemplified in the moderation or self-restraint of the aristocratic male as part of an effort to develop a gender- and status-specific ethic understood, accord-

---

8 Dumont, *Essays,* 29.
9 Foucault, *Use of Pleasure,* 6.
10 Foucault, *Use of Pleasure,* 28.

ing to Foucault, as "the elaboration of a form of relation to the self that enables an individual to fashion himself into a subject of ethical conduct."[11] The deliberate, calculated restraint of aristocratic male dominance was seen as the method by which the ethical self could be cultivated. Apparently this activity was deemed especially important, given the failures of the city-states to realize sustained success in statecraft. The cultivation of the ethical self among elite males seemed to represent an effort to redefine and relocate the agent of significant social and political change—from the form or structure of government to the ethically and morally disciplined individual. Such an effort should be understood as a response to the social and political situation in fifth-century Greece. But such a response should nevertheless not be understood as either the universal *conditio sine qua non,* or the sufficient explanation, for the rise of philosophic activity that was the turn inward. Among some Greek aristocrats, it is clear that the socio-political situation of the fifth and fourth centuries served as occasion, even catalyst, for, the turn inward.

Consideration of concrete examples from the classical period can help establish more clearly the origins of "worldly asceticism," or inwardness, as a type of philosophic activity that would come to represent a response in opposition to the socio-political order. For example, it is clear that during the period of the Hellenistic kingdoms and the early Roman empire, the "worldly asceticism" of aristocratic males seemed not only part of an effort to cultivate the ethical self, but also a response to the real dangers that the aristocratic Greek and Roman empires represented to some local aristocrats. Under these circumstances, aristocrats practiced self-restraint in order both to save themselves from peril and to cultivate the ethical self. About this development more is to be said below. At this point it is enough to hypothesize that the discovery of the self in ethical cultivation was the *conditio sine qua non* for the development of philosophically inspired inwardness in opposition to the world.

The prominence given to "self-knowledge and self-restraint" in Greek and Roman literature from the heroic and archaic periods to the patristic period in Helen North's comprehensive and fascinating study entitled *Sophrosyne* is significant. It establishes without doubt the importance of the term in efforts to articulate assumptions about what was required for the ethical cultivation of the self.[12]

According to North, in the archaic and heroic periods the term sophrosyne was on the whole little used and when used was, for the most part, without religious or moral connotations.[13] It primarily signalled the importance of

11 Foucault, *Use of Pleasure,* 251.
12 North readily admits that the issues that relate to "self-knowledge" and "self-restraint" cannot be limited to the occurrence of the term. But she does argue for the primacy or great popularity of the term (and its Latin equivalents) over a very long period of time. In referring to the term sophrosyne, I have followed North's practice of treating it as though it were an English word, without italics. This alleviates some of the pressure to define the term categorically.
13 *Sophrosyne,* 3.

"soundness of mind" on the part of the hero. Such a state entailed the capacity to discern and respect the boundaries between the gods and human beings, as well as the laws of human society in general.[14]

In the age of the tragic poets the term enjoyed its first important "flowering." What was developed was the understanding of the *consequence* of overstepping the boundaries that were understood to be set up between human beings and the gods as well as within human society. Sophrosyne is used to explore more deeply what is required to honor boundaries and restrictions—a proper sense of measure, balance, respect, self-knowledge. What was only implicit in the poets of the heroic and archaic periods became explicit in the tragic poets.[15]

The age of the sophists ushered in a new stage of development in the use of sophrosyne. At this time arose the sharpest focused questioning about what was and should be the relationship between the welfare of the πόλις ("city-state") and the individual possession of certain *virtues* (ἀρεταί). There was of course no consensus on the question among the sophists, as the diverse uses of sophrosyne clearly reflect. In many of the sophistic fragments sophrosyne is used to refer to the control of the appetite for the sake of the health of the individual.[16] In other sources sophrosyne is attacked as foolishness, the possession of the weak.[17] But in many other sources sophrosyne is used to refer to a combination of moral and political virtues, most of which were understood to be exhortations to moderation. Of signal importance is the constellation of related terms—εὐβουλία ("political prudence"), εὐνομία ("law-abiding conduct"), ἀπραγμοσύνη ("gentlemanly aloofness").[18]

A contemporary of the sophists, Socrates made special contributions to the history of the use of sophrosyne. Regardless of the extent to which Socrates can be entirely separated from his student biographers and placed within his own time and society, the picture of a man deeply concerned about the cultivation of the ethical self is clear. Socrates seemed to be convinced that what was important in life was self-knowledge, or the "care of the soul," which necessarily entailed the acquisition of certain virtues, *self-control* (ἐγκράτεια) being the most important. It was Socrates' consistent exercise of self-control that led his biographers and admirers to call him a σώφρων ἀνήρ ("temperate man").[19]

The influence of both the sophists and Socrates proved to be enormous. In the latter part of the fifth century and beyond, concerns about self-knowledge and personal ethical cultivation, and about the relationship between personal ethical cultivation and the welfare of the πόλις, became central concerns among aristocratic males.

14 *Sophrosyne*, 4–5.
15 *Sophrosyne*, 32–33.
16 *Sophrosyne*, 88–96.
17 *Sophrosyne*, 97–98.
18 *Sophrosyne*, 88–99.
19 *Sophrosyne*, 117–18.

In the speeches of the fourth century Attic orators and in the writings from the Socratic "schools" interest in the Socratic self-questioning and cultivation of moral values, as well as in the characterization of the σώφρων πολίτης ("temperate citizen") continued, although much of the actual radical social and political character of Socrates' questioning was toned down by, even lost upon, the next immediate generations of his admirers and students. Among the orators, with their special interest in the characterization of the σώφρων πολίτης, three arguments were dominant: that the σώφρων πολίτης always be a democrat with an aversion to oligrachy; that he be loyal, generous, always ready to serve the πόλις; and that in his private life—and, for some, also in public life and in international relations—he be self-effacing and peaceable in nature. In the writings of the philosophical schools, inspired by the lifestyle and teachings of Socrates, sophrosyne figured prominently, often used—along with ἐγκράτεια ("self-control") and αὐτάρκεια ("self-sufficiency")—in contexts of discussion about what values ought to be held by the sage and elite males.[20]

Due to the influence of Socrates, sophrosyne began almost immediately to be used primarily and consistently to point to the cultivation of the ethical self in relationship to the welfare of the *household* (οἶκος) and of *society* (πόλις). For this reason it is important to discuss some classical Greek writers in more detail. These writers, although hardly typical in any respect, do collectively represent and reflect the interrelatedness of three different contexts for self-cultivation—the self, the household, and public life—for the aristocratic males of the period. The three writers were all greatly influenced by Socrates and the arguments of the sophists about matters relating to the virtuous life. They were chosen for discussion here because they allow us to see clearly the development of ethical cultivation among the elite in different contexts.[21]

Xenophon is to be noted here for his attempt to recapture the charisma, teaching, and example of Socrates as related to the virtuous life. His *Oeconomicus* is especially important as a reflection of his concern for the application of sophrosyne as the key virtue for the domestic life. Isocrates is important as one among the first and most influential orators to attempt to establish individual ethics as important for the governance of the πόλις as well as for international relations. His writings about the ethical cultivation of the ruler and the ruler's role as a παράδειγμα ("example") would serve as model in rhetoric for centuries to come. His protreptic work entitled *Nicocles or the Cyprians* is an especially good example of his perspective because it attempts to characterize and idealize the ethical and moral qualities of a particular ruler. Plato, for all the obvious reasons, also needs to be discussed. He made the same connections that Isocrates made between individual ethics and public leadership, but his contribution was far more creative and extensive and his influence far greater. He is for purposes of discussion here especially important for his

20 *Sophrosyne*, 122–42.
21 Foucault, *Use of Pleasure*, 75–76.

creative extension of the scope of the meaning of sophrosyne as a key virtue in all subsequent discussion in the west about the ethical life.

Discussion of these writers will follow in the order of Xenophon, Isocrates, and Plato. Since it is the subject of the ethical cultivation of the self that commands the discussion of the whole essay, the effort to demonstrate the concrete application of such cultivation will proceed at the same time from what is (next to the self) the smallest sphere of application, the οἶκος, to the larger sphere, the πόλις. Because Plato's writings are so extensive, and because his influence is so far-reaching and creative, especially as regards thinking about the cultivation of the self as foundation for the development of the "worldly asceticism" under discussion, it is appropriate to end with him.

3. Xenophon and Self Cultivation in the Oikos

Xenophon's *Oeconomicus* has to do with the ethical cultivation of the aristocratic male in the context of the governance or management of the household or large estate. The latter included all property, a wife, children, and servants (I.5–8; VI.4). The ethical cultivation of the dominant male was understood to be an important part of the "science of household management" (ἐπιστήμη, τέχνη).

A number of responsibilities, challenges, and relationships that define the aristocratic land-owning male are considered; but none is more challenging for the success of the governance of the household and for ethical cultivation than the marital relationship, primarily because this relationship involves at once both domination and intimacy. The challenges are enormous.

> Husbands differ widely in their treatment of their wives, and some succeed in winning their co-operation and thereby increase their estates, while others bring utter ruin on their houses by their behaviour to them. (III.10)

It was understood that the best occupation for an aristocrat (καλός τε κἀγαθός ["fine and good"]) was husbandry, viz., all those outdoor responsibilities related to the management of the large estate. The wife's responsibilities were understood to fall under and complement those of her husband's. She was to spend her time indoors, attending to the affairs of the house (VII.3). It was assumed that she, typically no more than fifteen years of age at the beginning of the marriage relationship, would be instructed in wifely duties (VII.5–6); but the point is made by Xenophon that in the context of a relationship in which dominance is clearly understood to belong to the husband, the effort to establish a relationship reflective of mutuality of concerns was important. In the context of discussion with his wife about what expectations he had for her, Ischomachus began his remarks by stating that he thought that the gods had ordained married life—the *yoking* (τὸ ζεῦγος) of male and female—for the purpose of forming "a perfect partnership in mutual service" (ὅτι ὠφελιμώτατον ἦ αὑτῷ εἰς τὴν κοινωνίαν [VII.18]).

Although it is made quite clear that males and females are assigned different spheres of activities and responsibilities—indoors for females, outdoors for males (VII.23–43)—and although it is never questioned that males play the dominant role, a degree of mutuality of consideration and respect is nonetheless stressed by Ischomachus.

> Because both must give and take, [God] granted to both impartially memory and attention; and so you could not distinguish whether the male or the female sex has the larger share of these. And God also gave to both impartially the power to practise due self-control, and gave authority to whichever is the better—whether it be the man or the woman—to win a larger portion of the good that comes from it. And just because both have not the same aptitudes, they have the more need of each other, the one being competent where the other is deficient. (VII.260–28)

4. Isocrates and Ethical Self Cultivation in Public Life

As an aristocratic Athenian with training in rhetoric and philosophy, Isocrates was predisposed to leadership in practical politics and in ideas. He did in fact attempt to exert some leadership in both politics and public opinion from an outsider's perspective. But his love for the quiet life led him to the founding of a school of rhetoric, and to teaching and writing. He distinguished the rhetorical training that he offered students from that which was offered in the schools of the sophists and philosophers. His instruction combined reason, feeling, and imagination with structured expression. It was training by which public and private affairs could be ordered toward the civilized existence of the citizen (*Antidosis* 253–255; 270ff.).

When not attending to the affairs of his school, Isocrates was found writing. He wrote forensic speeches, encomia, essays on education, political treatises, letters, and protreptic addresses. The specifically political treatises dominate both in numbers and in their importance in antiquity, addressing as they did the pressing matters of statecraft and war and peace. The three protreptic addresses that deal with the education and virtues of the ideal political leader—*To Nicocles, Nicocles or the Cyprians, Evagoras*—reflect most clearly Isocrates' moral and ethical sensibilities.

As one of the three "Cyprian" orations, *Nicocles or the Cyprians,* composed sometime between 372 and 365 BCE, was addressed to the Cyprians as though written by King Nicocles, obviously from a pro-monarchy perspective. But what chiefly characterizes the document is its description and commendation of an ideal monarch. Isocrates' ideal monarch is the Nicocles who justifies his rule not simply on the basis of ancestry (27–28), but on the basis of his own virtuous character (29). Such character is described most consistently throughout the document with reference to sophrosyne. Even when other virtues are discussed, they are most often accompanied by, and placed under the category of, sophrosyne (cf. 30, 36, 38, 43, 44). Understood as self-restraint, sophrosyne refers to the limitations that Nicocles as monarch, as absolute ruler, imposes upon himself. Such self-restraint is embraced as the most important trait of the monarch, not only because it can lead to *better human relations* (τὰς χρήσεις τῶν πραγμάτων), but also because it is represents what Foucault describes as the cultivation of the ethical self, and what in Isocrates is referred to as a "personal benefit" (ἡμᾶς τὸ καθ αὑτὰς ὠφελοῦσιν [30]).

The sophrosyne of the monarch is demonstrated in the areas of judicial and political clemency for the citizenry (32), material goods (31), military might vis-à-vis foreign enemies (33–34), and sexuality and fidelity in the marriage relationship (36–42). Most attention is devoted to the subject of sexuality and marriage, apparently because lack of self-restraint in this area was thought by Isocrates to be the cause of most of what was wrong about the world (36).

Isocrates' Nicocles boasts of his consistent self-restraint in an area in which so many other monarchs and aristocrats had proved themselves without restraint. Of course, such men did not have to prove themselves so. Because he wanted to be a *model* (παράδειγμα [37]) for his people, and because he wanted to cultivate his ethical self:

> I wanted to show that I could be strong in those things in which I should be superior, not merely to people in general, but even to those who pride themselves on their virtue. (39)

Such sensitivity led Nicocles the king not only to practice fidelity in his marriage, but also to chastise other male aristocrats for their failure to cultivate a harmonious, partnership relationship with their wives.

> I had no patience with the perversity of men who take women in marriage and make them partners in all the relations in life, and then are not satisfied with the compacts which they have made, but by their own lawless pleasures bring pain to those whom they expect never to cause them pain; and who, though honest in all partnerships, are without conscience in the partnership of marriage, when they ought to cherish this relationship the more faithfully inasmuch as it is more intimate and more precious than all others. . . . If kings are to rule well, they must try to preserve harmony, not in the states over which they hold dominion, but also in their own household and in their places of abode; for all these things *are the works of temperance* (σωφροσύνης ἔργα ἐστίν). (40–41)

That Nicocles' self-restraint was considered by Isocrates to be status-specific is made clear by statements that address the question of motives.

> I saw that courage and cleverness and the other qualities which are held in high esteem are shared by many even among the *base* (κακῶν ἀνδρῶν), whereas *justice* (δικαιοσύνην) and *temperance* (σωφροσύνην) are the *possessions of the good and noble* (τῶν καλῶν κἀγαθῶν ὄντα) alone. (43)

Not only does Isocrates' Nicocles directly identify self-restraint with aristocratic character (44), he also expressly challenges his audience to consider the relevance of circumstance and social status as factors in the judgement about the virtuous character of a person.

We ought not to *test* (δοκιμάζειν) all the virtues *in the same set of conditions* (ἐν ταῖς αὐταῖς ἰδέαις ἁπάσας), but should test justice when a man is in want, *temperance* (σωφροσύνην) when he is in power, *continence* (ἐγκράτειαν) when he is in the prime of youth. (44)

What in self-restraint is admired by Nicocles is the fact that it is meaningful to, viz., can only be exercised by, powerful men. The latter, by definition—because so much is at stake—are the ones for whom self-restraint can be experienced most poignantly as virtue.

When I was *left* by my father *without means* (ἐνδεὴς ... χρημάτων καταλειφθείς), I was so just in my dealings as to injure not one of my citizens; but when *I gained the power to do whatever I pleased* (λαβὼν δ ἐξουσίαν ὥστε ποιεῖν ὅ τι ἂν βούλωμαι), I proved myself more temperate than men in private station; and *I showed my self-control* (ἐκράτησα) in both circumstances at an age in which we find that the great majority of men most frequently go morally astray. (45)

Nicocles' rule is therefore justified because he was willing to restrain himself, to limit his power. This self-limitation, however, was not cynical. It was not done merely to win over the people. According to Isocrates, it was part of the sage's life-long cultivation of the (ethical) self. To be sure, the aim was to insure successful statecraft [63–64], but successful statecraft was seen as the virtuous cultivation of the individual writ large. The extent to which the powerful man of politics and statecraft, or the military leader, was willing to limit his power over others, not initially and primarily so much for the sake of the welfare of others as for the sake of his own ethical formation—to this extent the state would be advantaged.

Along with many other aristocrats of Greek antiquity, Isocrates equated the virtue of the powerful aristocrat with the voluntary stylized restraint and moderation of his power. Such a view clearly reflects sensitive ruminations about the potential and real dangers of seemingly unlimited power. Among some of the powerful the cultivation of the ethical self required self-imposed restraint and moderation.

It can be concluded that insofar as he is typical of a certain group of aristocratic moralists, orators, and philosophers of Greek antiquity, Isocrates provides important, viz., fairly representative, evidence for the origins of a type of ethic and orientation that on account of its restraining and limiting character, can be classified as *proto-ascetic*. His writings would serve to challenge the self-understanding and orientation of the aristocratic male in western antiquity.

5. Plato and the Cultivation of the Self

There is no attempt here to provide anything approaching a comprehensive summary of Plato's system of thought; such knowledge on the part of the reader is presupposed. Plato enjoys such enormous influence in western culture in general that it seems unnecessary to justify his general inclusion in any argument that touches upon the constitution of the west. It seems important here only to demonstrate the degree to which he can help to establish or disestablish an argument.

In terms of the use of sophrosyne in connection with thinking about moral and ethical development, Plato's influence, as mentioned above, was important and far-reaching. He extended the scope of reference for the term much beyond the traditional popular notion of self-control, even beyond the contemporary philosophical and moralist notions of self-cultivation. Actually, the two notions were united and refocused to constitute a new Platonic synthesis of the understanding of the good life.

This new understanding was accomplished by making sophrosyne one of the four cardinal virtues, along with justice, wisdom, and courage (*Rep.* IV.), thereby focusing its meaning and function. It was still the case that these virtues were understood to be civic virtues. But justice, the chief of the four virtues, was analyzed by Plato as that which can be grasped and practiced first by the individual, in the soul.

> Justice is indeed . . . not in regard to the doing of one's own business externally, but in regard to that which is *within* (τὴν ἐντός) and in the true sense *concerns oneself and the things of one's self* (περὶ ἑαυτὸν καὶ τὰ ἑαυτοῦ)—it means that a man must not suffer the principles in his soul to do each the work of some other and interfere and meddle with one another, but that he should dispose well of what in the true sense of the word is properly his own, and having first attained to self-mastery and beautiful order within himself, and having harmonized these three principles . . . self-controlled and in unison, he should then and then only turn to practice if he find aught to do either in the getting of wealth or the tendance of the body or it may be in political action or private business, in all such doings believing and naming the just and honourable action to be that which preserves and helps to produce this condition of soul, and wisdom the science that presides over such conduct. (443D–E)

Sophrosyne emerged as the glue that held all the other virtues together, as the controlling element, the presence of which guaranteed the proper balance or harmony of all virtues in the soul, and all parts of the soul, now no longer thought to be unitary.

> *Soberness* (sophrosyne) is a kind of beautiful *order* (κόσμος) and a continence of certain pleasures and appetites, as they say, using the phrase "master of himself" I know not how. . . . Now the phrase "master of himself" is an absurdity, is it not? For he who is master of himself would also be subject to himself, and he who is subject to himself would be master. For the same person is spoken of in all these expressions. . . . The intended meaning of this way of speaking appears to me to be that the soul of a man within him has a better part and a worse part, and the expression self-mastery means the control of the worse by the naturally better part. (430E–431A)

Because he was convinced that the duty of the state was the realization of justice, and because he was also convinced that justice must first be realized in the individual, specifically the ruler class, or guardians, Plato was not content to leave the cultivation of justice to chance. A system of education was devised so as to insure the grasp and cultivation of ethical and moral sensibilities that would mark the guardians of the platonic republic. From the elementary to the advanced stage of training Plato's guardians were to be characterized by their sophrosyne. It is the latter that at the elementary stage of training fosters a harmonious relationship among the constitutive parts of the soul—the rational, the spirited, the appetitive (433A)—and enables it to make right decisions about the things of the world. At the advanced stage the guardian is expected to be a philosopher, capable of a deeper, metaphysical grasp of reality. At this level the guardian as philosopher king would mostly contemplate the Forms of each virtue, including the Good. A grasp of the Forms would convince him of their characteristic order and harmony and would inspire imitation.

> The man whose mind is truly fixed on eternal realities has no leisure to turn his eyes downward upon the petty affairs of men . . . but he fixes his gaze upon the things of the eternal and unchanging order, and seeing that they neither wrong nor are wronged by one another, but all abide in harmony as reason bids, he will endeavour to imitate them and, as far as may be, to fashion himself in their likeness and assimilate himself to them. . . . Then the lover of wisdom associating with the divine order will himself become orderly and divine in the measure permitted to man. (500C–D)

The importance of sophrosyne for the individual and the state is to be seen in the emphasis placed upon balance, proportion, and harmony. To the extent to which sophrosyne is present in the individual soul the state, through the sensibiliities and self-restraint of the individual, can be peaceful and just. The presence of sophrosyne represents the balancing of different and unequal elements in the soul and in society, led in the soul by the rational element, in society by the ruling guardian class (545D–560D).

Plato's teaching did not emphasize or require contempt for the world. Rather it emphasized the proper (rational) prioritizing of the things of the world. Above all other things, contemplation of the Forms must take priority for the true philosopher. The body, worldly activities and concerns are not evil; they simply must assume secondary importance vis-à-vis contemplation. They may on occasion even have to be rejected if they prove a hindrance to contemplation. But all of the references in Plato to the primacy of contemplation (of the Eternal, the Forms), on the one hand, and of detachment and renunciation, on the other hand, function to hold out the challenge "that the body be kept in its proper place, and that the philosopher attach no value to it."[22]

22 Swain, *Hellenic Origins*, 61.

The fundamental contribution and challenge of Plato in terms of the development of the type of asceticism under discussion is his emphasis on the cultivation of the interior, the self. By encouraging the development of the philosophically minded (aristocratic) individual, who would turn inward in order to develop himself into the type of person capable of assuming leadership in the republic, Plato also influenced a type of piety and cultural orientation that would succeed him. It would thereafter prove almost impossible in the west to conceive of a wise or pious individual without thinking also of the turn inward.

6. Conclusion

Isocrates, Xenophon, and Plato are writers from Greek antiquity whose writings encourage a type of personal and socio-political orientation. Such orientation was status- (aristocratic) and gender- (male) specific in its origins. It should be characterized as psychologically felt, rationally ordered experience developed in association with the increasing awareness of the self and the cultivation of the same into an ethical subject (Foucault). This concern with the ethical self was inspired or provoked by socio-political situations that were judged to be less than utopian. Xenophon is representative of the sensitive aristocratic male who attempts to define himself as a person in terms of his handling of the authority that he holds over others in the context of the household. Isocrates is somewhat representative of the sensitive male Greek aristocrat of the fourth century attempting to come to terms with the failure of the Greek city-states to realize peace and stability. What was judged to be lacking was not the best or appropriate form of government, but virtuous men in leadership positions. An ethic of moderation and self-restraint on the part of men of power was commended as the remedy. He represents the beginning of attempts on the part of the aristocratic male to develop himself as ethical subject through a self-imposed ethic of restraint. Plato provides the most elaborate and sophisticated prescription for the realization of a utopian social order through the cultivation of the ethical self of aristocratic males. All three writers commended an ethic, a social orientation, that was aristocratic, spiritual, or intellectualist and "ascetic." It was aristocratic in that it had to do with the full and absolute power assumed to be the prerogative of the free aristocratic male; it was spiritual and intellectualist in that it called for the development of the interior self; it was "ascetic" in the sense that it challenged the free aristocratic male to cultivate himself as an ethical subject by *limiting* or *renouncing* his assumed power and authority over others and by developing sensibilities for the contemplative or philosophic life.

To be sure, not all, but enough, evidence has been marshalled in this essay to establish the ethic of self-restraint on the part of the aristocratic male in Greek antiquity. The most important conclusion to be drawn for the purpose of this essay is that this ethic, by cultivating the individual as ethical subject, seems to have provided both historical precedent and ideological underpinning for the development of a type of ascetic piety that would be consistently inner-directed and rational.

The importance of this conclusion lies in its potential to help efforts to understand and explain the diversity of expressions of piety and self-understanding in Greek and Roman antiquity, thus to a large extent in contemporary Western culture. Because such efforts have characterized the research agenda of James M. Robinson and the Institute for Antiquity and Christiantity for decades, it is little wonder that both Robinson and the Institute have had such a great impact.

James M. Robinson on a panel with Bernadette Brooten and Hans Küng

viii

Liberating Death's Captives

RECONSIDERATION OF
AN EARLY CHRISTIAN MYTH

Harold W. Attridge

Extremely widespread in early Christian sources was the mythologou-menon of the descent of Christ to the underworld. Its numerous attestations have been frequently catalogued,[1] and its multifaceted motifs have been the subject of numerous studies. There have been two principle, and not unre-lated, foci for these investigations, the article in the creeds[2] with its prehistory and subsequent interpretation,[3] and the primary biblical text in which the confessional and dogmatic tradition has attempted to find its basis, 1 Pet 3:18–20; 4:6. This brief essay will not attempt to recapitulate the entire history of theological debate or modern historical scholarship on the topic. It will high-light what appears to be an important but neglected example of one type of the "descensus ad inferos" myth. In doing so this contribution honors a scholar long concerned with the existential significance of early Christian stories.

While it is neither possible nor desirable to treat the entire scholarly discus-sion of the descensus tradition, a brief review is useful as background for this essay. Much of the discussion may be usefully exemplified by three treatments. Jean Daniélou's classic study of Jewish Christianity reviewed some of the key texts with Jewish-Christian connections.[4] He understood the belief in the

---

1 Useful surveys remain Schmidt, "Der Descensus"; MacCulloch, *The Harrowing;* Bieder, *Die Vorstellung;* Grillmeier, "Gottessohn"; and Vogels, *Christi Abstieg,* 183–225, al-though they need updating in the light of more recent finds, especially the Nag Hammadi collection. Many of the relevant texts from that find are mentioned in Peel, "The Decensus."

2 The formula first is found in the creed of Sirmium of 359 CE. Vogels (*Christi Abstieg,* 207–9) offers a critical discussion of the theory of a Syrian origin for the formula, advanced by Kelly (*Early Christian Creeds,* 379) on the basis the work of Connolly, "Early Syriac Creed." The Latin formula, *descendit ad infera* (not, as later, *inferos*), is first attested in Rufinus, *Commentarius in symbolum* 28, on the basis of the creed of Aquileia.

3 For a survey of the earlier history of the dogmatic discussion, see Bieder, *Die Vorstellung,* 3–32.

4 Daniélou, *Theology,* 233–48=*Théologie,* 257–73. He cites GPet 41–42; an anonymous Presbyter in Irenaeus, *Adv. Haer.* 4.27.2; an apocryphal citation of Jeremiah—whether an interpolation, midrash, or apocryphon is unclear—cited in Justin, *Dial.* 72.4; and Irenaeus, *Adv. Haer.* 3.20.4; 4.22.1; 4.33.1; 4.33.12; 5.31.1 and *Demonstratio* 78; IgnMagn 9:2; HermSim 9:16; *Ep. Ap.* 26–27; TestLevi 4:1, TestDan 5:10–11; *Asc. Isa.* 4:21; 9:16–17; 10:8–14; SibOrac 8:310–12; OdesSol 17:8–11; 22:8–11; 42:15–26.

103

descent to consist of Christ's literal post-mortem involvement with the realm of the dead to announce there salvation to the just of the Old Testament. Only as the tradition develops in the second century, for the first time, according to Daniélou, in the Jeremiah apocryphon cited by Justin and Irenaeus, does the descent come to involve liberation of the dead. Daniélou understood the descent tradition to be not a scriptural doctrine,[5] but a belief of the Jewish-Christian community, with concerns that are primarily soteriological, not christological.

Heinz-Jürgen Vogels[6] agrees on one major point with Daniélou, namely that preaching is the primary activity ascribed to Christ in the underworld in the earliest layers of the tradition. He differs, however, by rooting the tradition firmly in 1 Peter. The tradition of the early Church he sees developing in three major types. (1) *Christ preaches and thereby liberates prisoners of Hades.*[7] As the tradition develops, various dogmatic questions are posed and answered in different ways by various authors and communities. So, for example, it becomes a problem whether liberation was proclaimed to all or only to the just of the Old Testament and whether it was immediate or only promised for the future. The earliest traditions seem to be less differentiated and precise on such matters. (2) *Christ baptizes.*[8] The texts recording this tradition are relatively few and express an obviously later ecclesiastical and dogmatic concern. (3) *Christ battles the powers of Hades in order to gain liberation.*[9] These texts sound the most "mythical" but are often merely colorful metaphor. The realm of apostolic teaching does not, virtually by definition, involve myth. As the tradition develops further the imagery becomes more extravagant.

Vogels rejected attempts to find a purely metaphorical doctrine in the image of the descent[10] or to accord any place to "myth" as a developmentally primitive or theologically fruitful category.[11] Hence, with many more recent stu-

---

5 In denying the presence of the notion of the descent into Hades in 1 Peter, Daniélou (*Théologie*, 257–59) follows Reicke, *Disobedient Spirits;* Schlier (*Christus*, 13–18); and, interestingly, Bultmann ("Bekenntnis," 5). Among others who have questioned the presence of the notion in 1 Peter are Spitta, *Christi Predigt;* Bieder, *Die Vorstellung;* and Dalton, *Christ's Proclamation.*

6 Vogels, *Christi Abstieg*, 184.

7 In this category Vogels (*Christi Abstieg*, 189–210) cites: IgnMagn 9:2; IgnPhld 5:2; 9:1; GPet 39–42; *Ep. Ap.* 27 (38); Marcion, in Irenaeus, *Adv. Haer.* 1.27.3; the Presbyter in Irenaeus, *Adv. Haer.* 4.27.1; the apocryphal Jeremiah citation in Justin, *Dial.* 72, and Irenaeus, *Adv. Haer.* 4.22.1–2; HermSim 9.16.5; SibOrac 8:310–17; Irenaeus, *Adv. Haer.* 4.22.1–2; 5.31.1; Tertullian, *De anima* 55.2; Clement of Alexandria, *Strom.* 6.6; Hippolytus, *De antichristo* 26; Origen, *De principiis* 2.5.3; *Contra Celsum* 2.43; then the creeds, on which see n. 2 above.

8 The theme appears as a secondary element in several of the sources listed in the previous note, *Epistula apostolorum*, Shepherd of Hermas, Sibylline Oracles.

9 Vogels (*Christi Abstieg*, 212–25) lists OdesSol 17:8–15; 22:8–9; 24:7–14; 42:11–20; Melito of Sardis, *Paschal Homily* 100–2 and Frag. 13; TestLevi 4:1; 5:10–12; Hippolytus' *Anaphora;* AcThom. 10, 156; the *Gospel of Nicodemus;* and traces in the fourth-century creeds of Sirmium, Nice, and Constantinople.

10 See Gschwind, *Niederfahrt Christi.*

11 For another rejection, from a different dogmatic tradition, of the descensus tradition as

dents of the descensus tradition, he rejected the earlier attempts of students of the history of religion to derive the tradition from any particular mythical complex.[12]

John Dominic Crossan represents a third position.[13] He would agree with Daniélou and Vogels on one point, namely the primacy of the preaching motif, and with Daniélou on the absence of the descensus motif in the New Testament. He differs on other important points. The apocryphal Gospel of Peter is a witness to the earliest text, a "Cross Gospel" which is the source of the passion narratives of the Synoptics as well as of the descensus tradition. Like some earlier historians of religion, Crossan is interested in popular piety, not dogmatic development. He sees the belief in the descent as an early Jewish-Christian formula, thoroughly mythical in character, giving expression to belief in the liberating power of Christ's death and exaltation. Its authentic continuation is found in those sources which continue to operate in the sphere of myth, including some texts that Vogels had seen as derivative.[14] Likewise, some of Vogels's primary texts become examples for Crossan of secondary dogmatic concerns.[15]

Despite their differences, these studies agree on certain key points: that the earliest form of the tradition posits a literal activity of Christ in the realm of the dead, and that this activity consisted primarily, if not exclusively, of preaching.[16] Other forms of the descensus tradition, including the notion that Christ engaged in combat with infernal powers, or the metaphorical identification of Hades with this world, are frequently seen to be derivative from the imagery of Christ preaching to the souls below.

On certain points the consensus does seem to be warranted. The earliest attestations of the tradition, including the one that I shall presently discuss, do involve a preaching mission of Christ in the realm of the dead, but, as Vogels suggests and Crossan ardently maintains, that preaching is liberating, and in the earliest attestation of the tradition the liberating act is metaphorically portrayed as a destruction of the infernal power. Hence, the combat motif is rooted within the framework of a descent tradition at a very early stage.[17]

myth unbecoming the lofty clarity of Pauline theology, see M. Werner, *Formation*, 99–104; *Entstehung*, 255–71.

12 See especially Kroll, *Gott und Hölle*.

13 See Crossan, *The Cross*.

14 Crossan (*The Cross*, 364–73) cites *Ep. Barn.* 11:1–4; Odes Sol 17; 22; 42; *Asc. Isa.* 3:15; 4:21; 9:7–18; 10:7–8, 14.

15 Crossan (*The Cross*, 373–81) cites IgnTral 9:1; IgnMagn 9:2; Justin, *Dial.* 72; Irenaeus, *Adv. Haer.* 3.20.4; 4.22.1; 4.33.1; 4.33.12; 5.31.1; *Demonstratio* 78; SibOrac 8:310–17; 1:376–82; *Ep. Ap.* 51; HermSim 9:16.

16 For expressions of this consensus see also, e.g., Grillmeier (*Christ*, 73–75, and Vogels (*Christi Abstieg*, 183). For the descent to preach as a "typical Jewish-Christian idea," see Grillmeier (*Christ*, 73).

17 All three exemplary treatments of the descensus tradition, Daniélou (*Theology*, 233–34) followed by Crossan (*The Cross*, 362–63) as well as by Vogels (*Christi Abstieg*, 211), admit the presence of combat imagery in the New Testament but see it independent of the descensus tradition, with which it merges only in the second century.

Moreover, the development of the combat tradition is correctly ascribed to the Hellenization of Christianity,[18] but its development is placed much too late. The consensus is, I believe, in error in its contention that the identification of earth with Hades, often assumed to be confined to gnostic sources,[19] is a late and derivative element of the tradition. Like the combat motif, the identification is present in one of the earliest attestations of the tradition.

A key to reassessing the current consensus on these points is to recognize that an early, if not the earliest, attestation of the motif of Christ's descent appears in the Epistle to the Hebrews, in a text generally overlooked or slighted in treatments of the theme.[20] The pericope, Heb 2:10–18, with its arresting title of Christ the ἀρχηγός ("pioneer"), and its notion of perfective suffering,[21] through which the Son leads many children to heavenly glory, has been the subject of considerable attention, particularly since the attempt by Käsemann to discover here a form of gnostic redeemer mythology. That derivation has frequently been disputed, e.g., by Müller, and is indeed unlikely, given the emphasis on suffering at the heart of the mythic imagery of the passage (Heb 2:10). Such a positive evaluation of suffering would be unusual, to say the least, in most of the ancient sources that might be labelled gnostic.[22] Nonetheless, alternative readings of the pericope—as an example, for instance, of an Exodus typology—fail to do justice to the importance of a coherent mythological scheme in the work.[23]

The mythical scheme is clear at the beginning (Heb 2:10) of the pericope:[24] "Now it was fitting for him, for whom and through whom all things exist, in bringing many sons and daughters[25] to glory, to perfect through sufferings the one who leads the way to salvation." Here the core image describes the way to heavenly glory (2:9) under the guidance of a leading guide or ἀρχηγός.[26] The

18 See, e.g., MacCulloch, *The Harrowing,* 253, and Peel, "The Decensus," 48.

19 See, e.g., Peel, "The Decensus," 36.

20 Bieder (*Die Vorstellung,* 90–92) at least canvasses the possible relationship of Hebrews to the tradition but minimizes its significance and does not discuss this passage. Vogels (*Christi Abstieg,* 220) refers to Hebrews 2:14 in passing as an example of the biblical (hence non-mythical) notion of overcoming the powers by Christ's death. He fails to see the mythical pattern underlying the whole pericope. The other recent treatments already noted quite neglect the passage.

21 On this theme, see in particular Peterson, *Hebrews.*

22 The point is often made, e.g., by Dey (*Intermediary World,* 215–16); and Vanhoye (*Situation,* 224–25). I prescind from a discussion of the definition of Gnosticism and Gnostics. While some Valentinians (see e.g., *Gos. Truth* 18,24; 20,11, and *Tri. Trac.* 115,3–11) might see the human suffering of Jesus in a positive light, their position is hardly characteristic of most Gnostics, and in any case it is different from the significance of suffering in Hebrews.

23 Grässer ("Die Heilsbedeutung," 183 n. 177) rightly insists on the mythical character of the pericope but continues to follow Käsemann's identification (*Wandering People*) of the myth as gnostic.

24 On the various grammatical and exegetical issues in the verse, and in the pericope as a whole, see Attridge, *Hebrews,* 78–96.

25 Literally "sons," but the term is certainly inclusive of all members of the community of faith.

26 For general semantic data on the term, see Delling, "ἀρχηγός," 487–88, and Müller, ΧΡΙΣΤΟΣ ΑΡΧΗΓΟΣ, 72–102).

imagery is most closely paralleled by those of the numerous descensus texts that describe some act of liberation, and not simply a promise of such. To cite but a few examples, Marcion in Irenaeus notes that "the Sodomites and Egyptians, and those who were like them, and in fact all the Gentiles who had walked in thorough wickedness, were saved by the Lord when he descended into the Underworld, and they had hastened to him, and he took them into his kingdom."[27] In the Odes of Solomon the psalmist records that "death ejected me and many with me. . . . And they cried out and said, Son of God, have pity on us. And deal with us according to Thy kindness, And bring us out from the bonds of darkness. And open for us the door by which we may come out to Thee."[28] The scene is familiar to gnostic sources such as the *Apocryphon of John*, which includes a poetic comment by the divine revealer:

> . . . and I who am leading you to the place of honor. Arise! Keep in mind that you are the person who has listened. Follow your root, which is myself, the compassionate. Be on your guard against the angels of poverty and the demons of chaos and all those who are entwined with you; and be wakeful, (now that you have come) out of heavy sleep and out of the garment in the interior of Hades.[29]

The scenario is also found among the orthodox, such as Melito's *Paschal Homily*, where Christ speaks: "I, said Christ, I am the one who destroyed death and led the enemy in triumph, who trampled Hades and bound the strong one, who snatched up mankind and led them to the heights of heaven."[30] In somewhat more elaborate form it is found in the Acts of Thomas: "Jesus Christ, the compassionate son and perfect savior, Christ, son of the living God, the undaunted power which has overthrown the enemy, and the voice which has been heard by the rulers, which has shaken all of their powers, the ambassador sent from on high who has descended as far as Hades, you who have opened the doors and led up from there those who for long ages have been locked in the storehouse of darkness, and have shown to them the way which leads on high. . . ."[31]

Myth is prominent in Heb 2:10 but is not confined to that initial verse. Also replete with clearly mythic imagery is Heb 2:14–15, "Now since the children share in blood and flesh, he too likewise partook of the same things so that through death he might break the power of the one who holds sway over death, that is, the devil, and might release those who by fear of death were subject to slavery through all their lives." These verses describe, in effect, the decisive moment when the "children" are released from bondage to begin their journey to glory on high. Although the passage does not have the

27 Irenaeus, *Adv. Haer.* 1.27.3.
28 OdesSol 42:12, 15–17. Translation by Charlesworth, *The Odes*, 145–46.
29 *Ap. John* (NHC II,*1*) 31,13–21. Translation by Layton, *The Gnostic Scriptures*, 51. Also from the Nag Hammadi collection, cf. *Teach. Silv.* (NHC VII,*4*) 110,27–29: "He brought up the poor from the Abyss and the mourners from the Underworld."
30 Melito of Sardis, *Hom. Pasch.* 102. Author's translation.
31 AcThom 10 (Greek). Author's translation. For further parallels, see MacCulloch, *The Harrowing*, 253–87.

dramatic imagery of some of the combat scenarios, the reference to the "destruction of the power" (καταργήσῃ τὸ κράτος) suggests a conflict between Christ and the adversary, in the restrained fashion that characterizes earlier "combat" texts.[32] Apart from the Christian, or perhaps Jewish-Christian, identification of the "one who holds sway over death" as the devil, the imagery here is that of the widespread and ancient pattern of heroic liberation of those held in bondage by death.

Recognition of that pattern, by the way, resolves another traditional exegetical crux in the pericope, the meaning of the verb ἐπιλαμβάνεται in the next verse (2:16). That verb does not mean blandly "help"[33] or, in a technical theological sense, "assume the nature of."[34] Instead it refers to the concrete act by which the *archegos* begins to guide his fellow "children" to heavenly glory. Like Orpheus holding the hand of Eurydice,[35] he "grasps" the "children of Abraham" as he leads them on the heavenly path.[36]

The only reason for doubting the presence of the mythical pattern—and no doubt the reason that this text has not played a more prominent role in the discussion of the Descensus tradition—is the fact that no descent into Hades is explicitly mentioned in the context. The only descending of any kind appears in the preceding passage, Heb 2:6–9, which describes the incarnation of the Son through a playful exegesis of Ps 8:5–7. That text had hymned the glory of human beings, made by God only "a little less than the angels." The affirmation stands in synonymous parallelism with a remark that human beings are "crowned with glory and honor." The exegetical comment in Hebrews drives a wedge between the two cola and thereby finds a reference to the incarnation. Christ was made "for a little while lower than the angels." Then, through suffering death, he was "crowned with heavenly glory." The abasement "below" the angels certainly implies a descent, though hardly to Sheol. If

---

32 Melito, *Hom. Pasch.* 102, cited above, offers a fairly close parallel. There is nothing here of the breaking of bars and doors, as in OdesSol 17:4, 10 or *Teach. Silv.* 110,19–21, much less of the extravagent imagery of the *Gospel of Nicodemus*.

33 This is the most common interpretation of the text, among both patristic and modern commentators. See, e.g., Moffatt, *Hebrews*, 36–37; Bruce, *Hebrews*, 41 n. 56; and Michel, *Hebräer*, 162. This understanding of the verb no doubt underlies the *RSV*'s translation, "is concerned with."

34 The term is related to the incarnation by such patristic authors as Ambrose, Chrysostom, Theodoret, and Oecumenius, and in the Reformation by Calvin. On the patristic interpretation, see Westcott, *Hebrews*, 55, and Hughes, *Hebrews*, 115–16. For a modern defense of this exegesis see Spicq, *Hébreux, ad loc.*

35 For this well-known myth, cf. Apollodorus, *Bibliotheke* 1.3.2; Pausanias 9.30.4; Virgil, *Georgica* 4.454–527; Ovid, *Metam.* 10.1–63.

36 An interesting parallel in the descensus tradition, although overlaid with dogmatic interpretation, is the account in *Ep. Ap.* 27, more clearly preserved in the Aethiopic version: "And on that account I have descended and have spoken with Abraham and Isaac and Jacob, to your fathers the prophets, and have brought to them news that they may come from the rest which is below into heaven, and *have given them the right hand* of the baptism of life and forgiveness and pardon for all wickedness as to you, so from now on also to those who believe in me" (ET in Hennecke-Schneemelcher, 209). See also Melito of Sardis, *Hom. Pasch.* 102, cited above.

descent is equivalent to incarnation, it is clear that the destruction of "the one who holds power over death" (2:14) is a metaphor for something that takes place in this world. That assessment is supported by the description of the means by which that inimical entity exercises its sway, not through a bondage which can only affect disembodied shades, but through "lifelong fear of death" (2:15).

That mythical imagery is used in Hebrews 2 seems to be clear. That it is used in a metaphorical way is also obvious. The metaphorical identification of the earth as the place where people are held in bondage to death might provide grounds for identification of the myth as "gnostic," since similar metaphors are common in gnostic sources.[37] It has already been noted that the emphasis on the importance of suffering makes the designation "gnostic" problematic. Equally significant is the fact that the bond to be loosed is not death itself but the fear of death. Such a fear is not a characteristic gnostic concern.[38]

The mythical plot in Hebrews is clearly being used in a metaphorical way, but it seems to be distinctive in comparison with other metaphorical uses. Can anything more be said about the source and character of the mythical imagery deployed here? The fact that one of the text's distinctive elements is the reference to the fear of death is suggestive. There are some texts from the Hebrew Bible that speak of the fear of death,[39] although they are relatively few and far between. On the other hand, references to such fear have long been recognized as common in Greco-Roman traditions. The Roman poet Lucretius[40] vividly describes the fear of death which haunts humankind and celebrates the liberation from that fear achieved by the philosophy of Epicurus. Stoics[41] recognize the debilitating dread of a mortal end and advise resolute endurance in the face of that eventuality. Jews influenced by that classical tradition can speak in a similar fashion. Philo, in a treatise on the very stoic theme "That every just man is free," maintains that "nothing is so calculated to enslave the mind as fearing death through desire to live."[42]

The prominence of the motif in Greco-Roman sources suggests that the

---

37 For identifications of this world as the place to which the savior descends, cf. *Naassene Hymn* (Hipp. *Ref.* 5.2); *Ap. John* (NHC II,*2*) 30,13–31,27; GEgy (NHC III,*2*) 56,22–58,22; *Teach. Silv.* (NHC VII,*4*) 103,23–104,14; 110,14–111,4; *Trim. Prot.* (NHC XIII,*1*) 35,12–13; 41,1–42,1; *Great Pow.* (NHC VI,*4*) 40,24–42,3; and possibly AcThom10.

38 Grässer ("Die Heilsbedeutung," 176) criticizes analyses that do not explain how the death of the Son overcomes fear of death and, following in Käsemann's footsteps, suggests that gnostic myth provides the answer. Evidence for the position is, however, hard to find. Death in and of itself or as a metaphor for the state of ignorance or "sleep" is regularly said to be overcome in the gnostic versions of the myth listed in the last note, but liberation from fear of death is not attested.

39 Cf. Hos 13:14; Qoh 9:4; Sir 41:1–4.

40 Lucretius, *De rer. nat.* 1.102–26.

41 Cf. Seneca, *Ep.* 24; 30.17; Epictetus, *Diss.* 1.17.25; 1.27.7–10; 2.18.30; 4.7.15–17. Cf. also Cicero, *Tusc. Disp.* 1 and Dio Chrysostom, *Or.* 6.42.

42 *Quod omnis probus liber sit* 22.

earlier allusion to heroic liberators such as Orpheus is not a simple phenome-
nological parallel. The storied musician, of course, was not the only figure to
whom a liberating descent to the underworld was ascribed. Of the several
figures who are supposed to have made such a descent, the one who most
closely approximates the action here predicated of Christ is, in fact, Herakles.[43] The parallel to traditions about Herakles consists not simply in the
combination of certain motifs characteristic of a mythical pattern but, more
importantly, in a psychologizing (or perhaps existentializing) reinterpretation
of the ancient story.

The two key foci of the comparison with the saga of Herakles are the role of
suffering (2:10: διὰ παθημάτων) in the "perfecting"[44] of the Son and the
liberation of death's captives from their "lifelong fear of death" (2:15: ὅσοι
φόβῳ θανάτου διὰ παντὸς τοῦ ζῆν ἔνοχοι ἦσαν δουλείας). It is precisely these
motifs that are highlighted in the Hellenistic and Roman philosophical
reinterpretations of myths about Herakles.

That the Herakles tradition might provide relevant parallels for the portrait
of Christ as savior has often been maintained, both in antiquity,[45] and among
modern scholars.[46] The response to such claims, often apologetic in tone,[47]
can easily point to differences between Christ and Herakles, given the diversity
of the myths about the latter. Herakles, the Paul Bunyan or perhaps the
Rambo of the heroic past, is in some ways a rather unlikely companion of or
model for Christ. Yet it was not the demi-god who had his way through
unbridled ferocity upon whom Hellenistic philosophers and poets concen-
trated, but rather the man who, through toils, sufferings, and wrestling with
his own passions, won immortal glory for himself and provided a model of
philosophical confrontation with death for any who cared to look to his
example.[48]

The clearest and most relevant example of this whole development is found
in the Hercules tragedies of Seneca,[49] where the end of Hercules the hero is
understood to be his glorification through his suffering. The final choral ode
of the *Hercules Oetaeus* summarizes the process of apotheosis, the journey *per
aspera ad astra* ("through rough ways to the stars"),[50] described throughout the
play: "Never to Stygian shades is glorious valor borne. The brave live on, nor
shall the cruel fates bear you o'er Lethe's waters; but when the last day shall

43 In general, see Malherbe, "Herakles."
44 On this complex image, see most recently Peterson, *Hebrews.*
45 See the sources collected by Malherbe, "Herakles," 576–81.
46 See Pfister, "Herakles"; Knox, "Divine Hero"; and Simon, *Hercule.* See Malherbe,
   "Herakles," 569–72, for further references.
47 See, e.g., the article of Rose, "Herakles."
48 On the Hellenistic reinterpretation of Herakles, see in general Hoistad, *Cynic Hero,* 22–
   68, and Galinsky, *The Herakles Theme.*
49 On Seneca's dramas in general see Pratt, *Seneca's Drama.*
50 Or as Seneca puts it (*Hercules Furens* 437), Non est ad astra mollis e terris via ("There is
   no easy way from earth to the stars"). Texts are cited from the critical edition by Leo.

bring the final hour, glory will open wide the path to heaven."[51] Hercules, once he achieves heavenly glory, becomes, like the heavenly High Priest of Hebrews, an object of cult.[52]

In the *Hercules Furens*[53] the chorus, upon hearing from Theseus of the hero's underworld exploit, sings of their fear of death and the liberation from that fear that Hercules' descent into Hades has brought them. "He has crossed the streams of Tartarus, subdued the gods of the underworld, and has returned. And now no fear remains; naught lies beyond the underworld."[54] The play is not, however, about the descent to Tartarus and the capture of its watchdog, but about the hell on earth, which Juno, the hero's mythological enemy, inflicts upon him.[55] The play ultimately suggests that Hercules' true victory over the powers of Hades is achieved in his conquest of his own irrational self, but only after he suffers through the madness of his passions. That conquest is finally completed when, in the *Oetaeus*, he accepts his own death. The Hercules plays of Seneca thus offer an existential interpretation or philosophical actualization of the Herakles cycle. Two important elements of that interpretation involve the story of the final self-sacrifice of the hero and the story of his descent to the underworld and confrontation there with the

---

51 *Hercules Oetaeus* 1983–88:

> Numquam Stygias fertur ad umbras
> inclita virtus. vivunt fortes
> nec Lethaeos saeva per amnes
> vos fata trahent, sed cum summas
> exiget horas consumpta dies,
> iter ad superos gloria pandet.

Doubts about the authenticity of the play have been frequently expressed. For a summary of the arguments and a review of pertinent literature, see Zwierlein, *Kritischer Kommentar*, 313–43, who dates the work in the early second century. In defense of the authenticity of the piece, see Pratt, *Seneca's Drama*, 28, 115–28.

52 Before the final choral ode (*Herc. Oet.* 1979–82) Alcmena, having witnessed the self-immolation and heard his subsequent voice from heaven, exclaims,

> misera mens incredula est.
> es numen et te mundus aeternum tenet,
> credo triumphis. regna Thebarum petam
> covumque templis additum numen canam.

("My wretched mind is incredulous. You are a divine power and the world of eternity holds you, in triumph, I believe. I shall seek the kingdom of Thebes and sing of the new deity added to the temples.")

53 In general see Shelton, *Seneca's Hercules Furens*, and, most recently, Fitch, *Seneca's Hercules Furens*.

54 *Hercules Furens* 889–92:

> Transvectus vada Tartari
> pacatis redit inferis;
> iam nullus superest timor;
> nil ultra iacet inferos.

55 *Herc. Fur.* 91, *hic tibi ostendam inferos*, ("I shall show you hell here.")

infernal powers. The two elements are intimately related. The descent and confrontation with Hades serve as a symbolic expression of the significance of the hero's encounter with his own death. The apotheosis or exaltation that ensues upon his death is a guarantee of the enduring effects of the encounter with death. In short, it is in confrontation with and acceptance of the reality of his own death that Hercules overcomes the lifelong fear of death, for himself and those who, through his philosophical cult, take him as a model, as what we might dub the "initiator and perfecter of the Stoic ideal."

The parallels between the reinterpreted myth of Herakles and the christological portrait of Heb 2:10–18 are striking. On the level of thematic or mythemic correspondences: (1) The savior figure in both cases is involved in a confrontation with the mysterious adversary who holds power over death.[56] (2) In both cases the result of the confrontation is the liberation of captives held in the infernal realm. (3) In both cases the savior figure is himself involved in educative suffering: Herakles' toils teach him about the meaning of his own human limitations; Jesus' sufferings prepare him to be a merciful High Priest (Heb 2:17–18). The theme of Christ's educative suffering is, by the way, taken up again explicitly in Heb 5:7–9, which uses a proverb long familiar in the classical tradition. (4) In both cases the hero attains, through his suffering, a heavenly glory. (5) Of equal importance is the correspondence at the level of interpretation of the basic mythical plot. As the plays of Seneca show, the liberating function of the hero's action is ultimately directed to the general human fear of death. This too, as we have seen, is the distinctive feature of the version in Hebrews of the deliverance effected by the Son.

There are, of course, obvious differences between the two accounts, and the parallel should not be construed as a harmonization. Hebrews does not present Jesus as simply a stoic sage, teaching a stalwart resolution in the face of personal extinction or overcoming fiercely destructive passion. Nor can any dependence of Hebrews on Seneca—or, for that matter, Seneca on Hebrews[57]—be demonstrated. The parallels suggest something about the generic source of the mythical imagery of at least part of the descensus tradition and, perhaps more clearly, about one of the ways in which mythical imagery was construed and appropriated at a very early stage of the Christian tradition.

To take these points in order, the appropriation of the myth of Herakles' descent as a forceful image in Greco-Roman literature of the first century should serve as a caution against too narrow a derivation of the descent traditions of early Christianity. Combat imagery stemming from Jewish apocalyptic traditions was clearly operative in some Christian accounts,[58] but it is

56 As already noted, the designation of the figure in Hebrews as the Devil (2:14) indicates that the mythical plot has developed in a Jewish-Christian milieu.

57 The hypothesis of Herrmann (*Sénèque*) that early Christian traditions influenced the Roman statesman and philosopher is highly unlikely, to say the least.

58 Cf. e.g., TestDan 5:10–11, where Christ and Beliar battle, but where there is no explicit descent. The classification of the Testaments of the Twelve Patriarchs as Jewish or Christian is, of course, a much disputed matter. For our purposes, it is sufficient to note

hardly the only possible inspiration for those traditions. What Seneca and Hebrews both in fact attest is a paradigm for discussing liberation or salvation of various sorts common in Hellenistic culture.[59] The use of this ancient mythical paradigm for metaphorical applications is well established practice, exemplified, for instance, in the story of the cave in Plato's *Republic.*[60] Hence the possibility should be left open that apocalyptic is not the mother of at least this Christian theologoumenon and that the inspiration for the account of Christ's liberation of those held by the power of death was the ancient heroic liberation story.

Under whatever influences the story first emerged, it is clear that Hebrews, like Seneca, is interested in it for its contemporary or existential significance. For both, the story of deliverance is not about the invasion of the nether world, but about the entrance into and grappling with the forces of evil in this cosmos, either through philosophy or through a life of fidelity to God. This understanding of the relevance of the mythical is not an isolated phenomenon in Hebrews. Despite all the language of Christ "entering the heavenly sanctuary," Hebrews finally, and somewhat surprisingly, locates the place where the "heavenly" covenant-inaugurating sacrifice takes place "in the cosmos," where Christ conforms himself to the divine will (10:1-10).[61] Similarly, the mysterious "altar" that Christians have (13:10), which is presumably connected with where Christ consummates his sacrifice, is the inimical world "outside the camp" where they follow Christ, "bearing his reproach" (13:13), and where they offer their "sacrifices of praise and deeds of loving kindness" (13:15-16).

There is one further contemporizing touch in the text of chapter 2 that may shed light on the form of the descensus tradition available to Hebrews. As I noted in our consideration of several recent studies, there is a general consensus that in the earliest phases of the tradition Christ, whatever else he does, is portrayed as preaching or proclaiming deliverance to the captives of Hades. Such a motif has not appeared in the discussion of the mythical pattern present in Hebrews. Yet the text does highlight an important proclamation that Christ is said to have made, apparently when he was about to make his descent "below the angels." In 2:12-13 Hebrews cites a series of scriptural texts, from the Psalms and Prophets, which give expression to Christ's intention upon

that the passage in question is clearly Christian, whether it be an interpolation into a Jewish source or part of a Christian composition reworking some traditional Jewish themes.
59 Cf. the remarks of J. Z. Smith ("The Prayer of Joseph") in connection with the mythological scheme of the *Prayer of Joseph.*
60 Cf. *Rep.* 7.514A-517A. The existence of people held in fetters at the bottom of the cave is a sort of living death. The hypothetical individual who ascends to the light of the real world and then descends would have a difficult time if he tried to proclaim truth to prisoners. But that is what the philosophical guardians of the state are called upon to do.
61 For a detailed analysis of the pericope and its function within Hebrews, see Attridge, "Antithesis in Hebrews."

becoming incarnate.[62] The first of these, Ps 21:23, cited in vs 12, reads, "I shall announce your name to my brethren, in the midst of the assembly I shall sing your praise." This text sounds two themes that are important for Hebrews, the solidarity between Christ and his brethren and the specific locale where Christ's proclamation is to be made, the "assembly" or church. The former theme is explicitly developed in the subsequent verses, including the final scriptural citation in the series, from Isa 8:18, in Heb 2:13. The theme is developed in the comment that immediately follows (2:14), and it leads to the characterization of Christ as the merciful (2:17) and sympathetic (4:15) High Priest. The second clause in the first citation ("in the midst of the assembly I shall sing your praise") is a brief hint that a major function of the paraenesis of the work as a whole is to keep the addressees from succumbing to the temptation to "leave the assembly" (10:25) and to induce them to renew their commitment to the "assembly of firstborn enrolled in heaven" (12:23). The vehicle for that commitment is defined by the second remark of Christ, cited from Isa 8:17, "I shall trust in him." Christ here declares that he will endeavor to exemplify the fidelity to which all in the assembly will be called in various exhortations throughout the work.[63] Thus the specific contents of the proclamation that Christ makes are adapted to the needs of the expository and hortatory programs of Hebrews. Yet it is significant that, upon his entry into that sphere where he is to confront the power behind death and liberate its captives, he is to make a proclamation of some sort. This item probably derives from the underlying mythical scheme.

It is extremely difficult in this case, as in numerous other instances in Hebrews where traditional material might be involved, to separate sources or traditions from redaction. In this case some tentative suggestions might be in order. Since the content of Christ's proclamation (2:12–13), quite unparalleled in descensus texts, is so heavily involved with important themes of Hebrews as a whole, that content is certainly part of the author's adaptation of traditional material. That much seems clear, but how much more literary stratigraphy can be detected is not as clear. There are probably two basic options. (1) The traditional material could have involved an uninterpreted and naive myth of the descent of Christ into Hades to proclaim and grant release to its captives. If so, then the metaphorical application of the myth to describe the incarnation of Christ and his liberation of his brethren from the fear of death is interpretation by our author and would be quite analogous to the handling of the saga of Herakles by Seneca. (2) Alternatively, it is possible that the available tradition already involved the "life is hell" metaphorical structure. The fact that the notion of the "fear of death" does not play an explicit role in the rest of the text may indicate that the latter scenario is more likely and that the author knows of

---

62 The conceit of putting scriptural words in the mouth of Jesus reappears at 10:5–6. These are the only passages that cite "sayings of Jesus" in Hebrews.

63 Cf. especially 3:6–4:11; 10:22–25; 11:1–12:3. On the theme in general see Grässer, *Der Glaube.*

a metaphorical "descent." Nonetheless, it may be argued that the text's concern with persecution and external threats[64] addresses precisely this issue and that therefore the theme of "liberation here from the fear of death" is part of the author's adaptation of a naive myth.

Whichever of the two scenarios is more likely, it is clear that Hebrews as it stands affords what may be the earliest attestation of the descensus tradition. The version of the tradition in Hebrews clearly involves features that many have taken to be much later, including the identification of this earth as the place where death holds its captives in thrall, and the destruction of the lord of death as means of liberation. Exploration of the specific features of this attestation of the descensus tradition indicate striking affinities not with the apocalyptic myths of Jewish tradition, often assumed to be at the root of the descensus tradition, but with Greco-Roman sources. What remains unclear is the extent to which these affinities are part of the most primitive layer of the tradition or are due to the sophisticated literary activity of the author of Hebrews.

64 Cf. Heb 10:32–36; 11:32–38; 12:1–13.

James M. Robinson hosts Gilles Quispel in the Institute for Antiquity and Christianity lecture series.

ix

"The Politics of Paradise"
Reconsidered

CHRYSOSTOM AND PORPHYRY

Kathleen O'Brien Wicker

It has been my pleasure and privilege over the last seventeen years to have been associated with several research projects sponsored by the Institute for Antiquity and Christianity, of which James M. Robinson has been Associate Director and then Director since its inception in 1967.[1] As a participant in the Corpus Hellenisticum project[2] and the Ascetic Behavior in Late Antiquity project, I have come to appreciate the importance of viewing the intellectual, literary, and social worlds of early Christianity as part of, rather than primarily in contrast to, the larger Greco-Roman world within which Christianity developed.

In this essay, which is devoted to examining aspects of sexual asceticism in the writings of John Chrysostom and of Porphyry, the third century Neoplatonist, I will argue the following: that the early Christians were not unique in advocating sexual asceticism, that they experimented with a variety of ascetic lifestyles before arriving by the fourth century at what have become traditional models of Christian asceticism, and that the earlier forms of Christian asceticism often imitated or paralleled ascetic practices within the larger cultural world of Greco-Roman antiquity. I will use the recent work of Elaine Pagels as a point of departure for this discussion.

1. Elaine Pagels on Sexual Asceticism

Elaine Pagels has argued[3] that the church fathers prior to Augustine held "that conversion and baptism convey above all the gift of liberty, by which they meant liberation internally from the rule of the passions and externally from

1 An earlier version of this paper was presented at the Institute for Antiquity and Christianity Continuing Education Lecture Series in May 1988.

This research has been supported by the Scripps College Faculty Research Fund and the John Anson Kittredge Educational Fund.

2 The Corpus Hellenisticum Novi Testamenti project, under the direction of Professor Hans Dieter Betz, is now located at the University of Chicago Divinity School.

3 *Adam, Eve, and the Serpent*; "The Politics of Paradise" (1988); "The Politics of Paradise" (1985).

116

enslavement to custom, convention, and from coercion by imperial author-ity."[4] She uses John Chrysostom's writings to illustrate the Christian "proc-lamation of *autexousia*—the moral freedom to rule oneself"[5] and to show that the early Christians imposed upon themselves strict codes of moral behavior, particularly in the area of sexual attitudes and practices, as expressions of their new *autexousia*.[6] However, under the influence of Augustine's argument that all humans are under bondage through original sin, Christianity, she claims, rejected the idea of *autexousia*, accepted the need for external control, both civil and ecclesiastical, and developed the negative views on sexuality and the body that have characterized subsequent Christian thought.[7]

I will not challenge Pagels' thesis regarding Augustine's influence on Chris-tian attitudes toward human nature and sexuality. I will argue, however, (1) that *autexousia* was not a distinctively Christian concept in antiquity; (2) that Christianity before Augustine, and Chrysostom in particular, did not accept completely the view that baptism conferred *autexousia* over the passions and freedom for self-rule; and (3) that the varieties of sexual asceticism practiced by early Christians were diverse; they often paralleled non-Christian ascetic practices; and they did not always resemble the forms of sexual asceticism that became traditional in Christianity after the fourth century.

After examining the familiar *topos* of freedom in the philosophic and reli-gious literature of antiquity, I will show that John Chrysostom, in his two treatises[8] against the practitioners of *syneisaktism* or "spiritual marriage"[9] clearly doubted that sexual passions could be controlled effectively in our present bodily condition, and that the rhetorical strategies he used against them did, in fact, constitute moral coercion. Then I will use the philosophic marriage of Porphyry and Marcella and the philosophic community gathered around Porphyry's teacher Plotinus[10] as examples of non-Christian ascetic lifestyles that had interesting parallels with the practice of *syneisaktism* and with the apotaktic communities[11] in early Christianity.

---

4 "The Politics of Paradise" (1985), 92.
5 "The Politics of Paradise" (1985), 68.
6 *Adam, Eve, and the Serpent*, 8: "All converts to this new movement, whether they had once been Jews or pagans tended to distinguish their 'new Israel' from the rest of the world by insisting upon strict, even extreme, moral practices. The most controversial aspect of this new moral austerity was the sexual attitudes and practices of its adherents."
7 *Adam, Eve, and the Serpent*, 98–154. However, the third-century penitential crisis suggests that *autexousia* was being questioned in the Christian community much earlier than Augustine. See Trigg, "Healing."
8 *Adversus eos* and *Quod regulares*.
9 *Syneisaktism* is the practice of heterosexual couples, committed to virginal asceticism, who lived together. See the discussion of this practice in Achelis, *Virgines Sub-introductae*; de Labriolle, "Le mariage"; Lea, *Sacerdotal Celibacy*; Clark, "John Chry-sostom," and *Jerome, Chrysostom, and Friends*; Rader, *Breaking Boundaries*, 62–71.
10 Porphyry, *Ad Marcellam*; *Vita Plotini*.
11 On the *apotaktoi*, or *apotaktikoi*, Christian ascetics who developed a lifestyle intermediate between that of the anchorites and coenobites, see the important article by Judge, "Earliest Use of Monachos."

118   •   Kathleen O'Brien Wicker

2. Freedom or Self-Rule in Antiquity

Several important and interconnected ideas are involved in the ancient concepts of freedom or self-rule.[12] *Autexousia* is, of course, only one of the terms used to describe this concept in the ancient literature. First, there is the Greek political paradigm of *isonomia*, the freedom of citizens to participate in the political process and to live as they wish in the state.[13] This freedom, which was rooted in the sophistic idea that all men are by nature free, connected the free individual to the community of the free.[14] The free state, engaged in self-rule, embodied *autonomia*.[15] This political paradigm changed, however, with the Roman concept of *libertas* as "the sum of civic rights granted by the laws."[16] The Roman concept was rejected by Christian church fathers and by Hellenistic-Roman philosophers, who held that the laws of nations were customary and were superseded by unchangeable divine law.[17]

A second paradigm, that of *eleutheria* ("freedom") and *douleia* ("slavery"), was applied not only to the political and social but also to the personal realm. True freedom in the latter context was regarded as the control of the passions. This paradigm, which generally required withdrawal from political life, was espoused by the Cynics, Stoics, Epicureans, and Neoplatonists. They sought to achieve a form of internal self-sufficiency or freedom, called variously *autarkeia* ("self-sufficiency"), *ataraxia* ("imperturbability"), or *apatheia* ("freedom from emotion").[18] The term *autexousia* also occurred in their discussions. Epictetus declared that what "makes a man free from hindrance and his own master (*autexousia*)" is "the knowledge of how to live."[19] And "the knowledge of how to live" consists in having "a harmonious and regulated desire for the things that are within the sphere of the moral purpose."[20] Plotinus claimed that *autexousia* inheres in human nature and moves humans to noble actions,[21] while Proclus attempted to reconcile individual autonomy and divine providence.[22]

A variation on the *eleutheria/douleia* paradigm viewed the whole world as under the control of *tyche* or "fate." Thus true freedom consisted in a flight or ascent of the soul to the deity, who alone was truly free. The mystery religions and Gnosticism offered guidance to souls seeking to negotiate the ascent to the divine.[23] Another form of this paradigm was also used by Paul, notably in

12 See Betz, *Paul's Concept of Freedom*.
13 Anderson in Betz, *Paul's Concept of Freedom*, 14.
14 Schol. Arist. *Rhet.* 1373b, cited in Betz, *Paul's Concept of Freedom*, 1, n. 3.
15 Anderson in Betz, *Paul's Concept of Freedom*, 14.
16 Ch. Wirszubski, *Libertas as a Political Idea*, 7, cited in Betz, *Paul's Concept of Freedom*, 3.
17 Porphyry, *Ad Marcellam* 25.384–402; Nörr, *Rechtskritik*.
18 Betz, *Paul's Concept of Freedom*; cf. esp. the discussion on p. 14.
19 Epictetus 4.1.62.
20 Epictetus 4.1.84.
21 Plotinus, *Enn.* 3.2.10.
22 Proclus, *Alcibiades 1* 143C.
23 Betz, *Paul's Concept of Freedom*, 4–5.

Galatians and *Romans*, to describe the present state of human unfreedom due
to "a series of mythicohistorical events in primordial time,"[24] as well as to the
new freedom that Christians achieved through faith in Jesus.[25]

Yet another form of the paradigm of freedom was the freedom from fear of
death. "In one way or another all forms of freedom eventually became forms of
suicide. The only remaining question was when and how to end one's life,
whether at once or by gradual 'mortification of the flesh.'"[26] This paradigm
was operative in the ascetic practices both of early Christianity and of Neoplatonism, as will become clear in the following discussion of John Chrysostom and Porphyry.

3. John Chrysostom

Pagels presents the argument of John Chrysostom (347–407 CE) that the
original human likeness to God consisted in the ability to govern, but that with
the fall humans lost this capacity and became subject to imperial rule in
immoral states. The capacity for self-government is restored through baptism,
however, and is reflected in the Christian community, where the moral freedom of the members for self-rule requires a leadership style of persuasion
rather than coercion.[27] She quotes John Chrysostom as saying:

> We do not have "authority over your faith," beloved, nor do we command these
> things as your lords and masters. We are appointed for the teaching of the word,
> not for power, nor for absolute authority. We hold the place of counsellors to
> advise you. The counsellor speaks his own opinions, not forcing his listeners, but
> leaving him full master of his own choice in what is said.[28]

This view of the *autexousia* of the believer in the community of faith is
reminiscent of the sophistic idea that all humans are free by nature, except, of
course, that in the Christian context what was originally true by nature is now
true by grace. And, as in the Greek political paradigm, the free individual is
connected to the community of the free, but in a spiritual rather than a secular
politeia. In adopting the Greek rather than the Roman political paradigm,
Chrysostom rejected, at least theoretically, the notion of the absolute authority
of those in leadership positions.

But Chrysostom's two treatises addressed to the male and to the female
virgins who practiced *syneisaktism* leave no doubt that Chrysostom had definite negative views of this practice and that he used all of his rhetorical skills to

24 Betz, *Paul's Concept of Freedom*, 6.
25 Betz, *Paul's Concept of Freedom*, 5–13. See also Betz, *Galatians*.
26 Betz, *Paul's Concept of Freedom*, 5.
27 Pagels, "The Politics of Paradise" (1985), 69–75. See also P. Brown, *The Body and
Society*, 305–22, for an eloquent description of Chrysostom's vision of a new community
based on the reform of the Christian household according to principles of subordination
outlined by Aristotle and continued in the NT "household codes."
28 *Homilia XI in Epistolam ad Ephesios*, 5; Pagels, "The Politics of Paradise" (1985), 74.

convince them to discontinue it. One of these strategies is not to use the word *syneisaktos*, a word he despises as much as the practice itself.[29] Instead he employs *synoikeo* ("to cohabit") and its cognates to refer to *syneisaktism*, though he says that this term also offends him in this context.[30] Another rhetorical strategy he draws upon is to contrast real and apparent virginity, with the result that physical integrity alone cannot demonstrate virginity.[31] In Chrysostom's view real chastity can be practiced only by those who forego any intimate contact with the opposite sex. Finally, he cites scriptural passages that require the strong to defer to the weak, a practice that sharply limits the benefits of the *autexousia* that he advocates.

It is uncertain when Chrysostom wrote the treatises against *syneisaktism* entitled "Instruction and Refutation Directed against Those Men Cohabiting with Virgins" and "On the Necessity of Guarding Virginity." One theory dates them to the 380's or early 390's when he was a deacon at Antioch. Another hypothesis is that they came from the period of Chrysostom's episcopacy in Constantinople after 398 CE. Yet a third suggestion is that the treatises were issued twice, once from Antioch and once from Constantinople.[32]

Chrysostom opens his argument to the male virgins by reviewing sexual arrangements after the fall.[33] The first of the two traditional modes of men and women living together is marriage, which he describes as "ancient, licit, and sensible, since God was its legislator."[34] The other, prostitution, of which he claims evil demons were the originators, is newer, unjust and illegitimate. He laments that in his day some people have dreamed up a third way of life, that of "spiritual marriage":

> There are certain men who apart from marriage and sexual intercourse take girls inexperienced with matrimony, establish them permanently in their homes, and keep them sequestered until ripe old age.[35]

This they do, not to have children by them or because they are licentious, but because there is pleasure in living with a woman, even in "cases which do not

---

29 *Quod regulares*, 3.
30 *Synoikeo* and its cognates occur twenty-six times in *Adversus eos* (as well as in the title): 1 (5 times), 2 (1), 3 (2), 4 (6), 5 (7), 6 (1), 9 (2), 11 (2). These terms also occur twenty-six times in *Quod regulares* (as well as in the title): 3 (2), 4 (6), 5 (2), 6 (9), 7 (1), 8 (4), 9 (2).
31 See Malina, "Social World," 71–119 for the ways in which rhetorical strategies such as this are used in Ignatius of Antioch.
32 Clark, "John Chrysostom," 175 and n. 46. Those who prefer an early dating of these texts may argue that they reflect a more stringent attitude toward asceticism than do his later writings. However, as I argue below on the basis of other texts, Chrysostom was fundamentally opposed to the kind of asceticism reflected in the practice of *syneisaktism* because he thought that it distorted the order of nature and gave women equality with men.
33 *Adversus eos* is translated by Clark, *Jerome, Chrysostom, and Friends*, 164–208. All English translations of this text are taken from this source. However, I have maintained the section divisions in Migne, PG.
34 *Adversus eos*, trans. Clark, *Jerome, Chrysostom, and Friends*, 164.
35 *Adversus eos*.

involve marriage and sexual intercourse."[36] In fact, these relationships may be even more pleasurable than marriage, he speculates, because the men are never totally satisfied, and the women, who don't have to bear and rear children, "retain their beauty until they are forty, rivalling the virgins being led to the nuptial chamber."[37]

Chrysostom's efforts to persuade these men "that this practice is not just disadvantageous, but positively malignant"[38] includes appeals to ancient mythology, to Scripture and to philosophy. The practitioners in the treatise protest that nothing terrible happens to them as a result of this lifestyle.[39] But Chrysostom expresses doubts that they can be in close contact with women and not be moved by desire for them, thus losing the virginity they claim to practice. When the men answer that perhaps Chrysostom is guilty of projecting his own problems onto them, he responds by referring to the words and example of Jesus and Paul and concludes that it is the obligation of the strong not to scandalize the weak, and that the battle with the flesh is lifelong.[40]

Chrysostom next appeals to male pride in the superiority of their sex in order to dissuade the male virgins from practicing *syneisaktism*. He states: "What man, if he were free from the compulsion to have a woman, would choose to put up with the delicacy, wantonness, and all the other faults of that sex."[41] God made women attractive to men, because without this attraction women would be totally despised by them.

The practitioners in the treatise then allege that the female virgins need the protection, assistance, comfort and security that was provided in their relationship. Chrysostom responds that the practice creates more problems than it solves, since it involves ascetics in too many worldly concerns. Further, there are needy men and older women to be taken care of as well. Purity of motive would suggest that attractive young women should not be the only recipients of these kindnesses.[42]

When Chrysostom reverts to the problem that the practice scandalizes others, the ascetics respond that they need the household services of these women.[43] Chrysostom retorts that it is much better to have a man do these tasks than a woman, since men have the same needs. Indeed, "one house, one pillow, one bed, and the same covers suffice for both of them,"[44] Chrysostom claims, carefully ignoring the issue of sexuality in homosocial relationships.

But Chrysostom's most serious objection to *syneisaktism* finally surfaces when he complains that a monk who lives with a woman is immersed in the

36 *Adversus eos*, trans. Clark, *Jerome, Chrysostom, and Friends*, 165.
37 *Adversus eos*, PG 47.496, trans. Clark, *Jerome, Chrysostom, and Friends*, 166.
38 *Adversus eos*, trans. Clark, *Jerome, Chrysostom, and Friends*, 167.
39 *Adversus eos*, 3, trans. Clark, *Jerome, Chrysostom, and Friends*, 170.
40 *Adversus eos*, 3–4.
41 *Adversus eos*, 5, trans. Clark, *Jerome, Chrysostom, and Friends*, 179.
42 *Adversus eos*, 6–7.
43 *Adversus eos*, 9.
44 *Adversus eos*, 9, trans. Clark, *Jerome, Chrysostom, and Friends*, 191–92.

female world and becomes too concerned with pleasing women. "It is the supreme unworthiness for a spiritual man to crave . . . [the] esteem"[45] of women. Men who do so are like warriors, outfitted for battle, who retreat instead to the women's quarters.[46] Chrysostom concludes the treatise with a rousing call to the male ascetics to give up slavery to women and to practice the virtues of their calling. If they do so, he promises them, women will admire them, men will crown them, God will accept them, and they will be regarded as martyrs.[47] And, as a final consolation to these men, he adds that men and women will be able to associate freely in heaven because they will be spiritual beings like the angels and the intellectual powers.[48]

When Chrysostom addresses the female virgins in his treatise "On the Necessity of Guarding Virginity,"[49] he rejects the validity of their lifestyle and compels them to regard their companions as adulterers who violate their commitment to Christ. He begins with the lament, "Alas, my soul," which becomes the theme song of the treatise. First he laments that virginity has been degraded from the most to the least esteemed state because of the *subintroductae*, the Latin term for the female virgins who practiced *syneisaktism*. He claims that virginity is a virtue practiced only by Christians,[50] but that it has become suspect, among both believers and unbelievers because of the practice of "spiritual marriage." Midwives who have been sent to ascertain the virginity of the *subintroductae* often establish their physical integrity, he claims, but they can not attest to their spiritual virginity as well.[51]

Chrysostom asserts that female virgins desire relationships with the male virgins because of the vanity involved in controlling men.[52] "As it is said, the whole human race is vain, but especially the female sex."[53] He charges that these virgins are more like prostitutes than married women.[54] When they object that they are weak and need a man, he reminds them that the men say they need women as well.[55] So, if they both need support, they should rely on their own sex. Actually, though, says Chrysostom, the result of these unions is that both partners get a bad reputation, because the proper order of nature is violated: "The upper assumes the position of the lower so that the head is below, the body is above."[56]

---

45 *Adversus eos*, 11, trans. Clark, *Jerome, Chrysostom, and Friends*, 198.
46 *Adversus eos*, 11.
47 *Adversus eos*, 12.
48 *Adversus eos*, 13.
49 *Quod regulares* is translated by Clark, *Jerome, Chrysostom, and Friends*, 209–48. All English translations of this text are taken from this source.
50 This is not the case, as will be evident in the discussion on Porphyry below. See Rouselle, *Porneia*, for a more comprehensive discussion of sexual restraint in non-Christian antiquity.
51 *Quod regulares* 1–3.
52 *Quod regulares*, 1.
53 *Quod regulares*, 5, trans. Clark, *Jerome, Chrysostom, and Friends*, 229.
54 *Quod regulares*, 3.
55 *Quod regulares*, 4.
56 *Quod regulares*, 6, trans. Clark, *Jerome, Chrysostom, and Friends*, 231.

Chrysostom concludes by attempting to persuade the virgins that their male companions really hate them for ensnaring them but can't leave them because they derive pleasure from the relationship.[57] He threatens them with the revelation of their behavior at the final judgment and their exclusion from the shining entourage of virgins in heaven.[58] He appeals to them to live in this world as aliens and sojourners in a foreign land, not attending to their outward apparel or being involved in relationships with men,[59] lest their virginity be destroyed.[60] He pleads with them to have God alone as lover and bridegroom and concludes with a magical incantation intended to bring about the reform of the virgins' lives.[61]

While Chrysostom may in theory have recognized the baptismal right of the practitioners of *syneisaktism* to determine for themselves the authenticity of their ascetic lifestyle, the passages I have cited demonstrate that he certainly felt no hesitation about employing powerful rhetorical strategies to dissuade them from the practice. In practice, he did not grant, contrary to Pagels, that baptism "meant liberation internally from the rule of the passions"[62] or from ecclesiastical rule. His exegetical and homiletic writings confirm this conclusion. A number of these texts reflect his notion that the Christian, while free from the fear of death and thus intent upon "mortification of the flesh," can never fully attain freedom from slavery to the passions while in the earthly state.

Chrysostom describes, in his treatise "On Virginity" the life of Adam and Eve before the fall as one of intimate but non-sexual relationship between themselves and with God.[63] He even goes so far as to suggest that, if the fall had not occurred, the human race could have been produced by God without sexual activity.[64] But, since we do live in a fallen state, God devised marriage as a way to avoid fornication. Outside of marriage, there is no way for sexual passion to be curtailed, other than by complete abstinence. "Spiritual marriage" is not a viable option, for even if a couple could maintain physical virginity, they would undoubtedly be guilty of sexual desire, thus violating their commitment to chastity.

Another of Chrysostom's strong objections to "spiritual marriage" is based on the assumption that, in the fallen state, women are to be subject to men, and not their superiors or even their equals. This, he argues in "Discourse Four on Genesis," was not the original order intended by God, but it came about as an abuse of power by Eve.[65] Since women, in their present fallen state, are to be

57 *Quod regulares*, 6.
58 *Quod regulares*, 6.
59 *Quod regulares*, 7.
60 *Quod regulares*, 8.
61 *Quod regulares*, 9, trans. Clark, *Jerome, Chrysostom, and Friends*, 246.
62 Pagels, "The Politics of Paradise" (1985), 92.
63 *De Virginitate*, 14.3, 5.
64 *De Virginitate*, 14.6; 15.1.
65 *In Genesim Sermo* 4.

subordinate to men, they can withdraw from the lordship of a husband only if Christ becomes their spiritual bridegroom.

Another consequence of the position that women are condemned by God to be subordinate to men and to be excluded from the public realm is that they should not teach publicly, according to Chrysostom in "Homily Nine on I Timothy":

> She taught the man once, upset everything, and made him liable to disobedience. Therefore God subjected her, since she used her rule, or rather, her equality of honor badly.[66]

Chrysostom further objects to "spiritual marriage" because it causes the men to become too entangled in the affairs of the household.[67] This, of course, does not justify Chrysostom's argument that if ascetics, men or women, need help, they should resort to another of their own sex to provide it. There are, apparently, some times when it is better to violate the doctrine of spheres than to threaten the observance of voluntary chastity.

These arguments make it even more clear that in Chrysostom's judgment the realm of sexuality and human social arrangements was not one in which baptism restored the original human integrity ordained by God. Christians will have to wait until heaven for that blessed state, where, as he promised the male virgins, "there will be no hindrance . . . to prevent man and woman from being together, for every evil suspicion is removed and all who have entered the Kingdom of Heaven can maintain the way of life of those angels and intellectual powers."[68]

Indeed, it was not Chrysostom, but rather the practitioners of *syneisaktism*, who thought it possible, through baptism, to be liberated from the tyranny of the passions and to be restored to the harmonious non-sexual and non-marital state that Adam and Eve enjoyed before the fall. The subordination of women to men, the restriction on women's teaching role, the division between private and public spheres, and other results of the fall were apparently also thought by them to be eliminated by the power of baptism. The understanding that baptism conferred *autexousia* upon believers undoubtedly contributed to the widespread and ongoing practice of *syneisaktism* in the Christian community, despite its prohibition by a number of synods and councils and the arguments advanced against it by John Chrysostom and other church fathers.[69]

---

66 *In Epistolam Primam Ad Timotheum Commentarius* 9, trans. Clark, *Women in the Early Church*, 157.

67 *Quales ducendae sint uxores* 4. The notion of male and female spheres and virtues is a *topos* of the ancient philosophical and religious literature. See Wicker, "Marriage Ethics," 141–53; Wicker "Mulierum Virtutes," 106–34.

68 *Adversus eos*, 13, trans. Clark, *Jerome, Chrysostom, and Friends*, 204.

69 For the history of the practice see Achelis, *Virgines Subintroductae*; de Labriolle, "Le mariage"; Lea, *Sacerdotal Celibacy*.

4. Neoplatonism

Neoplatonic social and sexual arrangements were also rooted in certain understandings about the human condition and the possibilities for human freedom. Neoplatonism, like Christianity, had a tradition about a fall.[70] But, unlike Christianity's view of fallen, embodied human existence as a state of domination by the passions, Neoplatonism regarded the fall as the experience of the soul alone[71] and as the state of embodiment itself. This resulted in a dualistic anthropology in which the body was viewed as an aspect of the material, divinely-created realm[72] but distinct from the intellectual realm. The body was not the real self, but only the shadow and visible form of the real self, the soul or intellect.[73] Even in its embodied state, however, the soul retained some memory of its former existence and of the perceptions that were implanted in it while it was in the spiritual realm.[74] Despite the forgetfulness that embodiment produced,[75] the soul needed to recollect those earlier perceptions in order to reascend to that realm.[76]

Philosophy, through its ascetic discipline, enabled the soul to be liberated from the power of bodily passions in order to turn in contemplation to the intellect.[77] The intellect, which is the mirror-image of God in the soul,[78] was then enabled through contemplation to be united with the divine.[79] This could happen either in ecstatic experience[80] while the soul was still embodied or when it was finally liberated from the body.[81] Through the practices of philosophical separation and ascent, the soul recovered its capacity for *autexousia*, which is inherent in its nature,[82] not, as in certain Christian writers,

70 In Porphyry's *Ad Marcellam*, the fall tradition is referred to in 33.501–02, 6.101, and 8.152–53. This raises the question about when Genesis. 2–3 were thought to describe a "fall." Did this terminology derive from earlier Greek mythical or philosophical traditions?
71 Porphyry, *Ad Marcellam* 29: "'Let us neither censure the flesh as cause of great evils nor attribute our distress to external circumstances.' Rather let us seek their causes in the soul, and, by breaking away from every vain yearning and hope for fleeting fancies, let us become totally in control of ourselves."
72 Since both the material and the intelligible worlds are divine creations, the fall of soul into body is not a fall into evil but into a different principle, which also manifests the divine. See Plotinus, *Enn.* 2.9. See also Armstrong, "Man in the Cosmos," chap. 22.
73 Porphyry, *Ad Marcellam* 10.174.
74 Porphyry, *Ad Marcellam* 10.183–85.
75 Porphyry, *Ad Marcellam* 6.112–14.
76 Porphyry, *Ad Marcellam* 8.152–53.
77 Porphyry, *Ad Marcellam* 31.481–83.
78 Porphyry, *Ad Marcellam* 26.412.
79 Porphyry, *Ad Marcellam* 13.233–35: "Let the intellect obey God since it is a mirror-image of God by its likeness to Him; let the soul obey the intellect; then, of course, let the body be subservient to the soul as far as is possible, pure body subservient to pure soul."
80 Porphyry, *Vita Plotini* 23.
81 Porphyry, *Vita Plotini* 22.
82 Plotinus, *Enn.* 3.2.10.

conferred through the cultic ritual of baptism. The soul that failed to reclaim its *autexousia* and liberate itself from the material realm was condemned to be reborn, possibly in another life form, until its purification was accomplished.[83]

Plotinus (205–270 CE), the leading Neoplatonic philosopher of late antiquity, is known to us through the writings of his student, Porphyry (232–ca. 305 CE).[84] Porphyry studied with Plotinus in Rome between 262 and 268 CE. One of his proudest achievements was to have been entrusted by Plotinus with the editing of his writings. These he edited into a collection of six books of nine treatises each, thus giving the collection the name *Enneads* (the "nines"). As a preface to the collection, Porphyry wrote the "Life of Plotinus."

> Porphyry's description of Plotinus was of a man who . . . sleeplessly kept his soul pure and ever strove towards the divine, which he loved with all his soul, and did everything to be delivered and "escape from the bitter wave of blood-drinking life here."[85]

Yet Porphyry also describes Plotinus's philosophic presence and union with other people as well, including a number of aristocratic Romans and *literati*. He discusses at length Rogatianus, a senator, whose renunciation of public life and indifference to physical needs exemplified the practice of the philosophic life.[86]

Porphyry also reports that Plotinus had several women disciples who were devoted to philosophy and that wealthy Romans frequently appointed him guardian of their minor children, whose education and financial affairs he supervised. Yet, though he shielded so many from the worries and cares of ordinary life, he never, while awake, relaxed his intent concentration upon the intellect.[87] He was gentle, too, and at the disposal of all who had any sort of acquaintance with him. Though he spent twenty-six whole years in Rome and acted as arbitrator in very many people's disputes, he never made an enemy of any of the officials.[88]

These accounts of Plotinus's own asceticism and his concern to assist others, both in the practical details of their lives and in attaining spiritual goals, provide us with a living example of the twofold freedom provided by Neoplatonic philosophy: the escape from the world through reasonable asceticism practiced for the sake of union within and with the divine and the awareness that being present to the self and the divine Intellect meant being present to others and connected to all of nature as well.[89]

83 Plotinus, *Enn.* 3.4.2. See Also Wolfskeel, "Augustin."
84 See the discussion of Porphyry's biography in Wicker, *Porphyry the Philosopher* (*s.v.* Porphyry), 1–4 and nn. 3, 12, p. 27, and in Valantasis, "Third Century Spiritual Guides," chap. 3.
85 Porphyry, *Vita Plotini* 23.
86 *Vita Plotini* 7.
87 *Vita Plotini* 11.
88 *Vita Plotini* 9.
89 Hadot and Saffrey, "Neoplatonist Spirituality," 230–33.

Plotinus's belief that freedom from the tyranny of the passions could be attained through asceticism and training of the intellect apparently allowed him to live in intimate contact with women, without apparent threat to his ascetic lifestyle, much as the practitioners of *syneisaktism* did. Porphyry mentions several women who were greatly devoted to Plotinus, including "Gemina, in whose house he lived"[90] and "Chione who lived with him, along with her children, continuing honorably in her widowhood."[91]

These references to Plotinus living with women, most likely widows, and caring for the orphans who filled his house, suggests an urban community lifestyle, possibly like that of the third–fourth century Christian *apotaktikoi*, who lived together, following an ascetic regimen including fasting and sexual abstinence, taught, and practiced acts of charity, while they maintained ownership of property.[92] It also has similarities to the Jewish Essene lifestyle that Porphyry, following Josephus, discussed in his *De Abstinentia*.[93]

Though Porphyry does not refer specifically to the sexual asceticism of the followers of Plotinus,[94] the evidence suggests that it was characteristic of the Neoplatonic life. Porphyry suggests that Plotinus lived celibately.[95] Porphyry tells us that he objected strongly to a suggestion by the rhetorician Diophanes that a student "should submit himself to carnal intercourse with his master if the master desired it."[96] And, interestingly, Porphyry uses the term *synoikos* ("cohabitor") to describe Plotinus's relationship with Chione.[97] This is the same term that Chrysostom employed for the practitioners of *syneisaktism*. Though *synoikos* and its cognates are general terms that can characterize various human relationships including marriage,[98] sexual liaisons,[99] and fellow-colonists and people who lived in close association,[100] as well as intimate non-sexual relationships, I believe that in this context it may well imply an

90 Porphyry, *Vita Plotini* 9.
91 Porphyry, *Vita Plotini* 11.
92 See n. 11 above. I owe the suggestion that the community of Plotinus has a parallel in Christian apotaktic communities to Richard Valantasis, whose "Third Century Spiritual Guides" contains an important chapter on Porphyry's *Vita Plotini*. This thesis is forthcoming from Fortress Press in the Harvard Dissertations in Religions Series.
93 *De Abstin.* 4.11; see Porphyrius, *Opuscula*, 245.
94 Peter Brown, *The Body and Society*, is correct that Porphyry does not stress the sexual asceticism of Plotinus's circle. But Judge, "Earliest Use of Monachos," 75–78, has argued persuasively that until the fourth century celibacy was not the guiding principle of male Christian ascetics either. Brown's conclusion that the "pagan sages . . . wished to snatch their charges away from the bustle of the forum, not the marriage bed" (179–80) relies too heavily on Porphyry's story about Rogatianus and does not consider the implications of Porphyry's description of Plotinus's relationship with the two Geminas, Amphicleia, and Chione or of the community created by the orphans who lived with him.
95 Porphyry, *Vita Plotini* 9.
96 *Vita Plotini* 15.
97 *Vita Plotini* 11.
98 Demosthenes, *Or.* 30.33–34.
99 Andocides, *De Myst.* 124. See also Macdowell's note in Andokides, *On the Mysteries*, 152.
100 Aristotle, *Pol.* 1303a27–29.

intimate, though non-exclusive and non-sexual relationship in a philosophical community.

Synoikos and its cognates are also used by Porphyry to describe a relationship that he himself had with a woman named Marcella.[101] Near the year 300, when he was almost seventy, Porphyry married a widow named Marcella who had seven children. He undertook the marriage, he says, because of a sense of duty to his friend, Marcella's deceased husband, and because Marcella showed an aptitude for the philosophic life. However, ten months after their marriage, he had to leave on a trip of indefinite duration. The letter "To Marcella" was written during Porphyry's absence and was intended to provide Marcella with a summary of the important Neoplatonic doctrines, and with encouragement to continue the practice of the philosophic life during his absence.[102]

The term that Porphyry uses to describe his relationship with Marcella is *synoikos*.[103] Initially, it appears to denote a conventional marriage relationship; but he denies that he has a traditional marriage, since he does not want what men usually look for in such a relationship: children, wealth, companionship, comfort for his old age.[104] Rather, their relationship is founded on very different principles. "I summoned you," he tells her, "to my own way of life, sharing philosophy and pointing out a doctrine consistent with that life."[105]

Porphyry and Marcella, though legally married, appear to have had an ascetic philosophical marriage.[106] They went through a conventional mar-

---

101 The terms occur in *Ad Marcellam* at 1.3 and 4.65–66.
102 Wicker, *Porphyry the Philosopher* (*s.v.* Porphyry), 17–21.
103 *Porphyry the Philosopher* (*s.v.* Porphyry), note to 1.3, 81.
104 *Ad Marcellam*, 1.5–17.
105 *Ad Marcellam*, 3.44–46.
106 P. Brown, *The Body and Society*, 180–83, believes that Porphyry advocated sexual restraint, not sexual abstinence. He bases his conclusion on one of the *Sentences of Sextus* (Chadwick, no. 239, p. 38), from which collection Porphyry drew maxims cited in the *Ad Marcellam*, and on a statement in *Adversos Christianos* (Harnack, *Gegen die Christen*, frag. 33, p. 60) that seems to suggest that Porphyry had a negative view of Christian virgins' renouncing marriage. On Brown's first argument: Porphyry did draw material from Sextus; but he does not cite no. 239 (*fidelium coniugium certamen habeat continentiae*, "Let the marriage of believers be a struggle for self-control") in the *Ad Marcellam*, where so much of this material is cited. And Brown has conveniently ignored other *sententiae* in Sextus, such as 230a (*coniugium tibi refutare concessum est, idcirco ut vivas indesinenter adhaerens deo*, "It is allowed to you to renounce marriage so that you might live as a companion to God), which do suggest the practice of total continence.
   Brown's other argument, which he derives from Demarolle, "Les Femmes chrétiennes," is based on a text from *Adversus Christianos*. Demarolle appears here to be advancing an argument over an apparent contradiction in Paul's thought, not about marriage per se. See "Les femmes chrétiennes," 45. I do not believe one can generalize from this passage that "demonstrative conversions to perpetual virginity among young Christian women . . . annoyed Porphyry greatly" (P. Brown, *The Body and Society*, 181) and that he "thought that it was positively inappropriate, if not impious, that young women of marriageable age should renounce their duty to society and to the 'gods that preside over generation,' by vowing their bodies to perpetual virginity" (*The Body and Society*, 181). The phrase, "gods that preside over generation," is found in the *Ad Marcellam* 2.23 where it is used ironically as a specious reason for Porphyry's marriage, though he has already made it clear that he does not intend to father children through this marriage. See my notes in Porphyry, *Ad Marcellam*, 82–84.

riage ritual, apparently for the sake of liberating Marcella from the influence of relatives who wanted her to remarry for economic reasons and who objected so strenuously to Porphyry that they tried to kill him.[107] But their primary relationship was that of student and teacher, thus similar in some ways to the relationships that Plotinus had with Chione and Gemina.

The letter "To Marcella" makes clear that Porphyry's and Marcella's was a celibate relationship. He admonishes her not to become attached to his physical person or presence, since that is only his bodily form, not himself. He tells her: "I am not this person who is tangible and susceptible to visible appearances, but rather a being completely separate from the body, without color and without form, totally incapable of being touched by hand but rather comprehended by thought alone."[108] But, he encourages her: "You could encounter me in complete purity, as one both present and united to you night and day in a pure and most beautiful form of union and not as one likely to be separated from you, if you would train yourself to ascend into yourself, gathering from the body all the parts of your soul which have been scattered and cut into many pieces from their former unity."[109] Further, he advised her: "Do not be overly concerned about whether your body is male or female; do not regard yourself as a woman, Marcella, for I did not devote myself to you as such. Flee from every effeminate element of the soul as if you are clothed in a male body."[110]

Their relationship, viewed in spiritual philosophical terms, imitates the relationship between God and the pure soul,[111] which Porphyry also describes as a *synoikia*. He is the image of the divine Intellect while she is soul. "For the most blessed offspring come from virginal soul and unmated Intelligence."[112]

Thus, Marcella must cease to identify herself and Porphyry in physical terms and realize that the inner spiritual unity that she can achieve interiorly between her soul and intellect, and then between her intellect and the divine Intellect, also creates a spiritual unity between herself and Porphyry. Sexual intimacy in this relationship is reduced to the level of metaphor, because sex involves its practitioners in carnality and therefore is hostile to the Neoplatonic philosophical life. The reality underlying this marriage and the philosophy which produced it is spiritual and intellectual, rather than physical and emotional, though it also recognizes that spiritual connection with the divine means being present and connected to other human beings as well.

5. Comparison and Conclusion

Our analyses of Christian "spiritual marriage," of *synikia* in Porphyry, and of John Chrysostom's critique of *syneisaktism* point to some interesting simi-

---

107 See my Introduction in Porphyry, *Ad Marcellam*, 4–10.
108 Porphyry, *Ad Marcellam* 8.147–50. See also the note to 8.147–50, pp. 91–92.
109 *Ad Marcellam*, 10.176–83. See also the note to 10.179–83, p. 95.
110 *Ad Marcellam*, 33.511–14. See also the note to 33.511–17, p. 121.
111 *Ad Marcellam*, 20.316.
112 *Ad Marcellam*, 33.515.

larities and differences among the Christians and the Neoplatonists of late antiquity in their ascetic behavior and in the ideas of freedom that inspired it.[113]

Both John Chrysostom and the Neoplatonists agreed that the material world was a divine creation. For the Neoplatonists, however, soul was part of the intellectual realm, and thus the soul needed to free itself from its engagement with the body to ascend to the divine Intelligence. Unfortunately, however, they did not think that this freedom could be attained by the majority of humans.[114] By John Chrysostom's time, the body was regarded as evil,[115] and thus freedom consisted in the liberation of the soul through ascetic practices. But Chrysostom did not believe that any amount either of grace or of human effort would achieve total *autexousia* over the passions in the earthly state. The practitioners of *syneisaktism* apparently held that it was possible to achieve *autexousia* in the present earthly state through a divine gift of God, which they tested through the practice of sleeping together but without sexual intimacy. They probably thought that this gift was bestowed not on all Christians but only on a selected few.

John Chrysostom regarded marriage as a social arrangement divinely ordained after the fall to enable humans to exercise restraint over their sexual passions. While he did not regard marriage as having the same dignity as virginity, the total denial of the expression of sexual passion, he believed that the sexual passions were so strong that the physical proximity of the sexes would certainly produce sexual desires, if not sexual activity. Thus he attempted to dissuade the practitioners of *syneisaktism* from this kind of ascetic lifestyle. Interestingly, however, in his two treatises against the practitioners of *syneisaktism*, he is not able to charge them, by and large, with sexual activity, so that he must instead accuse them of sexual desire, a charge much harder to substantiate. The Neoplatonists and the partners in "spiritual marriage," on the other hand, appeared to have acted on the assumption that human passions are controllable, either through the habitual exercise of self-restraint or through a divine gift. The latter perspective allows for a much greater emphasis on the freedom of the community of the free, found early in sophistic thought, except that the communities now are spiritual or philosophic rather than political.

Another assumption of Chrysostom's not shared by practitioners of *syneisaktism* and Neoplatonists is that male and female natures differ.[116] In our fallen state, Chrysostom argued, women are punished for Eve's role in the fall

---

113 For a discussion of differences between Neoplatonism and Christianity, see Armstrong, "Man in the Cosmos."
114 See Plotinus, *Enn.* 2.9.9.
115 See the discussion by Ruether ("Virginal Feminism," 150–83), who differs with Pagels on the origin of this view.
116 See Prusak, "Woman," 89–116 for the history of this attitude in the ancient Jewish-Christian literature.

by being subordinated to men.[117] One of the implications of this position was that of separate male and female spheres and roles. Christian women who committed themselves to an ascetic virginal lifestyle had an equal opportunity to strive for a life of perfection, but their behavior and lifestyle still had to conform to the unequal social arrangements that were imposed on women through a subordinationist interpretation of the tradition of the fall. It may have been the social equality of women and friendship between women and men resulting from *syneisaktism* rather than any theological principle that prompted the church fathers to attempt to eliminate the practice.[118]

The Neoplatonists came from a tradition in which Plato had Socrates argue in the *Republic* for the equality of the sexes in the ideal state. Plato made this case, not in the interests of women's liberation, but to make accessible to the state the total resources of its population. By the time we reach Plotinus in the third century CE, women as well as men are included in the community of his hearers and those who are committed to the philosophic life. It is probably significant that it is widows and virgins who are most free to pursue these philosophical aspirations, since the philosophic life demands an asceticism that would probably not be acceptable within most marriages. Once these women became members of philosophic communities, however, they appeared to enjoy greater freedom in their social arrangements as well.

The parallels between the Neoplatonists and the practitioners of *syneisaktism* are also evident in their attitudes toward women. Instead of assuming the subordinate relationship of women to men, as Chrysostom did, both of the former groups apparently did not believe in a separate path to salvation for women. Nor did they believe that living a spiritual life necessitated the segregation of the sexes. It happened that Porphyry was Marcella's superior in philosophical and spiritual attainment, and he wrote to her as such. However, a woman of like philosophical attainments, such as the later Neoplatonist Sosipatra, might similarly instruct a male neophyte.[119]

On the Christian side, perhaps the sublimation of Jesus' male sexuality made it easier to deny the importance of actual relationships with the opposite sex. When Chrysostom tried to persuade the female virgins to give up their special relationships, he appealed to them to think of themselves as spiritual brides of Christ. This set up their partners as people who made a competing claim to their loyalty to Jesus.

Porphyry's letter "Marcella" indicates that, while at the early stages of philosophic development it is easy to be attached to the physical person of one's teacher, this is not the goal of the partners of a philosophic marriage, who must pursue their individual paths of ascent to the divine. It is only in aspiring to attain union with their intellects and then the divine that they can truly be united to each other, in the real sense. The Christian practitioners of

---

117 *Quod regulares*, 6.
118 See Clark, "John Chrysostom," 182–85; Rader, *Breaking Boundaries*, 62–71.
119 Eunapius, *Philosophers and Sophists*, 467–71.

syneisaktism, on the other hand, appear to have been concerned about the quality of their relationship as well as about the spiritual support it provided them.

The Neoplatonists and the practitioners of *syneisaktism* seem also to have shared a greater sense of immediacy about the practical details of life, though in different ways. Plotinus responded to the needs of a number of people, and Porphyry was motivated by genuine concerns about Marcella and her family in establishing his special relationship with her. Chrysostom, in both of his treatises on *syneisaktism*, claimed that these couples alleged that they gave each other practical assistance, but he suggested that virgins dedicated to Christ should not have to worry about material affairs. Apparently alternatives for women were to remain in their families and be supported by them,[120] or to become servants in the homes of married couples.[121] Other options were for virgins of independent means to live independently or in communities with other women.[122] These options probably afforded virgins the greatest spiritual and temporal opportunities. But the bishops soon arranged to manage the financial affairs of the virgins,[123] in keeping with the principle of the necessary subordination of women. This system was probably not in the best interests of the virgins, who may have preferred to choose their own male protector and administrators, if they needed them, rather than being placed under the jurisdiction of an ecclesiastical official who may have resembled a bureaucrat more than a spiritual guide.

Marcella's situation also appeared to demand a male presence to counter the strong pressure of her relatives, if we read correctly the veiled references Porphyry makes in the letter "To Marcella" to people who suspected his motives, who made attempts on his life, and who threatened the safety of Marcella's children. Though a woman in Marcella's circumstances undoubtedly would have been legally independent after she was widowed, it may have been difficult for her to manage her affairs and pursue a philosophic life, due to the pressure of relatives on her to conform to the social and economic system that conventional marriage represented.[124] If, as Chrysostom suggests, *syneisaktism* was a convenient arrangement for male ascetics who needed housekeepers,[125] they would have done well to read Porphyry's profession of the altruistic motives that inspired his philosophic marriage. Some male virgins probably were motivated by the concerns ascribed to them by Chrysostom, but others may well have shared sentiments similar to those of Porphyry.

120 Rader, *Breaking Boundaries*, 62–64.
121 See Dumortier, "Le mariage," 149, cited in Clark, "John Chrysostom," 182, n. 102, and Achelis, *Virgines Subintroductae*, 28.
122 See the discussion of the alternatives in P. Brown, *The Body and Society*, 259–84; Castelli, "Virginity and Its Meaning," 61–88; Schmitz, "La première communauté."
123 Achelis, *Virgines Subintroductae*, 66
124 Wicker, in Porphyry, *Ad Marcellam*, 4–10.
125 *Adversus eos* 9.

"Spiritual marriage" as it was understood in *syneisaktism*, the close relationships with women enjoyed by Plotinus, and Porphyry's philosophic marriage to Marcella all assumed that control of the passions was possible and affirmed the importance of close bonds of human connectedness in the pursuit of spiritual goals and values, though in different ways. Chrysostom, on the other hand, believed that human passions, particularly sexual passions, were so strong that every energy must be devoted to curbing them, and that any contact between the sexes would be detrimental for those committed to virginity. Despite the models for engagement and transcendence afforded by the Neoplatonists and by the practitioners of *syneisaktism*, ultimately it was the ethic of transcendence through alienation from the body, from nature, and from the community of the opposite sex, which John Chrysostom as well as Augustine helped to shape, that prevailed in western culture.

X

The World Engaged

THE SOCIAL AND ECONOMIC WORLD
OF EARLY EGYPTIAN MONASTICISM

James E. Goehring

The discovery of the Nag Hammadi Codices and their publication gave impetus to the study of the Coptic language in many New Testament departments. While the majority of students produced as a result of this process have centered their research on the Nag Hammadi literature and Gnosticism, a few have moved into the more general field of Coptic studies. James Robinson's own efforts and those of his students reflect this development. His work in New Testament and gnostic studies is well known. His broader contribution to Coptic studies has been the result of his effort to establish the provenience of the Nag Hammadi Codices and the Dishna papers (Bodmer papyri). This effort has added considerable fuel to the debate over the relationship of these manuscript collections to the Pachomian monastic movement. While most Robinson students, like Robinson himself, remain close to New Testament and Nag Hammadi in their research, a few have moved more broadly into the study of Egyptian Christianity. The article that follows is offered as an example of such research fostered in part through the influence of James Robinson. It is a privilege to offer it in this collection in his honor.

Egyptian monasticism evokes images of the desert. Recluses withdrawn into their desert cells or pharaonic rock-cut tombs, assemblages of anchorites and their disciples far from the city, and coenobitic monks sharing the ascetic life in communities built on the edge of the desert have populated this image in the imagination of Christian authors and artists throughout the centuries. It received its clearest and surely most influential statement early in the *Vita Antonii*, where the author reports that "the desert was made a city by monks, who left their own people and registered themselves for citizenship in the heavens."[1] In the fifteenth century, the Italian artist Starnina, in his painting of the Egyptian Thebaid, transformed this desert city into a veritable megalopolis.[2] The centrality of the theme in modern scholarship is perhaps best

---

1 *Vita Antonii* 14; cf. Gregg, *Athanasius*, 42–43.
2 Barraclough, *The Christian World*, 36.

illustrated in the use of the phrase *The Desert a City* as the title of Derwas Chitty's 1966 history of early Egyptian and Palestinian monasticism.[3]

In an environment imbued with the visible separation of the black and red land, it is no mystery that the desert should serve as a symbol of death and distinction from the inhabited realm. As in ancient Egypt those who departed this life were entombed in the desert, so many early monks fled to the desert to symbolize while yet alive their chosen death to this life and citizenship in heaven. In the major sources of Egyptian monasticism that survive, separation from the *inhabited world* (οἰκουμένη) through *withdrawal* (ἀναχώρησις) into the *desert* (ἔρημος) or behind a monastery wall represents a central, unifying theme.

The symbolic significance of this desert imagery, seared into the mind by the physical geography of the land, is clear. Peter Brown has seen in it a causal factor that sets the practice of monasticism in Egypt apart from the other provinces, where the desert "was never true desert." There the holy man who withdrew to the desert did not "disappear into another unimaginable world," but wandered on the fringe of the οἰκουμένη and interacted with it. In Egypt, on the other hand, with its sharp antithesis between true desert and settled land, "the holy man . . . did not impinge on the society around him in the same way."[4]

While Brown's analysis is perceptive, one must be cautious lest the symbolic significance of the separation between ἔρημος and οἰκουμένη in the monastic literature of Egypt be translated into a reality that precludes too drastically the equally real social and economic interaction between the monks and the surrounding world. It is the symbolic importance of the theme of withdrawal or separation that makes it so central in the monastic literature of Egypt. While this same literature is replete with references to social and economic interaction with the inhabited world, such references appear only as elements within a larger story, the true purpose of which is to edify the reader in more spiritual matters. As a result, later interpretations of this literature often pass over such peripheral elements and emphasize the more spiritual, other-worldly goals. On occasion, in fact, the social and economic interaction of the monk and the world is not only passed over, but virtually denied as a result of this emphasis on the edificatory spiritual dimension of separation from the world.

The latter error is due to the continuing success of the rhetorical intent of the hagiographical literature. As sources designed for edification, for the encouragement of *imitatio patrum* ("imitation of the fathers"),[5] they naturally present the life of the monks in idealized form. They are concerned only marginally with the issues of economic and social interaction as facts of

3 Chitty, *The Desert a City*.
4 P. Brown, "Rise and Function," 82–83.
5 *Epistula Ammonis* (hereafter *EpAm*) 23; cf. Goehring, *Letter of Ammon*, 267–68.

everyday existence and stress instead separation from the world as indicative of the truer spiritual life. But that fact does not make the social and economic interaction any less real. Such interaction was not only possible; it was inevitable. The desert in Egypt, while sharply distinct from the inhabited land, was not remote.[6]

The *Vita Antonii,* which influenced greatly most subsequent representations of the monastic life, underscores the ideal of withdrawal as Antony moves ever further from the inhabited realm: from home to village boundary, to cemetary, to the near desert, to the distant desert.[7] Without denying such a process of withdrawal by Antony, one may still note that the manner of its formulation in the *vita* is the product of the propagandistic author.[8] Dörries long ago, through a comparison of the Antony of the *vita* with the Antony of the *Apophthegmata Patrum,* established the rather weak claim that the *vita* has to be historical.[9] Nonetheless it is still frequently used as indicative of the anchoritic life in most of its details.[10] It is where many historians begin their presentation of Egyptian monasticism. Withdrawal, central to the image of Antony in the *vita,* becomes the overriding image of the Egyptian monk.

Dörries's work, however, should caution one from such an uncritical use of the sources. It should raise the question not only in the case of the *Vita Antonii,* where a second source enabled Dörries's analysis, but in the case of all such literature, even when a second source is not available against which to judge an account. The need for such caution is underscored by the fact that in those cases where such sources do exist, Dörries's observation of the precedence of hagiographic concern over historical accuracy seems almost inevitably to hold true. The "mystical alphabet," which is noted in passing in the first Greek Life of Pachomius and explained simplistically in Palladius's *Historia lausiaca,* defies interpretation in the more direct witness of Pachomius's letters.[11] In the Shenutean corpus, the description in the Bohairic *vita*

6 Palamon, the anchorite under whom Pachomius began his career, is said to have lived in the inner desert. Lefort was the first to point out that this inner desert was not the remote desert situated far beyond the demarcation of the black land, but a small, barren, desert-like area of land within the confines of the irrigated fields near the village of Chenoboskeia. It is still present today and boasts the Coptic Monastery of Palamon, a stone's throw from the village. Lefort, "Les premiers monastères pachômiens," 383–84.

7 The influence of the *Vita Antonii* on the presentation of the Pachomian movement in its sources is clear. Pachomian Greek *Vita prima* (hereafter cited *G1*) 2, 99; cf. Goehring, *Letter of Ammon,* 188–89.

8 The question of the author of the *Vita Antonii* is currently under debate. T. D. Barnes, "Angel of Light or Mystic Initiate?" 353–68; Tetz, "Athanasius und die Vita Antonii," 1–30.

9 Dörries, "Vita Antonii," 359–410.

10 I am not suggesting that the *Vita Antonii* be discarded as valueless for historical inquiry into early anchoritic monasticism in Egypt. But one must use it with extreme caution. The ἀναγώρησις, emphasized in this influential source, should not be used indiscriminately as descriptive of Egyptian monasticism in all its forms, but should be seen in large part as hagiographical rhetoric.

11 *G1* 99; Halkin, *Sancti Pachomii Vitae Graecae,* 66; *Historia lausiaca* 32; cf. C. Butler, *The Lausiac History of Palladius,* 2.90–91, 206; Quecke, *Die Briefe Pachoms.*

of Shenute's destruction of the idols in the temple at the village of Pnueit, some fifteen miles north of his monastery at Sohag, differs dramatically from the abbot's own account. According to the *vita,* the non-Christian inhabitants, after failing to hinder Shenute's arrival through the use of magic, fled their village and left the monk to destroy the images of their gods. That is the end of the incident. But Shenute himself reports that the villagers brought charges against him to the authorities in Antinoe.[12] Considerably greater interaction with the surrounding societal order is implied. The letter of Ammon, which describes life in the Pachomian community of Pbow around 351 CE, clearly goes beyond the facts in its effort to align the Pachomian movement with Alexandrian "orthodoxy."[13] In similar fashion, the archaeological work at Kellia in Lower Egypt has dispelled, at least for the later period, the notion of the monastic cell as small and unpretentious. While one assumes that the first monks at Kellia were not so well furnished, it is indeed remarkable to find that later cells came to include a courtyard, a vestibule, a hallway, oratory, a bedroom for the ascete with a closet, an attached room, a room with closet for the novice or servant, an office, a kitchen, and a latrine. The cells were, in addition, finely decorated.[14]

A history of Egyptian monasticism needs to be more than a simple recounting of the lives of famous monks written by their faithful disciples. One must examine the texts with an eye to the brief references within them to other, often different, monastic movements, to interaction with secular and ecclesiastical authorities, and to practices that would necessarily lead to such interaction even if it is not expressly stated.[15] In addition one must gather the few shreds of non-monastic references to the monks that exist, as well as the archaeological evidence that is accruing. A critical history needs to explore all of these sources and interpret them not only in terms of content, but also in terms of intent. A tax receipt has at best marginal import in terms of the edificatory intent of a monastic *vita.* One cannot expect that the author of a *vita* would find the inclusion of tax information relevant.[16] Likewise, it is no wonder that the Bohairic "Life of Shenute" ignores the legal charges brought against the abbot in the Pnueit affair. The intent of the *vita* is to portray the power of Shenute as a man of God, not to detail his struggle with the secular authorities. The fact that it does ignore this struggle, however, leads one to suspect that such material is ignored or played down in most secondary monastic sources.[17]

---

12 *Sinuthii vita bohairice* 83–84 (CSCO 41.41); cf. Leipoldt, *Schenute von Atripe,* 179.

13 Goehring, *Letter of Ammon,* 103–22.

14 *Le site monastique des Kellia,* 22–23.

15 It is obvious that extreme caution must be used in such interpretation. But the nature of the hagiographic witness must be assumed to have slighted such evidence as unrelated to its intent of religious edification.

16 This fact would hold true for the oral stage of the tradition as well. Stories told for purposes of edification would develop themes that foster the edificatory goal. A list of monastic taxes would hardly be relevant.

17 The Shenutean corpus offers great possibilities in this regard, since we possess many

The very association of Egyptian monasticism with the desert must be kept in perspective. The prevalence of the motif in the literature is due as much, if not more, to its symbolic significance as to its actual predominance in practice. A careful reading of the sources betrays this fact. When Antony, who is often viewed as the father of the anchoritic flight to the desert, began his career, he gained insights into the ascetic life from an old man in a neighboring village who had lived the solitary life from his youth.[18] This ascetic had not found *anachoresis* to involve a literal flight to the desert. The centrality of that pattern awaited the hagiographic depiction of his student Antony. The Pachomian monasteries, both those established by Pachomius himself and those which chose to join his expanding community, were situated in the inhabited land. The monastic sources and church fathers know that monks lived in the cities, villages, countryside, and desert, though the fathers favor the last named category.[19] Before Ammon withdrew to the Pachomian monastery in Upper Egypt in 351 CE, he considered taking up apprenticeship with a monk in Alexandria.[20] The city of Oxyrhynchus was apparently bursting at the seams with the monastic presence, as every quarter was inhabited by monks.[21] A papyrus petition dated to 324 CE from the village of Karanis preserves the first known use of the term *monachos* as a title for an ascete, an individual named Isaac, who intervened in a village dispute over a cow. It has been suggested that Isaac represented an early pattern of ascetic practice that preceded the anchoritic and coenobitic developments. E. A. Judge defined it as the apotactic movement, "in which men followed the pattern long set for virgins and widows, and set up houses of their own in town, in which the life of personal renunciation and service in the church would be practiced."[22] Whatever the precise nature of the movement, it is clear that monks such as Isaac chose not to withdraw into the desert and in fact interacted readily with the secular world in which they lived.

The anchorite, who withdrew more dramatically from the inhabited world than his/her apotactic or coenobitic counterpart, had, of necessity, less contact with the secular realm. *Anachoresis* as a term had its origin among those in Egypt who withdrew to the desert to flee their responsibilities, such as taxation.[23] It was difficult for authorities to keep track of such persons, and the

writings by Shenute himself through which we can test the secondary monastic sources about Shenute and his movement. This is not the case for any other Egyptian monastic movement.

18 *Vita Antonii* 3.
19 Rufinus reports monks in the cities, countryside, and desert (*PL* 21.389–90). Jerome dismisses the remnuoth, who move about in the cities in small groups with no rule, with contempt (*Ep* 22.34–36). Palladius states in the prologue to his *Historia lausiaca* that he will leave unmentioned no one in the cities, in the villages, or in the desert.
20 *EpAm* 2. The local priest steered him clear of this Theban monk, whom he branded a heretic.
21 *Historia monachorum* 5 (cf. Festugière, *Monachorum in aegypto*).
22 Judge, "Earliest Use of Monachos," 85.
23 Rostovtzeff, *Roman Empire,* 2.677.

anchorite who withdrew to the desert was no exception. Such persons did not impinge upon the arable and hence taxable land, and it remains unclear whether or not they, like the coenobites, were taxed.[24] The necessities of life, however, meager as they may have been to the true anchorite, required contact with the external world, often in the form of trade. While flight from the world may be the predominant sentiment in the *Apophthegmata Patrum*, the collection contains numerous indications of commercial dealings.[25] Esias appears to have been involved in a sharecropping arrangement.[26] John the dwarf wove ropes and baskets and had an agreement with a camel driver who picked up the merchandise from his cell.[27] He also apparently left Scetis during the harvest season to work for wages.[28] Isidore the priest went to the market to sell his goods.[29] Lucius plaited ropes to earn the money with which he purchased his food.[30] In the collection of sayings associated with Abba Poemen, one reads of meetings with the village magistrate, of the plaiting and selling of ropes, of monks who went to the city, took baths, and were careless in their behavior, of a monk who worked a field, and of one who took his produce to the market.[31] The flight to the desert was real, but its spiritual significance did not preclude secular interchange.[32]

The early coenobitic communities in Egypt were in closer proximity to the inhabited world if not directly in its midst and, as a result, more readily defined in relationship to it by the people and the authorities. The Pachomian dossier offers numerous examples of the interaction of the Koinonia, a system of independent monasteries answerable to the central monastery at Pbow, with the surrounding society. While the hagiographic accounts do not dwell on this material, a careful reading reveals much.

According to the tradition, Pachomius received a vision in which he was instructed to build a monastery at the *deserted village* (κώμην τινά, ἔρημον οὖσαν) of Tabennesi on the shore of the Nile. He undertook this task, after which a number of monks joined him. It is then reported that "when he saw that many people had come to live in the village, he took the brothers and went to build them a church where they could assemble."[33] A number of intriguing

24 Winlock and Crum, *Monastery of Epiphanius*, 1.177.
25 Chitty, *The Desert a City*, 34.
26 *Apophthegmata Patrum* (hereafter cited *AP*) Esias 5.
27 *AP* John the Dwarf 5, 30–31.
28 *AP* John the Dwarf 82.
29 *AP* Isidore the Priest 7.
30 *AP* Lucius 1. Megethios obtained sufficient food by weaving three baskets a day (*AP* Megethios 1).
31 *AP* Poemen, 9, 10, 11, 22, 163.
32 One needs to note, as well, the interchange that took place in the opposite direction, namely the secular visitors who went to the cells and monasteries to meet the monks. This pattern is more frequently stressed in the literature since it corresponds more closely with the edificatory theme of withdrawal expressed in terms of movement of individuals from the worldly to the spiritual realm.
33 Bohairic Life of Pachomius (hereafter cited *Bo*) 17, 24–25 (cf. Lefort, *S. Pachomii vita*).

questions arise from this account. First it must be noted that the precise meaning of "deserted village" remains unclear. Pachomius's second foundation at Pbow is likewise described as a deserted village that he took over.[34] A canal being dug near the site of Pbow in 1976, however, unearthed evidence of a sizeable early Roman presence.[35] The nature of this presence is uncertain, but it clearly calls into question the image of a "deserted village." What can it mean? Wholesale depopulation of villages in Egypt as a result of economic exploitation is not unknown in this period.[36] Pachomius's "deserted villages" may indeed represent such a situation. Whatever the case, Pachomius's occupation of the site, besides drawing monks to his monastery, drew the people back to the village. They came in such numbers that his monks built a church in the village for them before constructing one within the monastery for themselves.[37] It is hard to imagine that such a process would not affect the economy of the area and come to the attention of the authorities, if for no other reason than taxation.

The coenobitic monasteries, as they grew in size and number, had not only a significant religious impact on the surrounding communities, but also a considerable economic impact. While the monastery wall represented the separated, spiritual calling of the monks, their physical needs were met by frequent forays outside the monastery wall to gather the materials needed for their livelihood. The plaiting of ropes and baskets required rushes gathered from the Nile.[38] Agricultural production was apparently carried on outside the monastery wall as well. A vegetable garden was situated near the Pachomian monastery of Tabennesi alongside the Nile.[39] The monks harvested grain from the islands in the Nile and fruit from orchards beyond the monastery gate.[40] One reads also of herdsmen and the shearing of goats for hair shirts.[41] The somewhat later Pachomian *Regulations of Horsiesi* have an extensive, though unfortunately incomplete, set of rules governing the agricultural enterprise of the monks. These include the existence of a housemaster over the monastic farmers, the regulation of time and leadership beyond the monastery walls, extensive discussion of canals and irrigation methods, and references to the raising of cattle and donkeys.[42] While one must posit stages of growth in such agricultural industry between the founding of Tabennesi in 323 CE and the death of Horsiesi (by 400 CE), the evidence certainly suggests

---

34 *Bo* 49.
35 Goehring, "Pachomian Studies," 256.
36 Rostovtzeff, *Roman Empire*, 2.677.
37 *Bo* 25; *G1* 29 suggests that the church was built in the deserted village for the shepherds of the surrounding region.
38 *G1* 23, 51, 71, 76; *EpAm* 19; *Paralipomena* (hereafter *Para*) 9 (cf. Halkin, *Sancti Pachomii Vitae Graecae*).
39 *G1* 24; *EpAm* 18.
40 *G1* 106; Pachomian Rule, *Praecepta* 76–77 (cf. Boon, *Pachomiana*); cf. also *Praecepta* 24.
41 *Praecepta* 108; *Epistula Pachomii* 8 (Quecke).
42 *Regulations of Horsiesi* 55–64 (cf. Lefort, *Oeuvres de S. Pachôme*).

that the monastery wall did not preclude activity that would involve the monks with the surrounding world. The *Regulations* even mention monks who undertook work in the village as well as in the fields.[43]

In addition to farming for their own needs, the coenobitic monastery also served as a production center for items of commercial value in the outside world. Certainly mats, baskets, and plaited ropes were the early products of the monks, but we also hear of sandals and other articles.[44] Monks were appointed from the beginning of the Pachomian movement to transact sales of the monks' handicrafts and to make the necessary purchases from the proceeds.[45] As the community obtained its own boats, the products were shipped down the Nile as far as Alexandria.[46] A late Pachomian source reports negotiations with a neighboring village for foodstuffs during a time of famine.[47]

The overseeing of such commerce, both within and outside the community, was the responsibility of the *steward* (οἰκόνομος) of the individual monastery and ultimately of the *great steward* (μέγας οἰκονόμος) for the Koinonia as a whole. By the time of Horsiesi, one hears of careful record keeping in the steward's office.[48] Each year, in August (the Egyptian year ended 28 August), the monks from the various monasteries in the Koinonia came together at the central monastery of Pbow for a financial and administrative reckoning.[49] Commercial dealings required careful control.

Shenute's White monastery likewise had considerable commercial exchange with the outside world. They sold, among other things, baskets, linen cloth, and books in exchange for money and/or items necessary for the cloister.[50] The trade was carefully controlled by the leadership of the monastery, and detailed records were kept.[51] Leipoldt has argued that Shenute developed the White Cloister, in part, as a great work co-operative (*Arbeitsgenossenschaft*) that served as a source of relief to the poor Coptic farmers by offering them at reduced prices such necessities as cloth, mats, and baskets.[52]

By Byzantine times, the monasteries had come to dominate the lives of the peasants both economically as well as religiously. They came to parallel in these functions the great Egyptian Byzantine estates. Frend notes that "the

---

43 *Regulations* 53; *Praecepta* 90.
44 *Para* 23. It has been suggested that the monasteries served as production centers for papyrus codices, both inscribed and uninscribed. J. M. Robinson, *The Nag Hammadi Library in English*, 16–17.
45 *Bo* 26; *G1* 28.
46 *G1* 113.
47 *Para* 21–22.
48 *Regulations* 29; cf. *Praecepta* 27; Ruppert, *Das pachomianische Mönchtum*, 320–23.
49 Early studies of Pachomian monasticism had assumed a fundamentally religious nature to this gathering in parallel with the only other such community-wide gathering during the Easter season. It is now clear that the August meeting was designed as a financial and organizational close of the old year. Veilleux, *La liturgie*, 366–70; Ruppert, *Das pachomianische Mönchtum*, 323–26.
50 Leipoldt, *Schenute von Atripe*, 136.
51 Leipoldt, *Schenute von Atripe*, 137.
52 Leipoldt, *Schenute von Atripe*, 174.

peasants were sharecroppers, leasing their seed and equipment from the central monastery stores and paying a perpetual rent."[53] The *Book of the Patriarchs* reports that in the sixth century some 600 monasteries existed in the vicinity of Alexandria together with "thirty-two farms called Sakatina, where all the people held the true path."[54] While the precise nature of these Sakatina remains unclear, their connection to the monasteries seems apparent.

The interaction of the monasteries with the surrounding world outlined above naturally had ramifications in public places. The monasteries were not above the legal system in Egypt. That one reads little of such interaction in the hagiographic sources is to be expected. Taxes, wills, legal disputes, and the like are hardly edifying. Nonetheless they did form part of the monastic scene in Egypt. A tax list from the Hermopolite nome dated 367–68 CE records the payment of land taxes by a certain Anoubion for the monastery of Tabennesi, the first Pachomian establishment.[55] One can only expect that the occupation of "deserted villages," the use of agricultural land, and the entry into the commercial life of the community would lead the authorities to apply the tax laws to the monasteries.[56] In a physician's will from Antinoe, land is left to a monastery with instructions to his other heirs to pay taxes on it.[57] Such an arrangement necessarily involved the monastery in the affairs of the outside world. Ownership and transfer of property by monks was relatively common. PLips 28 (381 CE) reveals a woman who left her orphaned grandson to his uncle Silvanus, an *apotaktikos*, to be his son and inheritor of his property. POxy 3203 (400 CE) records the lease of part of a house to Jose, a Jew, by two sisters, Theodora and Tauris, *monachai apotaktikai*.[58] Later wills seem to suggest the transfer of whole monasteries.[59] The laws of Justinian note the sale of monasteries as an abuse in Egypt, probably because there was little in the law's eyes to distinguish a monastic cell from a privately owned hut.[60]

As for legal disputes, Shenute's difficulties with the authorities in Antinoe as a result of his destruction of the images of the gods in the village of Pnuiet has already been noted. A fascinating example of such difficulties, though without clear evidence of legal ramification, is seen in the problem of children who entered the monastic life against their parents' will or without their knowledge. According to the earliest Greek Life of Pachomius, Pachomius

---

53 Frend, *The Rise of Christianity*, 844–45.
54 Evetts, *History of the Patriarchs*, 472; Frend, *The Rise of Christianity*, 845. The number of 600 monasteries may refer rather to individual cells: Hardy, *Christian Egypt*, 168.
55 Wipszycka, "Les terres de la congrégation," 623–36.
56 The coenobitic institutions were readily identifiable. Their growing wealth was also apparent. The anchorite, on the other hand, was less easily controlled by the authorities. It is still unclear whether anchorites were taxed.
57 P. Cairo 67151; cf. Hardy, *Christian Egypt*, 167–68.
58 Judge, "Earliest Use of Monachos," 82.
59 Winlock and Crum, *Monastery of Epiphanius*, 1.126–27, 2.343–48.
60 Hardy, *Christian Egypt*, 168; *Codex Theodosianus* 12.1.63. I am indebted to David Hunter for the latter reference.

tested the person who wished to join his monastery together with his parents.[61] This seems, however, to have been a later development based on problems that arose due to young persons who left their families to join the monastery. Theodore, Pachomius's ultimate successor, left his home to join the system at an early age. His mother came to the monastery with letters from the local bishop demanding to see her son. She was refused. There is no indication that Theodore's parents were informed or tested by the monastic authorities.[62] Ammon left Alexandria at age seventeen and joined the Pachomian movement in Upper Egypt without informing his parents of his plan. They were greatly grieved and searched throughout the monasteries in the delta for their son. Only by accident did they later learn of his whereabouts in the Thebaid.[63] An apothegm attributed to Pachomius records the futile efforts of a mother seeking to stop her son from joining the community.[64] The Arabic *vita* reports that Pachomius, after experiencing difficulties on this issue, relaxed his policy and permitted limited visitation.[65] One can only expect that such problems caused friction between the monasteries and the secular population from time to time. Cases of men deserting their families and of inheritances being given away to the monasteries would naturally add to such friction between monastery and community. Such friction may well lie behind the opposition of certain citizens of Panopolis to Pachomius's construction of a monastery in their community.[66] The practice of Shenute in requiring a written agreement from prospective monks that confirmed the donation of their property to the monastery surely had a legal basis.[67]

While interaction between the monasteries and the secular world became more complex over time, it seems clear that such interaction was part of the monastic self-understanding in Egypt from the beginning. While the image of separation from the world was definitive of the spiritual stance of the monk towards the world, it functions poorly as a metaphor of the monk's social and economic relationship to the world. Monasticism in Egypt was much more than a "city in the desert," separated from the *oikoumenē* as sharply as the red land is from the black. At times the monastic presence seemed an only too real source of friction as it disrupted traditional patterns of life; but more often it became an integral part of the landscape. Its significance and success in Egypt

---

61 *Gl* 24. The Bohairic version (*Bo* 23) does not include this statement.
62 *Gl* 33–37; *Bo* 31–37.
63 *EpAm* 2, 30. It is interesting to note that the first place they seem to have thought to look was the monasteries!
64 Lefort, *Oeuvres de S. Pachôme*, 28–29.
65 Amélineau, *Monuments*, 406.
66 *SBo* 54 (cf. Veilleux, *Pachomian Koinonia*, 1:1–4:73–74); *Gl* 81. There is no reason given for the opposition, which took the form of tearing down at night what the monks had built during the day.
67 Leipoldt, *Schenute von Atripe*, 106–7. A written document was not required in the Pachomian system.

lay not only in its religious import to the surrounding communities, but also in its social and economic interdependence with them. It enlivened dying villages, increased agricultural production and trade, and produced various necessities, e.g., baskets and ropes, for the peasants. Its leaders were the new holy men of antiquity, but its institutions were also among the new purveyors of social and economic power in the hinterland. Its success in Egypt was dependent on both elements.

James M. Robinson with Pope Shenonda III

Reconstructing a
Dismembered Coptic Library

Stephen Emmel

To study antiquity, or Christianity in antiquity, is to study archaeological remains, especially written records that have been preserved either by accident or by design. But the scholarship that has been devoted for centuries to these remains has filled our libraries with such a wealth of information that today a scholar engaged even in basic research in this field may never need to have direct contact with its artifactual basis—the architectural ruins, the utensils of war and peace, the potsherds, the ostraca, papyri, or other manuscripts. Such direct contact is a matter of choice. And those who choose to work at this fundamental level know that it entails an unusual responsibility. Not only must the fragile and often puzzling remains of the past be published in accordance with a rigorous method, but also they must be carefully preserved so that other scholars—perhaps centuries from now—can test and revise the published interpretations.

With his work on the Coptic gnostic manuscripts discovered near Nag Hammadi in Upper Egypt, James M. Robinson took on a very large share of this responsibility. He has devoted much of his career to the Nag Hammadi Codices, seeing to it not only that they would be made fully available to scholars through a variety of publications, but also that they would be physically restored and conserved as the precious artifacts they are. His work has resulted in fundamental contributions to the study of Gnosticism, early Christianity, Hellenistic Judaism, codicology, and Coptic language and literature. It has also drawn attention to one of the most pressing problems facing the entire field of Coptic studies: the need to reconstruct physically the remains of Coptic literature, remains which so knowledgeable a Coptologist as W. E. Crum described as "quite without parallel among the literatures of the Christian east in their fragmentariness and dilapidation."[1] Just as the physical restoration and publication of the thirteen Nag Hammadi Codices has led to significant advances in our knowledge of Gnosticism, so does progress in the wider study of Christian Egypt depend heavily on piecing together the scattered remains of very many more Coptic books.

---

1 Crum, *Catalogue British Museum*, xxii.

The manuscript fragments published below, with the permission of the American Oriental Society, are parts of three paper liturgical books, probably not older than the fourteenth century. They cannot claim anything like the manifold significance of the Nag Hammadi Codices. But they are more important than one might think at first, because it is known that they came from the library of a particular Egyptian monastery, the Monastery of Bishoi in the Wadi Natrun. Furthermore, knowing their provenance has made it possible to relate one of them to fragments preserved elsewhere, and thus to begin to reconstruct a codex. It was by such small steps that parts of the Nag Hammadi Codices were put back together, fragment by fragment, and it is by such small steps that Coptic literature is being reconstructed.

The Monastery of Bishoi is one of four monasteries that still survive as living institutions in the Wadi Natrun (ancient Scetis), deep in the desert northwest of Cairo. Three of them, including Bishoi, have histories that can be traced back into the later part of the fourth century.[2] No doubt the decay and despoliation of the monasteries' collections of books also began long ago. Old books wore out and fell apart; many were dismembered and used as scrap paper, or sponged clean and written over. Marauders pillaged them. Insects fed on them. Beginning in the fourteenth century all the monasteries suffered a severe decline,[3] from which they had not recovered when European antiquaries and scholars began in earnest to pick over what remained of their libraries early in the nineteenth century.

Manuscript collectors rescued much that otherwise might well have been lost forever. From a modern point of view their procedures were scientifically inadequate, but it is difficult to judge these collectors harshly. Archaeology was not yet a science; and in any case these libraries could hardly have been treated as archaeological sites, because they were parts of a living human reality, as they are still. Ideally, one of these ancient libraries ought to have been treated much like an archaeological site. A record of its contents and disposition, made in meticulous detail at a certain point in time, would have provided the basic data for reconstructing earlier states when the existing remains were integral books. Now that the sites have been disturbed and the artifacts scattered, many of the manuscripts and fragments have become more accessible than they would be otherwise, but the task of reconstruction has become more difficult. If it is to be achieved at all, such a reconstruction must begin with those manuscripts whose provenance is assured. In his monumental study of the monasteries of the Wadi Natrun, Hugh G. Evelyn-White gave particular attention to the libraries of the Monastery of Macarius and the Syrian Monastery.[4] Because his specific treatment of the library at Bishoi was much less detailed,[5] it may be useful to survey the relevant data here.

2 For the history of the Monastery of Bishoi, see Evelyn-White, *Monasteries*, 2:95–98, 111–15, and passim; for an architectural description, see 3:133–65.
3 Evelyn-White, *Monasteries*, 2:393–409.
4 Evelyn-White, *Monasteries*, 1:xxi–xlviii, and 2:439–58.
5 Evelyn-White, *Monasteries*, 1:271.

1. Dispersal of the Library of the Monastery of Bishoi

Europeans are known with certainty to have visited the Wadi Natrun in the early part of the seventeenth century.[6] From then on, the salient fact reported about the monasteries was that they possessed libraries full of manuscripts in an exciting variety of languages: Coptic, Arabic, Greek, Ethiopic, Syriac, Armenian. Although the earliest reports were exaggerated in some respects, these monasteries were rightly regarded as a preeminent source of valuable manuscripts, and during the following centuries many European libraries and museums were enriched by acquisitions from them.

The first manuscript from the library at the Monastery of Bishoi that is known to have left the country was transported by Tomkyns Hilgrove Turner, a British soldier with antiquarian interests.[7] How it left Bishoi in the first place is not known. In 1801, when the British defeated Napoleon Bonaparte's army in Egypt, Colonel Turner was put in charge of transporting to Britain the antiquities confiscated from the French. The most important object in his care was the Rosetta Stone, and according to Turner's inventory the spoils included "a chest of Oriental Manuscripts—sixty-two in number—in Coptic, Arabic, and Turkish."[8] Four Coptic manuscripts now in the British Library are said to have been brought thither by Turner,[9] and one of them (no. 27 in the list below) contains two statements indicating that it once belonged to the Monastery of Bishoi.

The first foreign visitor known to have removed a manuscript from Bishoi itself is the Coptologist Henry Tattam, during his second excursion to the Wadi Natrun, February 1839.[10] During his first visit, the previous month, Tattam had examined the monastery's manuscripts but had acquired none. His step-daughter and research assistant, Eliza Platt, had recorded in her journal entry for 14 January that in the church

> Mr. Tattam was examining their [the monks'] books, which were about 150 in number, and all Arabic and Coptic Liturgies; with the exception of one fine copy of the Four Gospels in Coptic, and an old and imperfect copy of the Book of Genesis.
>
> On the ground floor was a large vaulted apartment, very lofty, with arches at

6   The history of European visitors to the Wadi Natrun has been narrated by Evelyn-White, *Monasteries*, 2:417–35; cf. 1:xxxvii–xlii, 270–74, and 2:453–57; see also Gravit, "Peiresc et les études coptes," 13–15.

7   Vetch, "Turner"; Edwards, *Lives of the Founders*, 364–67; Dawson & Uphill, *Who Was Who*, 290.

8   Edwards, *Lives of the Founders*, 367.

9   Add. MSS. 5995–5998; see *Index to the Additional Manuscripts*, 461 under "Turner (Sir Tomkins Hilgrove)."

10 Crum (*Catalogue British Museum*, xii n. 4, followed by Evelyn-White, *Monasteries*, 1:271 with n. 2) thought that Robert Curzon, who visited the Wadi Natrun in March 1838, obtained one of his Coptic manuscripts from Bishoi, but this conclusion was unfounded. See Layton, *Catalogue British Library*, 7 (no. 2 [history (5)]). In fact, there are good reasons for believing that Curzon did not acquire this particular manuscript in the Wadi Natrun at all.

each end, perfectly dark; and so strewn with loose leaves of old Liturgies, that scarcely a portion of the floor was visible. And here we were all fully occupied in making diligent search, with each a lighted taper, and a stick to turn up old fragments. In some parts, the MSS. lay a quarter of a yard deep; and the amazing quantity of dust was almost choking, accompanied by a damp and fetid smell, nearly as bad as in the Tombs of the Kings. We did not find any thing really valuable here; or any thing on vellum, excepting one page.[11]

On 9 February, during their second visit to Bishoi, Tattam "successfully bargained for an old Pentateuch in Coptic and Arabic, and a beautiful copy of the Four Gospels in Coptic." And on the following day, his chief servant acquired several more manuscripts on Tattam's behalf, including "a very old and worm-eaten copy of the Pentateuch, from St. Amba Bischoi, exceedingly valuable, but not quite perfect at the beginning."[12]

The manuscript of the gospels (no. 10 in the list below) is now in the John Rylands Library. The "worm-eaten copy of the Pentateuch" can be identified as the part of no. 1 below that belongs to the British Library, except for the first leaf, which was added from a later acquisition by G. J. Chester. Probably the first of Tattam's acquisitions mentioned by Platt, the "old Pentateuch in Coptic and Arabic," was but a part of this same manuscript, because Tattam's collection was described later on as including only one Copto-Arabic Pentateuch.[13] Perhaps the "old and imperfect copy of the Book of Genesis" viewed during the first visit was again this same manuscript, or a part of it.

Judging by the accounts of later visitors, Platt was describing two separate places in the monastery. One of them was the church, but the "large vaulted apartment," which she described vaguely as being "on the ground floor," is on the second floor of the monastery's keep, or tower of refuge. Apparently her recollection of the location was confused by the fact that the keep can be entered only at the second floor level, by means of a drawbridge from the nearby gatehouse roof.[14] Although this spacious room was not the original library, which was a much smaller room on the same floor,[15] probably the heap of ruined books was the remains of what the library once contained. No doubt all the books still useful for worship services were kept in the church. The purpose of the remnants in the keep can be surmised from what a later visitor was told when he expressed an interest in purchasing a similar pile of loose leaves at one of the other monasteries: The monks needed the paper "to bind their new books, and all the paper in Cairo would not answer their purpose so well."[16]

11 Platt, *Journal*, 1:278–79. For the first name of "Miss Platt," see Layton, *Catalogue British Library*, 252 (no. 193[1] [history (11)]).
12 Platt, *Journal*, 2:47 and 49.
13 Tattam, "Catalogue" (see no. 1); see also Sotheby's *Catalogue*, 27–31 (see lot no. 406).
14 Evelyn-White, *Monasteries*, 3:139 (he refers to the two floors of the keep as "ground" and "first").
15 Evelyn-White, *Monasteries*, 3:140 and pl. 38 ("first [i.e., second] floor plan"); cf. 1:xliv–xlv.
16 A. J. Butler, *Ancient Coptic Churches*, 1:333.

Tattam's collection included two more manuscripts that can be identified as having come from Bishoi: nos. 303 and part of 304 (BM 858) in the list below; at least the latter probably was rescued from the pile of scraps in the keep. It is possible that Tattam acquired these two items in 1842, during his third visit to the Wadi Natrun, but his published account of that visit speaks only of his spectacular acquisition of Syriac manuscripts at the Syrian Monastery.[17]

Tattam's acquisitions at the Syrian Monastery aroused new interest in the Wadi Natrun. More than a century had passed since a comparable horde of manuscripts had been brought to Europe from that source. And so in 1844, when Constantin Tischendorf undertook the first of his famous Middle Eastern quests for ancient manuscripts of the Bible, he included the Wadi Natrun in his itinerary, visiting there in April, soon after his arrival in Egypt. His published accounts of the visit suggest that the only acquisitions that he made were at the Monastery of Macarius.[18] But among the manuscripts that he brought back to Europe in 1845 and donated to the Leipzig Universitäts-bibliothek is a lectionary (no. 28 below) that seems to have belonged to the Monastery of Bishoi,[19] where he might have acquired it.[20]

A few years later, in 1847, the Hofbibliothek in Vienna received a donation of oriental manuscripts and manuscript fragments from the Generalkonsul in Alexandria, Anton Laurin, who had been in Egypt since 1834.[21] Laurin's donation included seven Coptic manuscripts[22] and parts of a larger number of Christian Arabic manuscripts.[23] There is no published record of precisely when or how Laurin assembled this collection, but one of his Coptic manuscripts (no. 301 below) certainly comes from Bishoi.[24]

In 1870, it was said, the Egyptologist Heinrich Brugsch removed from the Monastery of Bishoi "the last remains" ("den letzten Rest") of its library, a collection of thirty-three manuscripts, which the Göttingen Universitätsbib-liothek acquired eight years later.[25] More than half of these manuscripts are in Arabic only; one is in Ethiopic. The Coptic portion of the collection is nos. 11, 29–35, 138–140, 305, and 306 in the list below.[26]

---

17 Cureton, "MSS from Egyptian Monasteries," 59–60.
18 Tischendorf, *Reise in den Orient*, 1:124–25; "Manuscripta Tischendorfiana," 71 (no. 24); cf. Evelyn-White, *Monasteries*, 1:xl–xli.
19 Evelyn-White (*Monasteries*, 1:271 with n. 7) interprets the colophon thus.
20 But Tischendorf's brief account of his visit to Bishoi does not mention either the library or its manuscripts (*Reise in den Orient*, 1:125–26).
21 Cramer, "Elf Codices," 113–14; Flügel, *Handschriften Wien*, 3:xiii.
22 Cramer, "Elf Codices" (nos. 2–8).
23 Flügel, *Handschriften Wien*, 3:7–26, 547 (nos. 1545–1547, 1549, 1553–1560, 1565–1569, 2013).
24 Of course it is possible, as Zanetti has suggested (*Les lectionnaires*, 321), that all of Laurin's manuscripts came from Bishoi; but see *P. Rainer Cent.*, p. 19 n. 113 (cf. Loebenstein, "Papyrus Erzherzog Rainer").
25 Wüstenfeld, "Coptisch-arabische Handschriften," 285–86, 289–325 (perhaps nos. 32 and 33 in his list did not come from Bishoi; no. 34 probably did not come thence, and nos. 35 and 36 certainly did not).
26 These thirteen manuscripts were described extensively by de Lagarde, *Die koptischen Handschriften*.

Even if Brugsch did remove from Bishoi the monks' last more or less complete codexes, which probably were books from the church, there still remained the great quantity of fragments in the large room in the monastery's keep. Greville J. Chester, a clergyman and avid antiquary, visited the monastery in January 1873 and saw this room "strewn with leaves of Coptic and Arabic MSS."[27] His report does not mention acquiring any of these leaves, but he did gain possession of a number of them, presumably on this occasion. Among the many items acquired from him by the British Museum are nine that can be identified as having come from Bishoi. In the list below, these items are nos. 137 and the British Library portions of 1 (first leaf), 12, 23, 26, 304 (BM 910), 432, 435, and 437.

A decade later, while writing his influential book on Christian Egypt, Alfred J. Butler toured the Wadi Natrun. In the keep at Bishoi in the winter of 1883–84, he too observed "the fragments of Coptic and Arabic volumes scattered about the floor."[28] Butler had with him a supply of gold with which he hoped to purchase manuscripts from the monasteries, but the dreams he harbored of recovering lost literary treasures were soon dashed. The only acquisition he was able to make, at the Monastery of Baramus, seemed to him disappointingly meager.[29] Curiously, one of the leaves that he brought back from Baramus is part of no. 26 in the list below, an unusual Holy Week lectionary in Coptic, Greek, and Arabic, of which other extant parts are known to have come from Bishoi.

Little had changed by February 1923, when the American biblical scholar William H. P. Hatch visited the Wadi Natrun. Like others before him, he hoped that important manuscripts might still be found there. "At Anbâ Bishôi," he reported,

> the prior conducted me to an upper room [i.e., in the keep] where there were fragments of paper manuscripts lying about on the floor in great profusion. I rummaged at will among the débris and picked up several leaves containing parts of Matthew, Luke, John, Acts, and James, as well as some liturgical fragments. All these were willingly given to me for the asking.[30]

Hatch published his acquisitions from Bishoi during the following years, identifying them as parts of five different manuscripts: see nos. 13, 20, 36, 141, and 307 in the list below. None of the fragments published by Hatch includes any passages from Luke, contrary to the expectation raised by his first account of the acquisition. The present whereabouts of these and Hatch's other manuscript fragments from the Wadi Natrun are not known.[31]

27 Chester, "Notes on the Coptic Dayrs," 110.
28 A. J. Butler, *Ancient Coptic Churches*, 1:315.
29 A. J. Butler, *Ancient Coptic Churches*, 1:316, 326, 333; Evelyn-White, *Monasteries*, 1:272 n. 11. Butler's manuscript fragments are now in the Bodleian Library.
30 Hatch, "Visit to the Coptic Convents," 99; see also his "Three Liturgical Fragments," 94.
31 See the Excursus below.

In February 1939, the orientalist L. Th. Lefort returned to Louvain with a few paper manuscript leaves as souvenirs from a similar visit.[32] He did not record the provenance of any of these leaves precisely, but one leaf belongs to no. 13 in the list below and thus can be traced to Bishoi.

The heap of manuscript fragments was finally sorted and cleared of Coptic items in 1959, by O. H. E. Burmester and O. F. A. Meinardus. Finding that on the second floor of the keep "the loose leaves of MSS. had been collected together and placed in a large stone bin," they took away with them "the residue of all that was found of Coptic texts in the said bin."[33] This enormous collection of fragments, now in the Hamburg Staats- und Universitätsbibliothek, has been catalogued as consisting of parts of some five hundred manuscripts.[34]

Four more items complete this survey of manuscripts known to have been alienated from the library at the Monastery of Bishoi: (1) A leaf in the British Library, said by Crum to have come from Cairo, apparently is part of no. 105 in the following list; (2) in the Library of the Coptic Patriarchate in Cairo there is an euchologion (no. 431 below) that was copied for a hegumenos at Bishoi; (3) in the Papyrussammlung of the Österreichische Nationalbibliothek in Vienna there is another leaf of the trilingual Holy Week lectionary (no. 26 below); and (4) there is in the Handschriftensammlung of the same library a hymnal (no. 302 below) that belonged to the monastery.[35]

2. List of Coptic Manuscripts from the Monastery of Bishoi

The following classified list includes only the Coptic (or Copto-Arabic) manuscripts that are currently known to have come from the Monastery of Bishoi. There are four grounds for accepting Bishoi as the assured provenance of these manuscripts or their constituent parts: (1) colophons; (2) marginal notes (some of them modern) stating the provenance; (3) other records indicating that they were acquired from the monastery; or in a few cases (4) simply the fact of being part of a codex, other parts of which can be traced to Bishoi.

32 Lefort, "Coptica Lovaniensia," 53:65–66. Lefort's entire collection of manuscripts was destroyed when the university library in Louvain was bombed during World War II.
33 Burmester, *Koptische Handschriften*, 12.
34 Burmester, *Koptische Handschriften*; see the reviews by Quecke and by Devos. Some of the items in Burmester's supplementary section do not come from Bishoi (Suppl. 1–14), and some are in only Arabic or Greek (Suppl. 16, 19A, 21, 25, 26, 30), while many of the remaining items in this section consist of unsorted fragments. Burmester ("Greek Synaptè and Lectionary Fragment") has also published three leaves from two Greco-Arabic liturgical manuscripts that apparently were part of his acquisition from Bishoi, but that are not included in his catalogue of the Hamburg collection.
35 This same collection also includes a medical miscellany in Arabic that was copied by a monk at Bishoi; see Flügel, *Handschriften Wien*, 2:533 (no. 1464). Flügel did not record the source of this manuscript, but that it might well have been part of Laurin's collection is suggested by the fact that its call number (Mxt. 489) comes just before a series of numbers assigned to part of his donation (Mxt. 490–494). See also the Addendum below.

I have assumed that all of Burmester's identifications of related fragments are correct, even though some of these identifications were made tentatively (nos. 1, 12, 23, 432, 437). Probably other identifications have yet to be discovered. The accompanying bibliographical references do not repeat information that is implied in the references to the manuscripts themselves or that has already been provided above. Parchment manuscripts are specially noted. Manuscript collections are referred to as follows:

ANB = Österreichische Nationalbibliothek, Vienna, Papyrussammlung; cited by call number.

ANBH = Österreichische Nationalbibliothek, Vienna, Handschriftensammlung; cited according to Cramer, "Elf Codices."

DDRLU = Universitätsbibliothek, Leipzig; cited according to Leipoldt, "In koptischer Sprache."

DGN = Niedersächsische Staats- und Universitätsbibliothek, Göttingen; cited according to Meyer, *Handschriften in Göttingen*, vol. 3.

DHB = Staats- und Universitätsbibliothek, Hamburg; cited according to Burmester, *Koptische Handschriften*.

EGCP = Library of the Coptic Patriarchate, Cairo; cited according to Simaika, *Catalogue*, vol. 2.

UKBL = British Library, London; BM indicates citation according to Crum, *Catalogue British Museum*.

UKMR = John Rylands University Library, Manchester; cited according to Crum, *Catalogue Rylands Library*.

UKOB = Bodleian Library, Oxford; cited by call number.

USAOS = American Oriental Society, the manuscripts published in the present article.

A. Biblical Books
   Pentateuch
   1. UKBL BM 712 + DHB Bibl. 1 + DHB Illum. 1.[36]
   2. DHB Bibl. 2.
   Psalms
   3–9. DHB Bibl. 3–9.
   Gospels
   10. UKMR 422.[37]
   11. DGN Kopt. 1.[38]
   12. DHB Bibl. 13 + UKBL BM 746.[39]
   13. DHB Bibl. 12 + Lefort, "Coptica Lovaniensia," no. 63 + Hatch, "Six Coptic Fragments," no. 5.[40]

36 De Lagarde, *Pentateuch koptisch*; M. K. H. Peters, *Coptic Pentateuch* (his MS "D").
37 Horner, *Coptic Version*, 1:cxii–cxiv (his MS "M").
38 Horner, *Coptic Version*, 1:cxi–cxii (his MS "L").
39 Horner, *Coptic Version*, 1:cxxiv (Mark).
40 The relationship between DHB Bibl. 12 and Lefort's leaf was discovered by Burmester. Hatch's leaf (fol. 134) immediately follows Lefort's leaf (fol. 133).

14–19. DHB Bibl. 10, 11, 14–17.
20. Hatch, "Six Coptic Fragments," no. 4 (lectionary?).
Epistles
21–22. DHB Bibl. 18, 19.
Revelation
23. UKBL BM 763 + DHB Bibl. 20.
24–25. DHB Bibl. 21, 22.

B. Lectionaries[41]
26. DHB Lect. 1 + UKBL BM 775 + ANB K 11346 + UKOB Copt.c.3 (Coptic-Greek-Arabic).[42]
27. UKBL BM 767.
28. DDRLU 1080.[43]
29. DGN Kopt. 2 (composed of two separate manuscripts dated thirty-nine years apart).
30–35. DGN Kopt. 3–8.
36. Hatch, "Six Coptic Fragments," no. 6.
37–103. DHB Parchm. 6 (parchment); DHB Lect. 2–16; DHB Lect. Frag. 1–50; DHB Suppl. 29.
104. USAOS Th/F84 no. 2.

C. Prayer Books (Horologia)
105. DHB Horol. 3 + UKBL BM 722 (parchment).[44]
106–107. DHB Horol. 1, 2.
108. DHB Horol. 4.[45]
109–116. DHB Horol. 5–12.
117. DHB Horol. 13.[46]
118–136. DHB Horol. 14–32.

D. Hymnals (Psalmodias, etc.)
137. UKBL BM 866.
138. DGN Kopt. 9.
139. DGN Kopt. 10.[47]
140. DGN Arab. 120 (in part).[48]
141. Hatch, "Three Liturgical Fragments," nos. 2+3.

---

41 See Zanetti, *Les lectionnaires*, passim (his MSS. "E 8, 12–14"; "J 34–37, 41"; "L 767"; "Tischendorf 18").
42 Evelyn-White, *Monasteries*, 1:271 with nn. 12–14; Burmester, "Holy Week Lectionary," and "Bodleian Folio," 35–48 and pl. 3; Cramer, "Koptische Pascha-Büchern," pls. 11–12, and "Vienna Folio." Concerning the provenance of ANB K 11346, see *P. Rainer Cent.*, p. 19 n. 113 (cf. Loebenstein, "Papyrus Erzherzog Rainer").
43 Tischendorf, "Rechenschaft," 12 (kopt. no. 2); "Manuscripta Tischendorfiana," 71–72 (no. 25); *Anecdota Sacra et Profana*, 68 (no. 18).
44 Burmester, "Bodleian Folio," 49–56 and pls. 1–2.
45 Burmester, "Bodleian Folio," 51–52; Quecke, *Stundengebet*, 41–42 n. 160.
46 Burmester, "Bodleian Folio," 52.
47 O'Leary, *Coptic Theotokia*, 61–65.
48 Zanetti (*Les lectionnaires*, 294 [no. E 10]) has pointed out that the text published by de Lagarde (*Die koptischen Handschriften*, 16) is from a hymnal; to be precise, it is parallel to Labib, *Psalmodia*, 45–47.

142–299. DHB Psalmod. 1–158.

300. USAOS Th/F84 no. 3.

301–302. ANBH 4, 10.

E. Liturgical Works

303. UKBL BM 856.

304. USAOS Th/F84 no. 1 + UKBL BM 858 + DHB Rituale 21 + UKBL BM 910.

305–306. DGN Arab. 117, 119.

307. Hatch, "Three Liturgical Fragments," no. 1 (horologion?).

308–430. DHB Eucholog. 1–53; DHB Pontificale 1–3; DHB Rituale 1–20, 22–28; DHB Liturg. Frag. 1–38; DHB Suppl. 19B, 24.

431. EGCP 766.

F. Homilies

432. UKBL BM 913 + DHB Parchm. 5 (parchment).

433–434. DHB Parchm. 2, 4 (both parchment).

G. Biographical Works

435. UKBL BM 917 + DHB Parchm. 1 (parchment; Life of Samuel of Kalamon).

436. DHB Parchm. 3 (parchment; homily?).

H. Philological Works

437. DHB Scala 1 + UKBL BM 926.

438–444. DHB Scala 2–8.

I. Unidentified

445–448. DHB Suppl. 31; DHB Illum. 2; DHB Bind. 1, 2.

Unsorted fragments: DHB Suppl. 15, 17, 18, 20, 22, 23, 27, 28.

3. The American Oriental Society's Manuscripts from Bishoi

The American Oriental Society's collection of manuscripts currently is stored in Yale University's Beinecke Rare Book and Manuscript Library, where the fragments from Bishoi bear the call no. AOS/Th/F84. These fragments were bequeathed to the Society by its first president, John Pickering, upon his death in 1846.[49] In the catalogue of the Society's library published in 1930, they are described as "Gliddon, G. R. [Fragments of Coptic and Arabic Christian missals]."[50]

George R. Gliddon (1809–1857) was the son of a British merchant, John Gliddon, who became the first U.S. consular agent in Egypt. The son accompanied his father to this post at an early age, and himself later served as U.S. vice-consul in Egypt. His experiences there nurtured an enthusiasm for ancient Egyptian things. In December 1842 he began an extensive tour of the

---

49 Gardner, "Donations to the Library," xvii ("Fragments of Coptic and Arabic Manuscripts"). On Pickering, see *National Cyclopaedia of American Biography* 7 (1892): 294; Pickering, *Life of John Pickering*.

50 Strout, *Catalogue*, 126.

United States, delivering lectures that aroused the first popular Egyptological craze in America.[51]

Gliddon's lecture tour began in Boston, where he met and impressed John Pickering and gave him the manuscript fragments published below.[52] The evidence for the latter transaction is a memorandum, written by Gliddon, that is kept with the manuscripts. It is headed in a different handwriting, presumably Pickering's: "Mr. Gliddon's memorandum—January 24, 1843—at Boston." The memorandum itself reads as follows:

> Fragments of Coptic and Arabic Christian missals—picked up by Geo. R. Gliddon in November 1840, from the floor of the now-ruined Library[53] of the Coptic Convent of "Amba-Beshōwee"—at the Natron Lakes—Western Desert—Lower Egypt—See for details "Sonnini's Travels"[54]—The Library was destroyed and plundered about 100 years ago by the Western Arabs—"Mogharba"[55]—The Books were torn and lying on the floor, when I visited the place, in a Dromedary excursion I made in that direction—These Manuscripts are perhaps as old as the invention of Paper, or soon after?[56] Dr. Henry Tattam, in 1839, got from the adjacent Convent "Sooriān"[57] several good manuscripts—and from the Patriarch of Cairo a Copy of the great Arabic & Coptic Lexicon wherewith he has improved his last Edition of his Dictionary 1840 or 1841[58]—Dujardin also obtained in Egypt in 1838 or 37 several good and new Manuscripts now at Paris, but he is dead.[59]

On the basis of this evidence, Gliddon's name must be added to the list of early European visitors to Bishoi who are known to have removed manuscripts from its library; he was there within two years after Tattam's second visit. To my knowledge, Gliddon's visit to the Wadi Natrun is not documented apart from this memorandum.

Gliddon's fragments, all of them paper, derive from seven different manuscripts in Bohairic Coptic and/or Arabic. Four are in Arabic only and will not

---

51 C. R. Williams, "American Interest in Egyptology," 6–8; Dinsmoor, "American Studies of Mediterranean Archaeology," 97–98; J. A. Wilson, *Signs and Wonders*, 41–43; Dawson & Uphill, *Who Was Who*, 117; Pickering, *Life of John Pickering*, 488–89, 492, 509–10.

52 Pickering (*Life of John Pickering*, 488–89) speaks of her father's interest in Gliddon's activities, but there is no mention of Gliddon's Egyptian manuscripts.

53 I.e., the large room on the second floor of the monastery's keep.

54 Reference is to C. S. Sonnini, *Travels in Upper and Lower Egypt, Undertaken by Order of the Old Government of France* (3 vols.; trans. Henry Hunter; London: John Stockdale, 1799), 2:142–87.

55 This sentence seems to reflect a confused recollection of events that occurred in the tenth century; see Evelyn-White, *Monasteries*, 1:xxxvi n. 3, and 2:339 with n. 7. But cf. Wright, *Catalogue of Syriac Manuscripts*, 3:ii.

56 This opinion need not be taken seriously.

57 I.e., the Syrian Monastery.

58 In fact, Tattam prepared but never published a second edition of his *Lexicon Aegyptiaco-Latinum* (1st ed. Oxford 1835). See Sotheby's catalogue of Tattam's library (n. 13 above), p. 31, where lot 407 is Tattam's printer's copy for the second edition.

59 Dujardin was also mentioned by Platt (*Journal*, 1:87 and 94) but is unknown to me otherwise.

be described here.[60] In the following descriptions of the Coptic fragments, the leaf dimensions are the maximum dimensions at present, height by width. Most of the other measurements are approximate, the results of careful averaging or estimation.[61]

1. Service of the Holy Oil.[62] A codex sheet; leaf size 172 x 131 mm. Paper (.176 mm thick) laid (?) and unmarked; wire and chain lines not visible. Minor stains, especially at inner head and fore-edge; first and last pages have penciled note at top: "Copy this page."

Two columns, one Coptic, the other an Arabic translation, 11 lines. Ruled, probably with a mastara (pattern uncertain; similar to Leroy, *Les types de réglure*, no. 00D1); inscription hangs from ruling. Dimensions of written area 120 x 90 mm; Coptic column 120 x 62 mm. No page numbers, signatures, headlines, or catchwords. Script in the style of Layton, *Catalogue British Library*, pls. 28.5 and 31.5, but not so elegant; liturgical directions in a smaller hand. Old-style *jinkim*. Space separates clauses; paragraphs marked by initials in ekthesis. No colors or ornamentation.

These leaves preserve part of the third section of the service of the holy oil, corresponding to Tuki, *Metrefšemši*, 178:25–183:22 and 185:1–14, and to Labib, *Thōhs ethouab*, 47:9–55:7 and 57:7–58:5, but quite variant throughout. The priest's and deacon's parts are given in full, with abbreviated biblical lections (1 Cor 12:27–13:8, Psalm 51:1 [50:3 LXX ed. Rahlfs], Matt 10:1–8). The text missing between the two leaves would have filled four pages; hence this is the second sheet out from the center of a quire.

This sheet belongs to the same codex (no. 304 above) as BM 858, BM 910,[63] and DHB Rituale 21.[64] BM 858 is quire 5 of the codex, five sheets signed on the first page only. The Yale sheet comes from quire 4, probably with four pages missing between it and the first page of quire 5. If this calculation is correct, then quire 4 consisted of four sheets, of which the innermost and the two outermost sheets are missing. Of the two leaves in Hamburg, one is signed as the beginning of quire 6, with text continuing from BM 858, and probably the other is its conjugate. To judge by Crum's description, what he called fol. 1 of BM 910 belongs just before the latter Hamburg leaf. It is likely that his fol. 2 is the conjugate of fol. 1, in which case it ought to be the second leaf of quire 6, with text continuing from the former Hamburg leaf and corresponding to Tuki, *Metrefšemši*, 213:19ff. (Labib, *Thōhs ethouab*, 97:7ff.), but presum-

---

60 I am indebted to Leo Depuydt for examining all the Arabic texts and sharing his observations with me. I also extend my thanks to Bentley Layton and Hans Quecke, who offered advice and encouragement.

61 The method of description used here owes much to Layton, *Catalogue British Library*, liv–lxvi.

62 For the character and structure of this service, see Burmester, *Egyptian Church*, 144–51.

63 The British Library provided me with a photocopy of BM 858 but was unable to find the two leaves of BM 910. The relationship between BM 858 and 910 was Crum's discovery.

64 The Hamburg Universitätsbibliothek provided me with photographs of these two leaves.

ably variant enough to disguise the parallel. It is difficult to determine whether two or three sheets are missing from the center of this quire.

2. Lectionary. A codex sheet, the center of a quire;[65] leaf size 271 x 184 mm. Paper (.165 mm thick) laid and unmarked; chain lines not distinct. Folded and torn around the edges; lower outer corner of second leaf missing with a few letters. Outer spine guarded with two adjacent paper strips 25 mm wide, one inscribed in Greek, the other in Syriac.[66]

One column, 21 lines on first two pages, then 20 lines. Ruled, probably with a mastara (pattern uncertain; similar to Leroy, *Les types de réglure*, no. 00D1); inscription hangs from ruling. Dimensions of written area 206 x 120 mm. Leaves numbered in cursive characters on versos, apparently 61 and 64. No signatures, headlines, or catchwords. Script similar to Layton, *Catalogue British Library*, pls. 14.1 and 30.2; some touching in with red. Old-style *jinkim* (with errors). A few corrections in a later hand. Headings in red. The lections from Acts and Mark begin with large decorative capitals, partly colored with red, and in the latter case also with yellow; here too there are in the outer margins brief indications of the content in Arabic. Within the lections there are some initials in ekthesis, touched in with red. Clauses are separated by red decorative marks.

The passages preserved are Jas 1:11–12, Acts 1:1–11, Ps 22:26 (21:27 LXX ed. Rahlfs), and Mark 9:33–34.

3. Hymnal (Psalmodia). The two inner sheets of one quire and the innermost sheet of another, still attached to the remains of a leather binding; leaf size 154 x 108 mm, but the width of the leaves in the final quire has been trimmed. From the last two quires of the codex, which originally probably consisted of twenty quires, but perhaps only ten (see below, on headband tie-downs).

The last quire is represented by four consecutive leaves. Paper (.273 mm thick) laid and unmarked; chain lines not visible. Insect damage and breakage at bottom; lower outer corner of first leaf missing with about half of five lines. One column, 13–15 lines, except last leaf, where text ends on recto line 12 and verso is blank. No ruling. Dimensions of written area 116 x 88 mm. No page numbers, signatures, headlines, or catchwords. Script similar to Layton, *Catalogue British Library*, pl. 12.9. Old-style *jinkim*. A few corrections, apparently by the copyist, but many errors remain uncorrected. An entire strophe (no. 12), omitted between fifth and sixth pages, was added by a different scribe around bottom and outer margins of fifth page, where part of the text along the outer margin has been trimmed away. First two lines of first page are a heading in Arabic. Strophes marked by initials in ekthesis; the four verses of each strophe

---

65 The text is continuous from the first leaf to the second.
66 Cf. Burmester, *Koptische Handschriften*, 57 (Lect. 6) and 68 (Lect. 14), both of which include leaves similarly guarded with scraps from paper manuscripts in Syriac; so also Hatch, "Six Coptic Fragments," 104 (no. 4).

158 • Stephen Emmel

separated by colons, with short lines at ends of strophes partly filled out with decorative lines. No colors or ornamentation.

The text on these four leaves is a communion hymn for the Saturdays and Sundays of Lent, the same as Labib, *Psalmodia*, 544–48 (incipit ογνιϣϯ ⲙⲙⲩⲥⲧⲏⲣⲓⲟⲛ: ⲉϥⲥⲁⲡ̄ϣⲱⲓ ⲉ̇ⲛⲓⲛⲟⲩⲥ ⲛ̄ⲣⲱⲙⲓ: "A great mystery, beyond human comprehension"), from which the Yale copy varies only slightly, mostly in matters of spelling.

The penultimate quire of the codex is represented by two consecutive leaves. Paper (.186 mm thick) laid and marked with a simple form of the hand watermark pattern.[67] One column, 13 lines. No ruling. Dimensions of written area 116 x 73 mm. No page numbers, signatures, headlines, or catchwords. Script in the style of Layton, *Catalogue British Library*, pl. 13.9; some touching in with red. Old-style *jinkim*. One correction (see n. 71 below). Strophes marked by initials in ekthesis, touched in with red; verses separated by red and/or black decorative marks, with short lines at ends of strophes filled out with decorative lines in red or black.

The text on these two leaves is a hymn about the resurrection. Because I have not been able to identify it precisely, I offer the text and a translation here. The division into strophes follows the manuscript; I have transcribed the decorative verse markers as colons.

[– – –] ⲛⲉⲙⲟⲩⲛⲓϣϯ ⲛ̄ⲁⲱⲣⲉⲁ̇: ϫⲉⲛⲧⲉϥⲁ̇ⲛⲁⲥⲧⲁⲥⲓⲥ:
ⲛⲟⲕ ⲛⲉ ⲛⲓⲫⲏⲟⲩⲓ̇: ⲫⲱⲕ ⲟⲛ ⲡⲉ ⲡⲓⲕⲁϩⲓ: ⲛⲉⲙⲡⲉⲥⲙⲟϩ ⲉ̇ⲃⲟⲗ:[68] ⲱ̇ ⲡⲓⲗⲟⲅⲟⲥ ⲛ̄ⲛⲟⲩϯ:
ⲁⲛⲓⲣⲉⲙⲛ̄ⲕⲁϩⲓ: ⲛⲉⲙⲛⲓⲣⲉⲙⲙ̄ⲫⲉ: ⲁⲩⲉⲣⲟⲩⲁⲓ ⲛⲉⲙⲡⲓϩⲱⲥ: ϫⲉⲛⲧⲁ̇ⲛⲁⲥⲧⲁⲥⲓⲥ:
ⲟⲩⲣⲁϣⲓ ⲛⲁϣⲱⲡⲓ: ϫⲉⲛϯⲟⲓⲕⲟⲙⲉⲛⲓ: ⲉⲑⲃⲉⲭⲉⲁ̇ϥϯ: ϣⲱⲡⲓ ⲛⲉⲙⲛⲓⲣⲱⲙⲓ:
ⲙⲉⲛⲉⲛⲥⲁⲉⲑⲣⲉϥⲉⲣⲣⲱⲙⲓ:[69] ⲛ̄ϫⲉⲡϣⲏⲣⲓ ⲙ̄ⲫϯ: ⲁϥⲟⲩⲱⲛ[70] ⲛ̄ⲧⲉϥⲙⲉⲑⲛⲟⲩϯ: ϫⲉⲛⲧⲉϥⲁ̇ⲛⲁⲥⲧⲁⲥⲓⲥ
ⲡⲓϩⲓⲏⲃ ⲡⲉ ⲡⲓⲗⲟⲅⲟⲥ: ⲛ̄ⲧⲉⲡⲓⲡⲁⲛⲧⲟⲕⲣⲁⲧⲱⲣ: ⲁϥⲧⲱⲛϥ ⲛ̄ⲑⲟϥ[71] ⲙ̄ⲫⲟⲟⲩ: ⲉ̇ⲃⲟⲗ ϫⲉⲛⲛⲏ ⲉⲑⲙⲱⲟⲩⲧ:

67 Cf. Briquet, *Les filigranes*, nos. 10706, 10723, 10777. In our example, the tips of the fingers are trimmed away at the top margin.
68 ⲛⲟⲕ (i.e., ⲛⲟⲩⲕ) to ⲡⲉⲥⲙⲟϩ ⲉ̇ⲃⲟⲗ: a quotation from Ps 89:11 (88:12 LXX ed. Rahlfs), from which ϯⲟⲓⲕⲟⲩⲙⲉⲛⲏ (or ⲟⲓⲕⲟⲙⲉⲛⲓ, as the word is spelled farther on) has dropped out by error between ⲕⲁϩⲓ and ⲛⲉⲙ. In the Bohairic version of this verse (according to the editions by Ideler, Schwartze, de Lagarde, and Labib), τὸ πλήρωμα αὐτῆς is translated by ⲡⲉⲥⲭⲱⲕ ⲉⲃⲟⲗ. Elsewhere in the Bohairic OT, πλήρωμα in this phrase is translated either by ⲭⲱⲕ ⲉⲃⲟⲗ (Ps 23:1 LXX; Ezek 19:7, 30:12), or ⲙⲟϩ ⲧⲏⲣ⳽ (Ps 95:11, 97:7 LXX), or simply ⲙⲟϩ (Ps 49:12 LXX; Jer 8:16); the NT adds to this list only ⲭⲱⲕ without ⲉⲃⲟⲗ (Rom 11:12, 11:25, 13:10; Eph 3:19). Crum (*Dictionary*, 209 *b*) gives only one example of ⲙⲟϩ ⲉⲃⲟⲗ used as a noun, but with a meaning different from that in the present passage.
69 ⲉⲑⲣⲉϥ: emend to ⲑⲣⲉϥ.
70 ⲟⲩⲱⲛ: probably for ⲟⲩⲱⲛϩ.
71 After ⲛ̄ⲑⲟϥ, at the end of the last line of a page, ⲉⲃⲟⲗ has been cancelled with four diagonal strokes, and the cancellation is noted in the margin in Arabic.

ⲛ̅ⲑⲟϥ ⲁϥ†ϣⲓⲡⲓ: ⲛ̅ⲛⲏ ⲉⲑⲙⲟⲥ†ⲙ̅ⲙⲟϥ: ϩⲉⲛ†ⲕⲩⲣⲓⲁⲕⲏ: ⲛ̅ⲧⲉⲧⲉϥⲁ̀ⲛⲁⲥⲧⲁⲥⲓⲥ:
ⲥⲟⲗⲥⲉⲗ ⲛ̅ⲛⲉⲧⲉⲛⲁⲓⲟ̇:⁷² ⲱ̀ ⲛⲓϩⲓⲟ̀ⲙⲓ ⲙ̅ⲡⲓⲥⲧⲟⲥ: ⲉⲧϥⲁⲓ ⲙ̅ⲡⲓⲥⲟϫⲉⲛ: ⲛⲉⲙⲡⲓⲁⲗⲗⲟⲏ̀:
ⲥⲱⲧⲉⲙ ⲉ̇†ⲥⲙⲏ ⲛ̅ⲧⲉⲡⲓⲁⲅⲅⲉⲗⲟⲥ ⲉϥϩⲓϣⲉⲛⲛⲟⲩϥⲓ ⲛⲱⲧⲉⲛ: ⲛ̅ⲧⲉϥⲁ̀ⲛⲁⲥⲧⲁⲥⲓⲥ:⁷³
ⲧⲱⲛⲕ ⲁ̀ⲙⲟⲩ ⲉⲑⲙⲏ†: ⲱ̀ ⲡⲓϩⲩⲙⲛⲟⲇⲟⲥ: ⲟⲩⲟϩ ⲡⲓⲯⲁⲗⲙⲟⲧⲟⲥ: ⲇⲁⲩⲓⲇ
ⲡⲓⲡⲣⲟⲫⲏⲧⲏⲥ:
ⲣⲁϣⲓ ⲟⲩⲟϩ ⲑⲉⲗⲏⲗ: ϩⲱⲥ ⲁ̀ⲣⲓⲯⲁⲗⲓⲛ: ϩⲉⲛⲡⲁⲓϣⲁⲓ ⲙ̅ⲃⲉⲣⲓ:⁷⁴ ⲛ̅ⲧⲉ†ⲁ̀ⲛⲁⲥⲧⲁⲥⲓⲥ
ⲫⲁⲓ ⲡⲉ ⲡⲓⲉ̇ϩⲟⲟⲩ: ⲉ̇ⲧⲁⲡⲟⲥ̅ ⲑⲁⲙⲓⲟϥ:⁷⁵ [- - -]

"[. . .] a great gift, by means of his resurrection.
The heavens are yours, the earth also is yours, ⟨the world⟩ and all that is in it,⁷⁶ o divine Word.
The earthly beings and the heavenly beings have united in song, by means of the resurrection.
There will be joy in the world because God has dwelt with mankind.
After the son of God became human, he revealed his divinity, by means of his resurrection.
The lamb is the Word of the Almighty. He rose today from the dead.
He shamed those who hate him, on this Sunday of his resurrection.
Console your . . .s, o faithful women who carry the ointment and the aloe!⁷⁷
Listen to the voice of the angel as it announces to you the good news of his resurrection!
Rise, come forward, o singer and psalmist, David the prophet!
Be joyful and rejoice! Sing hymns and psalms on this new festival of the resurrection!
This is the day which the Lord has made; [let us rejoice. . .⁷⁸]!"

The binding shows that the codex was originally 170 x 125 mm, and 50 mm thick.⁷⁹ The spine linings, tattered headbands, the back board with its attachment, very slight remains of the front board, and about three quarters of a cover survive. The book was sewn with fine, S-twist thread at three sewing stations. At present, the remains of the quires are held together by yarn and held in the binding by headband tie-downs.

The back board is made up of at least six paper leaves (inscribed in Arabic) pasted together between two pieces of leather. An interlace design is painted

---

72 ⲁⲓⲟ̇: corrupt?
73 Two verse division marks are missing from this strophe, presumably after ⲥⲙⲏ and after ⲁⲅⲅⲉⲗⲟⲥ.
74 The MS has ⲙ̅ⲃⲉ:ⲣⲓ:, by error.
75 This strophe is a quotation from Ps 118:24 (117:24 LXX ed. Rahlfs), which continues with ⲙⲁⲣⲉⲛⲑⲉⲗⲏⲗ ⲟⲩⲟϩ ⲛ̅ⲧⲉⲛⲟⲩⲛⲟϥ ⲙ̅ⲙⲟⲛ ⲛ̅ϩⲏⲧϥ. Cf. Labib, *Psalmodia*, 603:5–7, another instance of this verse's being incorporated into a hymn, where the following verse is simply ⲙⲁⲣⲉⲛⲑⲉⲗⲏⲗ ⲙ̅ⲫⲟⲟⲩ.
76 Ps 89:11.
77 Cf. Mark 16:1; Luke 23:55–24:1; John 19:39.
78 Ps 118:24.
79 I am indebted to Jane Greenfield for preparing a description of the binding, which served as the basis for the following paragraphs. This binding is described briefly in its historical-typological context in Shailor, *The Medieval Book*, 55 (no. 52).

near the center of the inside of the board. Three attachments of fairly heavy, Z-twist thread are wound three times into the back board and joined vertically at the ends of the windings. The spine is lined first with paper cartonnage (inscribed in Greek and Coptic), then with a coarse, plain-weave, natural-color cloth (of which only a fragment remains), and finally with blue and white striped, plain-weave cloth.

Three small S-twist headband cores were anchored twice in each board and tied down with S-twist threads through all the spine linings. The cores are embroidered with blue and natural color threads, mostly untwisted, in a double chevron pattern. Tie-downs still pass through the folds of the two surviving quires, holding them in place. There are ten pairs of tie-downs at the head and ten pairs at the tail. Pairing of the tie-downs is obvious on the outside of the spine, where they are almost perfectly preserved, but only single threads now pass through the two surviving quires.

A cover of strong, heavy leather, originally brick red (judging by the surviving turn-ins), followed the outline of the headbands. Each headband is outlined on the cover's spine with a sharply incised line about 5 mm in from the edge, and the leather thus delineated along the edges at the head and tail has been abraded so as to set it off by a different color and texture from the rest of the spine. At present, the cover extends only 50 mm in both directions beyond the spine, but traces of the turn-in along the fore-edge of the back board survive, indicating that the cover originally extended fully over both boards, as expected.

4. Excursus: William H. P. Hatch's Coptic Manuscripts

Despite information courteously provided by the Rt. Rev. Robert M. Hatch, I was unable to find his father's Coptic manuscripts (or any of his books and papers) at the institutions where he expected them to be. They are not in Cambridge, MA, at the Episcopal Divinity School, where W. H. P. Hatch taught from 1917 until 1946, nor in Atlanta, GA, at Emory University—neither in the Pitts Theology Library, nor in the Robert W. Woodruff Library —to which Rev. Hatch recalls his father leaving his library. In addition to his fragments from Bishoi, Hatch owned fragments from the Monastery of Macarius; see his "Visit to the Coptic Convents," 97; "Three Coptic Fragments"; "Lost Work on Dioscorus"; and "Six Coptic Fragments," 99–103 (nos. 1–3). To my knowledge, he never published the most interesting item in this part of his collection, three leaves from a Bohairic manuscript of apocryphal Acts of the Apostles (for a brief description, see his "Six Coptic Fragments," 99 n. 1). Evelyn-White (*Monasteries*, 1:27–50) had already published a large group of leaves that Hatch judged to belong to the same manuscript to which his leaves belonged. Discovering the whereabouts of Hatch's small collection remains a desideratum.

5. Addendum: More Missing Fragments from Bishoi

After this article was already in press, I chanced upon some unpublished evidence for the existence of additional manuscript fragments brought from the Monastery of Bishoi by G. R. Gliddon. In a penciled first draft of an unpublished catalogue of the Egyptian antiquities collected by Mendes I. Cohen (1796–1879), there occurs the following entry (part of item no. 470): "specimens of Arabic Christian Missals very old—from the Convent of Amba-Beshówée Lower Egypt, G. R. Gliddon" (Cohen, Mendes I., Travels, MS. 251.3, box 3, folder labelled "Catalogue of Egyptian Antiquities," Manuscripts Division, Maryland Historical Society Library, Baltimore; cf., in the same collection, a revised copy of this catalogue written in ink, item no. 644). Relations between Gliddon and Cohen are well-documented and may have begun as early as 1832, when Cohen made his tour of Egypt. In any case, the two men certainly were in close touch after Gliddon's American lecture tour began in 1842. Apparently, the manuscript fragments that Gliddon gave to Cohen were transferred to the Historical Museum of the Johns Hopkins University in 1884, along with the rest of Cohen's collection (see the unpublished "Catalogue of the Historical Museum of the Johns Hopkins University," p. 26 [item no. 644], accession no. 89.2.1, Department of University Collections, Evergreen House, Johns Hopkins University, Baltimore). This collection is now housed in the Johns Hopkins University Archaeological Museum, but nothing like the manuscript fragments described in Cohen's catalogue could be found there when I visited in July 1989.[80]

---

80 On Cohen and his activities, see Cohen, "The Cohen Collection"; Caroline Williams, "American Interest in Egyptology," 5–6; Poole, "Cohen's First"; Cooney, "Acquisition of the Abbott Collection", 17–19; Oliver, *Beyond the Shores of Tripoli*; Ellen Reeder Williams, *The Archaelogical Collection*.

Works Consulted

Abrahams, Roger D., "A Rhetoric of Everyday Life: Traditional Conversational Genres." *Southern Folklore Quarterly* 32 (1968): 44–59.

———, "Introductory Remarks to a Rhetorical Theory of Folklore." *Journal of American Folklore* 81 (1968): 143–58.

———, "The Complex Relations of Simple Forms." *Genre* 2 (1969): 104–28.

———, "Personal Power and Social Restraint in the Definition of Folklore." *Journal of American Folklore* 84 (1971): 16–30.

———, "Proverbs and Proverbial Expressions." Pp. 117–27 in *Folklore and Folklife: An Introduction.* Ed. Richard M. Dorson. Chicago: The University of Chicago Press, 1972.

Achelis, Hans, *Virgines Subintroductae. Ein Beitrag zum VII. Kapitel des I. Korintherbriefs.* Leipzig: J. C. Hinrichs, 1902.

Albig, William, "Proverbs and Social Control." *Sociology and Social Research* 15 (1931): 527–35.

Allen, Willoughby C., *A Critical and Exegetical Commentary on the Gospel According to St. Matthew.* 3d ed. Edinburgh: T. & T. Clark, 1912.

Amélineau, E., *Monuments pour servir à l'histoire de l'Egypte chrétienne au IVᵉ siècle. Histoire de saint Pakhôme et de ses communautés.* Annales du Musée Guimet 17. Paris: Leroux, 1889.

Andocides, *De Mysteriis.* In K. J. Maidment, ed. and trans., *Minor Attic Orators.* Vol. 1. LCL. Cambridge, MA: Harvard University Press, 1941.

Andokides, *On the Mysteries.* Ed. Douglas Macdowell. Oxford: The Clarendon Press, 1962.

Apollodorus, *Bibliotheke:* cf. Apollodorus, *The Library.* Trans. J. G. Frazer. LCL. London: Heinemann, 1921.

Apophthegmata Patrum. PG 65. Paris: Migne, 1862.

Arbeitskreis für die koptisch-gnostische Schriften, "Die Bedeutung der Texte von Nag Hammadi für die moderne Gnosisforschung." Pp. 13–76 in *Gnosis und Neues Testament: Studien aus Religionswissenschaft und Theologie.* Ed. Karl-Wolfgang Tröger. Berlin: Evangelische Verlagsanstalt; Gütersloh: Gerd Mohn, 1973.

Arewa, E. Ojo, "Proverb Usage in a Natural Context and Oral Literary Criticism." *Journal of American Folklore* 83 (1970): 430–37.

———, and Alan Dundes, "Proverbs and the Ethnography of Speaking Folklore." *American Anthropologist* 66 (1964): 70–85.

Aristotle, *Politics*. Trans. and ed. H. Rackham. LCL. Cambridge, MA: Harvard University Press, 1959.

Armstrong, A. H., "Man in the Cosmos: A Study of Some Differences between Pagan Neoplatonism and Christianity." Chap. 22 in *Plotinian and Christian Studies*. Ed. A. H. Armstrong. London: Variorum Reprints, 1979.

Attridge, Harold W., "The Uses of Antithesis in Hebrews 8–10." Pp. 1–9 in *Christians among Jews and Gentiles: Essays in Honor of Krister Stendahl on His Sixty-Fifth Birthday*. Ed. George W. E. Nickelsburg and George W. MacRae. Philadelphia: Fortress Press, 1986=*Harvard Theological Review* 79 (1986): 1–9.

―――, *Hebrews*. Hermeneia. Philadelphia: Fortress Press, 1989.

Barc, Bernard, *L'Hypostase des Archontes. Traité gnostique sur l'origine de l'homme, du monde et des archontes*. Bibliothèque copte de Nag Hammadi, Section "Textes" 5. Québec: Les Presses de l'Université Laval; Louvain: Editions Peeters, 1980.

―――, "Samael-Saklas-Yaldabaoth. Recherche sur la génèse d'un mythe gnostique." Pp. 123–50 in *Colloque International sur Les Textes de Nag Hammadi (Québec 22–25 août 1978)*. Ed. Bernard Barc. Bibliothèque copte de Nag Hammadi, Section "Etudes" 1. Louvain: Editons Peeters; Québec: Les Presses de l'Université Laval, 1981.

Barnes, J. A., *Three Styles in the Study of Kinship*. Berkeley, CA: University of California Press, 1971.

―――, "Kinship Studies: Some Impressions of the Current State of Play." *Man* 15 (1980): 293–303.

Barnes, Timothy D., "Angel of Light or Mystic Initiate? The Problem of the *Life of Antony*." *Journal of Theological Studies* 37 (1986): 353–68.

Barraclough, Geoffrey, ed., *The Christian World: A Social and Cultural History*. New York: Abrams, 1981.

Bascom, William R., "Four Functions of Folklore." *Journal of American Folklore* 67 (1954): 279–97.

Bauman, Richard, "Verbal Art as Performance." *American Anthropologist* 77 (1975): 290–311.

―――, *Verbal Art as Performance*. Prospect Heights, IL: Waveland Press, 1977.

Beardslee, William A., "Uses of the Proverb in the Synoptic Gospels." *Interpretation* 24 (1970): 61–73.

―――, *Literary Criticism of the New Testament*. Philadelphia: Fortress Press, 1970.

―――, "Parable, Proverb, and Koan." *Semeia* 12 (1978): 151–73.

―――, "Saving One's Life By Losing It." *Journal of the American Academy of Religion* 47 (1979): 52–72.

Ben-Amos, Dan, "Analytic Categories and Ethnic Genres." *Genre* 2 (1969): 275–301.

―――"Toward a Definition of Folklore in Context." *Journal of American Folklore* 84 (1971): 3–15.

Berliner Arbeitskreis für koptisch-gnostische Schriften, "Die dreigestaltige Protennoia." See Gesine Schenke.

Betz, Hans Dieter, *Paul's Concept of Freedom in the Context of Hellenistic Discussions about the Possibilities of Human Freedom*. Protocol of the 26th Colloquy. Berkeley, CA: The Center for Hermeneutical Studies, 1977.

―――, *Galatians: A Commentary on Paul's Letter to the Churches in Galatia*. Hermeneia. Philadelphia: Fortress Press, 1979.

Bianchi, Ugo, "Docetism. A Peculiar Theory about the Ambivalence of the Presence of the Divine." Pp. 265–77 in *Myths and Symbols. Studies in Honor of Mircea Eliade.* Ed. Joseph M. Kitagawa and Charles H. Long. Chicago and London: The University of Chicago Press, 1969.

Bieder, Werner, *Die Vorstellung von der Hollenfahrt Jesu Christi: Beitrag zur Entstehungsgeschichte der Vorstellung vom sog. Descensus ad inferos.* Abhandlungen zur Theologie des Alten und Neuen Testaments 19. Zurich: Zwingli-Verlag, 1949.

Blaszczak, Gerald R., *A Formcritical Study of Selected Odes of Solomon.* Harvard Semitic Monographs. Atlanta: Scholars Press, 1985.

Boadi, Lawrence A., "The Language of the Proverb in Akan." Pp. 183–91 in *African Folklore.* Ed. Richard M. Dorson. Bloomington, IN: Indiana University Press, 1972.

Boon, Amand, *Pachomiana Latina. Règle et épîtres de S. Pachôme, épître de S. Theodore et "livre" de S. Orsiesius. Texte latine de S. Jerome.* Bibliothèque de la revue d'histoire ecclésiastique 7. Louvain: Bureau de la Revue, 1932.

Brashler, James, "The Coptic 'Apocalypse of Peter': A Genre Analysis and Interpetation." Ph.D. diss., Claremont Graduate School, 1977.

Briquet, C. M., *Les filigranes: Dictionnaire historique des marques du papier dès leur apparition vers 1282 jusqu'en 1600.* 4 vols. Jubilee (3d) ed. Amsterdam: The Paper Publications Society, 1968.

Brown, Peter, "The Rise and Function of the Holy Man in Late Antiquity." *Journal of Roman Studies* 61 (1971): 80–101.

———, "The Philosopher and Society in Late Antiquity." Pp. 1–17 in *Protocol of the Thirty-Fourth Colloquy of the Center for Hermeneutical Studies.* Ed. Edward C. Hobbs and Wilhelm Wuellner. Berkeley, CA: The Center for Hermeneutical Studies in Hellenistic and Modern Culture, 1980.

———, *The Body and Society: Men, Women, and Sexual Renunciation in Early Christianity.* New York: Columbia University Press, 1988.

Brown, Raymond E., Karl P. Donfried, and John Reumann, *Peter in the New Testament.* Minneapolis, MN: Augsburg Publishing House; New York: Paulist Press; Toronto: Paramus, 1973.

Bruce, Frederick F., *The Epistle to the Hebrews: The English Text with Introduction, Exposition and Notes.* New International Commentary on the New Testament. Grand Rapids, MI: Wm. B. Eerdmans Publishing Co., 1964.

Bullard, R. A., *The Hypostasis of the Archons. The Coptic Text with Translation and Commentary. With a Contribution by Martin Krause.* Berlin: Walter de Gruyter & Co., 1970.

Bultmann, Rudolf, *Das Evangelium des Johannes.* 10th ed. Kritisch-exegetischer Kommentar über das Neue Testament. Göttingen: Vandenhoeck & Ruprecht, 1941.

———, "Bekenntnis- und Liedfragmente im ersten Petrusbrief." *Conjectanea Neotestamentica* 2 (1947): 1–14.

———, "General Truths and Christian Proclamation." Pp. 153–62 in *History and Hermeneutic=Journal for Theology and Church* 4. Ed. Robert W. Funk. Tübingen: J.C.B. Mohr (Paul Siebeck); New York: Harper & Row, 1967.

Burke, Kenneth, "Literature as Equipment for Living." Pp. 100–109 in *Perspectives by Incongruity.* Ed. Stanley Edgar Hyman. Bloomington, IN: Indiana University Press, 1964.

Burkert, Walter, *Ancient Mystery Cults.* Cambridge, MA: Harvard University Press, 1987.

Burmester, Oswald Hugh Ewart, "A Greek Synaptè and Lectionary Fragment from Scetis." *Bulletin de la Société d'Archéologie Copte* 16 (1961–62): 73–82.

———, "The Coptic-Greek-Arabic Holy Week Lectionary of Scetis." *Bulletin de la Société d'Archéologie Copte* 16 (1961–62): 83–138.

———, "A. The Bodleian Folio and Further Fragments of the Coptic-Greek-Arabic Holy Week Lectionary from Scetis. B. Four Parchment Folios of a Bohairic Horologion from Scetis." *Bulletin de la Société d'Archéologie Copte* 17 (1963–64): 35–56.

———, *The Egyptian or Coptic Church: A Detailed Description of Her Liturgical Services and the Rites and Ceremonies Observed in the Administration of Her Sacraments.* Publications de la Société d'Archéologie Copte, Textes et documents. Cairo: Printing Office of the French Institute of Oriental Archaeology, 1967.

———, *Koptische Handschriften 1: Die Handschriftenfragmente der Staats- und Universitätsbibliothek Hamburg, Teil 1* [*Catalogue of Coptic Manuscript Fragments from the Monastery of Abba Pišoi in Scetis, Now in the Collection of the Staats- und Universitätsbibliothek Hamburg*]. Verzeichnis der orientalischen Handschriften in Deutschland 21,1. Wiesbaden: Franz Steiner Verlag GmBH, 1975.

Butler, Alfred J., *The Ancient Coptic Churches of Egypt.* 2 vols. Oxford: The Clarendon Press, 1884.

Butler, Cuthbert, *The Lausiac History of Palladius. A Critical Discussion Together with Notes on Early Egyptian Monasticism.* Cambridge: Cambridge University Press, 1898. Repr. ed., Hildesheim: Olms, 1967.

Camp, Claudia V., *Wisdom and the Feminine in the Book of Proverbs.* Sheffield: Almond Press, 1985.

Campbell, J. K., "Honour and the Devil." Pp. 139–70 in *Honor and Shame. The Values of Mediterranean Society.* Ed. J. G. Peristiany. Chicago: The University of Chicago Press, 1966 (reprint 1970).

Carney, T. F., *The Shape of the Past. Models and Antiquity.* Lawrence, KA: Coronado Press, 1975.

Castelli, Elizabeth, "Virginity and Its Meaning for Women's Sexuality in Early Christianity." *Journal of Feminist Studies in Religion* 2 (1986): 61–88.

———, "A Response to Sex Education in Gnostic Schools." Pp. 361–66 in *Images of the Feminine in Gnosticism.* Ed. Karen L. King. Studies in Antiquity and Christianity 4. Philadelphia: Fortress Press, 1988.

Caulley, Thomas S., "The Idea of 'Inspiration' in 2 Peter 1:16–21." Th.D. diss., Tübingen University, 1982.

Chadwick, Henry, ed., *The Sentences of Sextus: A Contribution to History of Christian Ethics.* Texts and Studies, NS 5. Cambridge: Cambridge University Press, 1959.

Charlesworth, James H., "Les Odes de Salomon et les manuscrits de la Mer Morte." *Revue Biblique* 77 (1970): 522–49.

———, "Qumran, John and the Odes of Solomon." Pp. 107–36 in *John and Qumran.* Ed James H. Charlesworth. London: Geoffrey Chapmann, 1972.

———, *The Odes of Solomon.* SBL Texts and Translations 13, Pseudepigrapha Series 7. Missoula, MT: Scholars Press, 1977.

———, "A Prolegomenon to a New Study of the Jewish Background of the Hymns and Prayers in the New Testament." *Journal of Jewish Studies* 33 (1982): 265–85.

———, ed., *The Old Testament Pseudepigrapha*, Vol. 1: *Apocalyptic Literature and Testaments*. Garden City, NY: Doubleday & Company, Inc., 1983.

———, trans., "Odes of Solomon." Pp. 725–71 in *The Old Testament Pseudepigrapha*. Vol. 2. Ed. James H. Charlesworth. Garden City, NY: Doubleday & Company, Inc., 1985.

———, and R. A. Culpepper, "The Odes of Solomon and the Gospel of John." *Catholic Biblical Quarterly* 35 (1973): 298–322.

Chester, Greville J., "Notes on the Coptic Dayrs of of the Wady Natrûn and on Dayr Antonios in the Eastern Desert." *Archaeological Journal* 30 (1873): 105–16.

Chitty, Derwas J., *The Desert a City: An Introduction to the Study of Egyptian and Palestinian Monasticism under the Christian Empire*. London: Blackwells, 1966.

Chrysostom, John, *Adversus eos qui apud se habent subintroductas virgines*. PG 47. Paris: Migne, 1862.

———, *De Virginitate*. In Herbert Musurillo, ed. and trans., *Jean Chrysostome "La Virginité."* Paris: Les Editions du Cerf, 1966.

———, *Homilia XI in Epistolam ad Ephesios*. PG 62. Paris: Migne, 1862.

———, *In Epistolam Primam Ad Timotheum Commentarius*. PG 62. Paris: Migne, 1862.

———, *In Genesim Sermo*. PG 54. Paris: Migne, 1862.

———, *Quales ducendae sint uxores*. PG 51. Paris: Migne, 1862.

———, *Quod regulares feminae viris cohabitare non debeant*. PG 47. Paris: Migne, 1862.

Cicero, *Tusculanae disputationes*. Trans. J. E. King. LCL. London: W. Heinemann; New York: G. P. Putnam's Sons, 1927.

Clark, Elizabeth A., "John Chrysostom and the *Subintroductae*." *Church History* 46 (1977): 171–85.

———, *Jerome, Chrysostom, and Friends. Essays and Translations*. Studies in Women and Religion 2. New York: The Edwin Mellen Press, 1979.

———, *Women in the Early Church*. Message of the Fathers of the Church Series 13. Wilmington, DE: Michael Glazier, Inc., 1983.

Cohen, Mendes, "'The Cohen Collection of Egyptian Antiquities' and Its Collector, Colonel Mendes I. Cohen." *Johns Hopkins University Circulars* 4 (1885): 21–23.

Collier, Jane Fishburne, "Women in Politics." Pp. 89–96 in *Woman, Culture, and Society*. Ed. Michelle Zimbalist Rosaldo and Louise Lamphere. Stanford, CA: Stanford University Press, 1974.

Colpe, C., "Gnosis, I: Religionsgeschichtlich." *Die Religion in Geschichte und Gegenwart*. 3d ed. 2 (1958): cols. 1648–52.

———, "Heidnische, jüdische und christliche Überlieferung in den Schriften aus Nag Hammadi III." *Jahrbuch für Antike und Christentum* 17 (1974): 109–25.

Connolly, R. H., "The Early Syriac Creed." *Zeitschrift für die Neutestamentliche Wissenschaft* 7 (1906–7): 202–23.

Cooney, John D., "Acquisition of the Abbott Collection." *Bulletin of the Brooklyn Museum* 10, 3 (1949): 16–23.

Cramer, Maria, "Elf unveröffentlichte, koptisch arabische Codices der Österreichischen Nationalbibliothek zu Wien: Ihre inhaltliche und paläographische Wertung." *Etudes de papyrologie* 8 (1957): 113–45.

———, "Studien zu koptischen Pascha-Büchern: Der Ritus der Karwoche in der koptischen Kirche." *Oriens Christianus* 47 (1963): 118–28; 49 (1965): 90–115; 50 (1966): 72–130, pls. 3–12.

———, "The Vienna Folio and Fragments of the Coptic-Greek-Arabic Holy Week Lectionary from Scetis." *Bulletin de la Société d'Archéologie Copte* 19 (1967–68): 49–56.

Crenshaw, James L., "Wisdom." Pp. 225–64 in *Old Testament Form Criticism.* Ed. John H. Hayes. Trinity University Monograph Series in Religion 2. San Antonio: Trinity University Press, 1974.

———, *Old Testament Wisdom: An Introduction.* Atlanta: John Knox Press, 1981.

———, "The Acquisition of Knowledge in Israelite Wisdom Literature." *Word and World* 3 (1987): 245–52.

Crossan, John Dominic, *In Fragments: The Aphorisms of Jesus.* San Francisco and elsewhere: Harper & Row, 1983.

———, *The Cross That Spoke: The Origins of the Passion Narrative.* San Francisco and elsewhere: Harper and Row, 1988.

Crum, W. E., *Catalogue of Coptic Manuscripts in the British Museum.* London: British Museum, 1905.

———, *Catalogue of the Coptic Manuscripts in the Collection of the John Rylands Library, Manchester.* Manchester: University Press; London: Bernard Quaritch, and Sherratt and Hughes, 1909.

———, *A Coptic Dictionary.* Oxford: The Clarendon Press, 1939.

Crüsemann, Frank, "The Unchangeable World: The 'Crisis of Wisdom' in Koheleth." Pp. 57–77 in *God of the Lowly: Socio-Historical Interpretations of the Bible.* Ed. Willy Schottroff and Wolfgang Stegemann. Maryknoll, NY: Orbis Books, 1984.

Cullmann, Oscar, *Christ and Time: The Primitive Christian Conception of Time and History.* Trans. Floyd V. Filson. Philadelphia: The Westminster Press, 1950.

———, *Peter: Disciple, Apostle, Martyr.* London: SCM Press; Philadelphia: The Westminster Press, 1953.

———, *The Johannine Circle.* Philadelphia: The Westminster Press, 1976.

Cureton, William, "British Museum—MSS. from the Egyptian Monasteries." *Quarterly Review* 77,153 (December 1845): 39–69.

Curran, Leo C., "Rape and Rape Victims in the Metamorphoses." Pp. 263–86 in *Women in the Ancient World. The Arethusa Papers.* Ed. John Peradotto and J. P. Sullivan. Albany, NY: State University of New York Press, 1984.

Curzon, L. B., *Roman Law.* London: MacDonald and Evans, 1966.

Dalton, W. J., *Christ's Proclamation to the Spirits.* Analecta Biblica 23. Rome: Pontifical Biblical Institute, 1965.

Daniélou, Jean, *The Theology of Jewish Christianity.* London: Darton, Longman & Todd; Chicago: Regnery, 1964=*Théologie du Judéo-Christianisme.* Tournai: Desclée, 1958.

Darnton, Robert, *The Great Cat Massacre.* New York: Basic Books, 1984.

Dawson, Warren R., and Eric P. Uphill, *Who Was Who in Egyptology.* 2d ed. London: Egypt Exploration Society, 1972.

de Labriolle, Pierre, "Le mariage spirituel dans l'antiquité chrétienne." *Revue Historique* 136 (1921): 204–25.

de Lagarde, Paul, *Der Pentateuch koptisch.* Leipzig: B. G. Teubner, 1867.

———, *Die koptischen Handschriften der Göttinger Bibliothek.* Abhandlungen der Akademie der Wissenschaften in Göttingen, philologisch-historische Klasse 24,1. Göttingen: Dieterichsche Buchhandlung, 1879.

de Ste. Croix, G. E. M., *Class Struggle in the Ancient Greek World*. Ithaca, NY: Cornell University Press, 1981.

Delling, Gerhard, "ἀρχηγός." *Theological Dictionary of the New Testament* 1 (1964): 487–88.

Demarolle, Jeanne-Marie, "Les femmes chrétiennes vues par Porphyre." *Jahrbuch für Antike und Christentum* 13 (1970): 42–47.

Demosthenes, *Private Orations*. Ed. and trans. A. T. Murray. LCL. Cambridge, MA: Harvard University Press, 1936.

Devos, Paul, Review of Burmester, *Koptische Handschriften*. *Bibliotheca Orientalis* 35 (1978): 128–29.

Dey, L. Kalyan K., *The Intermediary World and Patterns of Perfection in Philo and Hebrews*. SBL Dissertation Series 25. Missoula, MT: Scholars Press, 1975.

Dinsmoor, William B., "Early American Studies of Mediterranean Archaeology." *Proceedings of the American Philosophical Society* 87 (1944): 70–104.

Dio Chrysostom. Vol. 1. Trans. J. W. Cohoon. LCL. London: William Heinemann Ltd.; New York: G. P. Putnam's Sons, 1932.

Dodds, E. R., *Pagan and Christian in an Age of Anxiety: Some Aspects of Religious Experience from Marcus Aurelius to Constantine*. New York: W. W. Norton and Company, 1965.

Donaldson, Mara, "Kinship Theory in the Patriarchal Narratives." *Journal of the American Academy of Religion* 49 (1981): 77–87.

Dörries, Hermann, "Die Vita Antonii als Geschichtsquelle." Pp. 357–410 in *Nachrichten der Akademie der Wissenschaften in Göttingen, phil. hist. Klasse* 14. Göttingen: Vandenhoeck & Ruprecht, 1949.

Dubois, Jean-Daniel, "Le préambule de l'Apocalypse de Pierre (Nag Hammadi VII, 70,14–20). Pp. 384–92 in *Gnosticisme et monde hellénistique: Actes du Colloque de Louvain-la-Neuve (11–14 mars 1980)*. Ed. Julian Ries. Louvain: Université Catholique, 1982.

———, "L'Apocalypse de Pierre (NHC VII,3) et le Nouveau Testament." Pp. 117–25 in *Ecritures et traditions dans la littérature copte: Journée d'études coptes Strasbourg 28 mai 1982*. Ed. Jacques E. Ménard. Cahiers de la bibliothèque copte 1. Louvain: Editions Peeters, 1983.

Dumont, Louis, *Essays on Individualism: Modern Ideology in Anthropological Perspective*. Chicago: The University of Chicago Press, 1986.

Dundes, Alan, "Metafolklore and Oral Literary Criticism." Pp. 50–58 in *Analytic Essays in Folklore*. By Alan Dundes. The Hague: Mouton, 1975.

———, "On the Structure of the Proverb." Pp. 43–64 in *The Wisdom of Many: Essays on the Proverb*. Ed. Wolfgang Mieder and Alan Dundes. New York: Garland, 1981.

Edwards, Edward, *Lives of the Founders of the British Museum; with Notices of Its Chief Augmentors and Other Benefactors. 1570–1870*. London: Trübner and Co.; New York: J. W. Bouton, 1870.

Eldredge, Niles, and Joel Cracraft, *Phylogenetic Patterns and the Evolutionary Process*. New York: Columbia University Press, 1980.

Eldredge, Niles, and Stephen Jay Gould, "Punctuated Equilibria: An Alternative to Phyletic Gradualism." Pp. 82–115 in *Models in Paleobiology*. Ed. Thomas J. M. Schopf. San Francisco: Freeman, Cooper and Co., 1972.

Epictetus. 2 vols. Trans. W. A. Oldfather. LCL. Cambridge, MA: Harvard University Press, 1966.

Eunapius, *Lives of the Philosophers and Sophists,* in Wilmer Cave Wright, ed. and trans., *Philostratus and Eunapius. The Lives of the Sophists.* LCL. New York: G. P. Putnam's Sons, 1922.

Evans, Craig A., "On the Prologue of John and the Trimorphic Protennoia." *New Testament Studies* 27 (1980-81): 395-401.

Evans-Pritchard, E. E., *"Sanza,* a Characteristic Feature of Zande Language and Thought." Pp. 330-54 in *Social Anthropology and Other Essays.* By E. E. Evans-Pritchard. New York: Free Press, 1962.

Evelyn-White, Hugh G., *The Monasteries of the Wadi 'n Natrûn.* 3 vols. Vols. 2 and 3 ed. Walter Hauser. Publications of the Metropolitan Museum of Art Egyptian Expedition 2, 7, 8. New York: Metropolitan Museum of Art, 1926-33.

Evetts, B., ed. and trans., *History of the Patriarchs of the Coptic Church of Alexandria.* Vol. 2: *Peter I to Benjamin I (661).* Patrologia orientalis 1, 2. Paris: Didot, 1948.

Fallon, Francis T., *The Enthronement of Sabaoth. Jewish Elements in Gnostic Creation Accounts.* Nag Hammadi Studies 10. Leiden: E.J. Brill, 1978.

———, "The Gnostics: The Undominated Race." *Novum Testamentum* 21 (1979): 271-88.

Festugière, A. J., *Monachorum in Aegypto. Edition et critique du texte grec et traduction annotée.* Subsidia hagiographica 53. Brussels: Société des Bollandistes, 1971.

Finnegan, Ruth, *Oral Literature in Africa.* Oxford: University Press, 1970.

Fiorenza, Elisabeth Schüssler, "Wisdom Mythology and the Christological Hymns of the New Testament." Pp. 17-41 in *Aspects of Wisdom in Judaism and Early Christianity.* Ed. Robert L. Wilken. Notre Dame and London: University of Notre Dame Press, 1975.

Firth, Raymond, "Proverbs in Native Life, with Special Reference to Those of the Maori." *Folk-Lore* 37 (1926): 134-53, 245-70.

Fisher, J. L., and Teigo Yoshida, "The Nature of Speech According to Japanese Proverbs." *Journal of American Folklore* 81 (1968): 34-43.

Fitch, John G., *Seneca's Hercules Furens: A Critical Text with Introduction and Commentary.* Ithaca, NY, and London: Cornell University Press, 1987.

Flügel, Gustav, *Die arabischen, persischen und türkischen Handschriften der Kaiserlich-Königlichen Hofbibliothek zu Wein im Auftrage der vorgesetzten K. K. Behörde geordnet und beschrieben.* 3 vols. Herausgegeben und in Correctur besorgt durch die K. K. Orientalische Akademie in Wien. Vienna: Druck und Verlag der K. K. Hof- und Staatsdruckerei, 1865-67.

Fontaine, Carole, *Traditional Sayings in the Old Testament.* Sheffield: Almond Press, 1982.

Fortes, Meyer, *Kinship and the Social Order: The Legacy of Lewis Henry Morgan.* Chicago: Aldine Publishing Company, 1969.

Foucault, Michel, *The Archaeology of Knowledge.* Trans. A. M. Sheridan Smith. New York: Pantheon, 1972.

———, *The Use of Pleasure.* Vol. 2 of *The History of Sexuality.* Trans. Robert Hurley. New York: Pantheon Books, 1985.

Fox, Robin, *Kinship and Marriage: An Anthropological Perspective.* Cambridge: Cambridge University Press, 1967.

Frend, W. H. C., *The Rise of Christianity.* Philadelphia: Fortress Press, 1984.

Gager, John G., *The Origins of Anti-Semitism*. New York and elsewhere: Oxford University Press, 1983.

Galinsky, Gotthard K., *The Herakles Theme. The Adaptations of the Hero in Literature from Homer to the Twentieth Century*. Oxford: Basil Blackwell, 1972.

Gardner, Francis, "Donations to the Library." *Journal of the American Oriental Society* 1 (1849): xii–xviii.

Geertz, Clifford, *The Interpretation of Cultures*. New York: Basic Books, 1973.

———, "Common Sense as a Cultural System." Pp. 73–93 in *Local Knowledge*. By Clifford Geertz. New York: Basic Books, 1983.

Gero, Stephen, "The Seduction of Eve and the Trees of Paradise—A Note on a Gnostic Myth." *Harvard Theological Review* 71 (1978): 299–301.

Gilhus, Ingvild Saelid, "The Nature of the Archons. A Study in the Soteriology of a Gnostic Treatise from Nag Hammadi." Ph.D. diss., Universitetet i Bergen, 1982.

Goehring, James E., "New Frontiers in Pachomian Studies." Pp. 236–57 in *The Roots of Egyptian Christianity*. Ed. Birger A. Pearson and James E. Goehring. Philadelphia: Fortress Press, 1986.

———, *The Letter of Ammon and Pachomian Monasticism*. Patristische Texte und Studien 27. Berlin: Walter de Gruyter & Co., 1986.

Goodenough, Erwin R., *The Political Philosophy of Hellenistic Kingship*. Yale Classical Studies 1. New Haven, CT: Yale University Press, 1928.

Goody, Jack, "Kinship: Descent Groups." *International Encyclopedia of the Social Sciences* 8 (1968) 401–8.

Gossen, Gary H., "Chamula Genres of Verbal Behavior." Pp. 145–67 in *Toward New Perspectives in Folklore*. Ed. Americo Paredes and Richard Bauman. Austin, TX: University of Texas Press, 1972.

Gould, Stephen Jay, *Ever Since Darwin. Reflections in Natural History*. New York and London: W. W. Norton & Company, Inc., 1977.

Gravit, Francis W., "Peiresc et les études coptes en France au XVIIᵉ siècle." *Bulletin de la Société d'Archéologie Copte* 4 (1938): 1–22.

Grässer, Erich, *Der Glaube im Hebräerbrief*. Marburg: Elwert-Verlag, 1965.

———, "Die Heilsbedeutung des Todes Jesu in Hebräer 2, 14–18." Pp. 165–84 in *Theologia Crucis—Signum Crucis: Festschrift für Erich Dinkler zum 70. Geburtstag*. Ed. C. Andresen and G. Klein. Tübingen: J.C.B. Mohr (Paul Siebeck), 1979.

Green, Henry A., *The Economic and Social Origins of Gnosticism*. SBL Dissertation Series 77. Atlanta: Scholars Press, 1985.

Gregg, Robert C., ed. and trans., *Athanasius. The Life of Antony and the Letter to Marcellinus*. Classics of Western Spirituality. New York: Paulist Press, 1980.

Griffiths, J. Gwyn, "Apocalyptic in the Hellenistic Era." Pp. 273–93 in *Apocalypticism in the Mediterranean World and the Near East: Proceedings of the International Colloquium on Apocalypticism, Uppsala, August 12–17, 1979*. Ed. David Hellholm. Tübingen: J.C.B. Mohr (Paul Siebeck), 1983.

Grillmeier, Alois, "Der Gottessohn im Totenreich: Soteriologische und christologische Motivierung der Descensuslehre in der älteren christlichen Überlieferung." *Zeitschrift für katholische Theologie* 71 (1949): 1–53, 184–203. Reprinted as pp. 76–174 in idem, *Mit ihm und in ihm*. Freiburg i. Br., 1975.

———, *Christ in the Christian Tradition*. 2d ed. 2 vols. London: Mowbray; Atlanta: John Knox Press, 1975.

Gschwind, Karl, *Die Niederfahrt Christi in die Unterwelt: Ein Beitrag zur Exegese des*

Neuen Testamentes und zur Geschichte des Taufsymbols. Neutestamentliche Abhandlungen 2. Münster: Aschendorff, 1911.

Hadot, Pierre, and Saffrey, H. D., "Neoplatonist Spirituality." Pp. 230–65 in *Classical Mediterranean Spirituality: Egyptian, Greek, Roman.* Ed. A. H. Armstrong. World Spirituality: An Encyclopedic History of the Religious Quest 15. New York: Crossroad, 1986.

Halkin, F., *Sancti Pachomii Vitae Graecae.* Subsidia hagiographica 19. Brussels: Société des Bollandistes, 1932.

Hardy, Edward Rochie, *Christian Egypt: Church and People. Christianity and Nationalism in the Patriarchate of Alexandria.* New York and elsewhere: Oxford University Press, 1952.

Harnack, Adolf, ed., *Porphyrius "Gegen die Christen" 15 Bücher.* Berlin: Verlag der Königl. Akademie der Wissenchaften, 1916.

Hatch, William H. P., "A Visit to the Coptic Convents in Nitria." *Annual of the American Schools of Oriental Research* 6 (1925): 93–107.

_____, "Three Coptic Fragments from Nitria." *Annual of the American Schools of Oriental Research* 6 (1925): 108–11.

_____, "A Fragment of a Lost Work on Dioscorus." *Harvard Theological Review* 19 (1926): 377–81.

_____, "Three Liturgical Fragments from the Wâdi Natrûn." *Annual of the American Schools of Oriental Research* 7 (1926): 94–99.

_____, "Six Coptic Fragments of the New Testament from Nitria." *Harvard Theological Review* 26 (1933): 99–108.

Hecht, Max K., Niles Eldredge, and Stephen Jay Gould, "Morphological Transformation, the Fossil Record, and the Mechanisms of Evolution: A Debate." *Evolutionary Biology* 7 (1974): 295–308.

Helderman, Jan, "'In ihren Zelten . . .': Bemerkungen zu Codex XIII Nag Hammadi p. 47:14–18 im Hinblick auf Joh. i 14." Pp. 181–211 in *Miscellanea Neutestamentica.* Vol. 1. Ed. T. Baarda, A. F. J. Klijn, W. C. van Unnik. Leiden: E.J. Brill, 1978.

Hennecke, Edgar, and Wilhelm Schneemelcher, *New Testament Apocrypha.* Ed. R. McL. Wilson. Philadelphia: Westminster Press, 1963.

Herrmann, Leon, *Sénèque et les premiers chrétiens.* Brussels: Latomus, 1979.

Herskovits, Melville J., and S. Tagbwe, "Kru Proverbs." *Journal of American Folklore* 43 (1930): 225–93.

Herzog, George, *Jabo Proverbs from Liberia.* London: Oxford University Press, 1936.

Hofrichter, Peter, *Im Anfang war der "Johannesprolog": Das urchristliche Logosbekenntnis—die Basis neutestamentlicher und gnostischer Theologie.* Regensburg: Friedrich Pustet, 1986.

Hoistad, Ragnar, *Cynic Hero and Cynic King: Studies in the Cynic Conception of Man.* Lund: Bloms, 1948.

Horner, George, *The Coptic Version of the New Testament in the Northern Dialect Otherwise Called Memphitic and Bohairic.* 4 vols. Oxford: The Clarendon Press, 1898–1905.

Horowitz, Maryanne Cline, "Aristotle and Woman." *Journal of the History of Biology* 9,2 (Fall 1976): 183–213.

Hughes, Philip E., *A Commentary on the Epistle to the Hebrews.* Grand Rapids, MI: Wm. B. Eerdmans Publishing Co., 1977.

Hymes, Dell, "The Ethnography of Speaking." Pp. 13–53 in *Anthropology and Human*

Behavior. Ed. T. Gladwin and W. C. Sturtevant. Washington, DC: Anthropological Society of Washington, 1962.

Index to the Additional Manuscripts, with Those of the Egerton Collection, Preserved in the British Museum, and Acquired in the Year 1783–1835. London: British Museum, 1849.

Isocrates. 2 vols. LCL. Trans. G. Norlin. London: William Heinemann, Ltd.; New York: G. P. Putnam's Sons, 1928.

Jackson, Howard M., *The Lion Becomes Man. The Gnostic Leontomorphic Creator and the Platonic Tradition.* SBL Dissertation Series 81. Atlanta: Scholars Press, 1985.

Janssens, Yvonne, "Le codex XIII de Nag Hammadi." *Le Muséon* 78 (1974): 341–58.

———, "Une source gnostique du Prologue?" Pp. 355–58 in *L'Evangile de Jean: Sources, rédaction, théologie.* BETL 44. Leuven: University Press, 1977.

Johannesen, Stanley K., "The Holy Ghost in Sunset Park: Piety, Place, Ethnicity, and the American City." *Historical Reflections/Réflexions Historique* 15 (1988): 543–77.

Jolles, André, *Einfache Formen.* 2d ed. Darmstadt: Wissenschaftliche Buchgesellschaft, 1958.

Jonas, Hans, *The Gnostic Religion.* 2d ed. Boston: Beacon Press, 1963.

Judge, E. A., "The Earliest Use of Monachos for 'Monk' (p. Coll. Youtie 77) and the Origins of Monasticism." *Jahrbuch für Antike und Christentum* 20 (1977): 72–89.

Käsemann, Ernst, *The Wandering People of God: An Investigation of the Letter to the Hebrews.* Trans. Roy A. Harrisville and Irving L. Sandberg. Minneapolis, MN: Augsburg Publishing House, 1984 = *Das Wandernde Gottesvolk: Eine Untersuchung zum Hebrerbrief.* 2d ed. Forschungen zur Religion und Literatur des Alten und Neuen Testaments 55. Göttingen: Vandenhoeck & Ruprecht, 1957.

———, "An Apologia for Primitive Christian Eschatology." Pp. 169–95 in *Essays on New Testament Themes.* By Ernst Käsemann. Trans. W. J. Montague. Studies in Biblical Theology 41. London: SCM Press, 1964.

Kelly, J. N. D., *The Early Christian Creeds.* 2d ed. London: Longmans, 1960.

Kippenberg, Hans G., "Versuch einer soziologischen Verortung des antiken Gnostizismus." *Numen* 16 (1970): 211–31.

———, "Verländlichung des Gnostizismus als Folge seiner staatlichen Unterdrückung." Pp. 307–20 in *Geisteshaltung und Umwelt. Festschrift zum 65. Geburtstag von Manfred Büttner.* Ed. Werner Kreisel. Aachen: Alano, 1988.

Kirk, G. S., *Myth: Its Meaning and Functions in Ancient and Other Cultures.* Berkeley, CA: University of California Press, 1970.

Kirshenblatt-Gimblett, Barbara, "Toward a Theory of Proverb Meaning." *Proverbium* 22 (1973): 821–27. Reprinted: Pp. 111–21 in *The Wisdom of Many. Essays on the Proverb.* Ed. Wolfgang Mieder and Alan Dundes. New York: Garland Publishing, 1981.

Klijn, A. F. J., *Seth in Jewish, Christian, and Gnostic Literature.* Leiden: E.J. Brill, 1977.

Kloppenborg, John, *The Formation of Q: Trajectories in Ancient Wisdom.* Studies in Antiquity and Christianity. Philadelphia: Fortress Press, 1987.

Knox, W. L., "The 'Divine Hero' Christology in the New Testament." *Harvard Theological Review* 41 (1948): 229–49.

Koschorke, Klaus, *Die Polemik der Gnostiker gegen das kirchliche Christentum.* Nag Hammadi Studies 12. Leiden: E.J. Brill, 1978.

Krause, Martin, "Das literarische Verhältnis des Eugnostosbriefes zur Sophia Jesu Christi: Zur Auseinandersetzung der Gnosis mit dem Christentum." Pp. 215–23 in *Mullus: Festschrift Theodor Klauser. JAC,* Ergänzungsband 1. Ed. A. Stuiber and A. Hermann. Münster: Aschendorffsche Verlagsbuchhandlung, 1964.

Kroll, Josef, *Gott und Hölle: Der Mythos vom Descensuskampfe.* Studien der Bibliothek Wartburg 20. Leipzig and Berlin: Teubner, 1932. Repr. Darmstadt: Wissenschaftliche Buchgesellschaft, 1963.

Küchler, Max, *Frühjüdische Weisheitstraditionen: Zum Fortgang weisheitlichen Denkens im Bereich des frühjüdischen Jahweglaubens.* OBO 26. Fribourg: Universitäts-Verlag; Göttingen: Vandenhoeck & Ruprecht, 1979.

Labib, Claudius Johannes, *Pjōm nte tipsalmodia ethouab ntemrompi mphrēti etauthašs nje nenioti ntiekklēsia nremnkhēmi.* Cairo 1908.

———, *Pjōm nte pithōhs ethouab nem pišlēl nte abba Stherpou.* Cairo 1909.

Lattke, Michael, *Die Oden Salomos in ihrer Bedeutung für Neues Testament und Gnosis.* 3 vols. OBO. Freiburg (Schweiz): Universitätsverlag; Göttingen: Vandenhoeck & Ruprecht, 1979–86.

Layton, Bentley, "The Hypostasis of the Archons or The Reality of the Rulers." *Harvard Theological Review* 67 (1974): 351–425; 69 (1976): 31–101.

———, *Catalogue of Coptic Literary Manuscripts in the British Library Acquired Since the Year 1906.* London: British Library, 1987.

———, *The Gnostic Scriptures. A New Translation with Annotations and Introductions.* Garden City, NY: Doubleday & Company, Inc., 1987.

———, ed., *The Rediscovery of Gnosticism: Proceedings of the International Conference on Gnosticism at Yale, New Haven, Connecticut, March 28–31, 1978.* Vol. 2: *Sethian Gnosticism.* Studies in the History of Religions (Supplements to *Numen*) 41. Leiden: E.J. Brill, 1981.

Lea, Henry Charles, *History of Sacerdotal Celibacy in the Christian Church.* 4th ed. rev. U. S. A.: University Books, 1966.

Leach, Edmund, *Genesis as Myth and Other Essays.* London: Jonathan Cape, 1969.

Lefort, L. T., "Coptica Lovaniensia." *Le Muséon* 50 (1937): 5–52; 51 (1938): 1–32; 53 (1940): 1–66.

———, "Les premiers monastères pachômiens: Exploration topographique." *Le Muséon* 52 (1939): 379–407.

———, *Oeuvres de S. Pachôme et de ses disciples.* Corpus scriptorum christianorum orientalium 159–60. Louvain: Secrétariat du CorpusSCO, 1956.

Leipoldt, Johannes, *Schenute von Atripe und die Entstehung des National Ägyptischen Christentums.* Leipzig: J. C. Hinrichs, 1903.

———, "[Christliche Literatur] In koptischer Sprache." Pp. vii–viii, 383–427 in *Katalog der islamischen, christlich-orientalischen, jüdischen und samaritanischen Handschriften der Universitäts-Bibliothek zu Leipzig.* Katalog der Handschriften der Universitäts-Bibliothek zu Leipzig 2. Ed. K. Vollers. Leipzig: Otto Harrassowitz, 1906.

Leo, Friedrich, *L. Accaei Senecae Tragoediae.* Berlin: Weidmann, 1879; repr. 1962.

Leroy, Julien, *Les types de réglure des manuscrits grecs.* Institut de Recherche et d'Histoire des Textes: Bibliographies, colloques, travaux préparatoires. Paris: Editions du Centre National de la Recherche Scientifique, 1976.

Lévi-Strauss, *The Elementary Structures of Kinship.* Rev. ed. trans. James Harle Bell and John Richard von Strumer. Ed. Rodney Needham. Boston: Beacon Press, 1969.

Lichtheim, Miriam, *Ancient Egyptian Literature*. Vol. 1: *The Old and Middle Kingdoms*. Berkeley and Los Angeles: University of California Press, 1975.

Lieber, Michael D., "Analogic Ambiguity: A Paradox of Proverb Usage." *Journal of American Folklore* 97 (1984), 423–41.

Little, Lindsay, *West African Urbanization: A Study of Voluntary Associations in Social Change*. Cambridge: Cambridge University Press, 1965.

Loeb, Edwin, "The Function of Proverbs in the Intellectual Development of Primitive Peoples." *Scientific Monthly* 74, 2 (1952), 100–104.

Loebenstein, Helene, "Vom 'Papyrus Erzherzog Rainer' zur Papyrussammlung der österreichischen Nationalbibliothek. 100 Jahre Sammeln, Bewahren, Edieren." Pp. 3–39 in *Festschrift zum 100-jährigen Bestehen der Papyrussammlung der österreichischen Nationalbibliothek: Papyrus Erzherzog Rainer*. Vol. 1. Vienna: Verlag Brüder Hollinek, 1983.

Luck, George, "σώφρων, κτλ." *Theological Dictionary of the New Testament* 7 (1971): 1097–1104.

Lucretius, *De rerum natura*. Trans. W. H. D. Rouse. LCL. London: W. Heinemann; New York: G. P. Putnam's Sons, 1937.

MacCulloch, J. A., *The Harrowing of Hell: A Comparative Study of an Early Christian Doctrine*. Edinburgh: T. & T. Clark, 1930. Repr. New York: AMS, 1983.

MacMullen, Ramsay, *Enemies of the Roman Order: Treason, Unrest, and Alienation in the Empire*. Cambridge, MA: Harvard University Press, 1966.

———, *Roman Social Relations 50 B.C. to A.D. 284*. New Haven and London: Yale University Press, 1974.

MacRae, George W., "The Jewish Background of the Gnostic Sophia Myth." *Novum Testamentum* 12 (1970): 86–101.

———, "Seth in Gnostic Texts and Traditions." Pp. 17–24 in *Society of Biblical Literature: 1977 Seminar Papers*. Ed. P. K. Achtemeier. Missoula, MT: Scholars Press, 1977.

———, "Nag Hammadi and the New Testament." Pp. 144–57 in *Gnosis: Festschrift für Hans Jonas*. Ed. Barbara Aland. Göttingen: Vandenhoeck & Ruprecht, 1978.

———, "Gnosticism and the Church of John's Gospel." Pp. 89–96 in *Nag Hammadi, Gnosticism, and Early Christianity*. Ed. Charles W. Hedrick and Robert Hodgson, Jr. Peabody, MA: Hendrickson, 1986.

Maine, Henry Sumner, *Ancient Law*. London: John Murray, 1861; repr. New York: Charles Scribner's Sons, 1871 (first American edition=2d English edition); repr. New York: Dorset Press, 1986.

Malherbe, Abraham, "Herakles." *Reallexikon für Antike und Christentum* 108–9 (1988): 559–83.

Malina, Bruce J., "The Social World Implied in the Letters of the Christian Bishop-Martyr (Named Ignatius of Antioch)." Pp. 71–119 in *Society of Biblical Literature Seminar Papers*. Ed. Paul J. Achtemeier. Vol. 2. Missoula, MT: Scholars Press, 1978.

———, *The New Testament World: Insights from Cultural Anthropology*. Atlanta: John Knox Press, 1981.

———, "'Religion' in the World of Paul." *Biblical Theology Bulletin* 16 (1986): 92–101.

_____, *Christian Origins and Cultural Anthropology: Practical Models for Biblical Interpretation.* Atlanta: John Knox Press, 1986.
Man, E. H., *On the Aboriginal Inhabitants of the Andaman Islands.* London: Anthropological Institute of Great Britain and Ireland, 1932.
Martin, Luther H., *Hellenistic Religions: An Introduction.* New York and elsewhere: Oxford University Press, 1987.
_____, "Artemidorus: Dream Theory in Late Antiquity," unpublished paper.
Mayr, Ernst, *Systematics and the Origin of Species.* New York: Columbia University Press, 1942.
McGuire, Ann, "Virginity and Subversion: Norea Against the Powers in the *Hypostasis of the Archons.*" Pp. 239–58 in Images of the Feminine in Gnosticism. Ed. Karen L. King. Studies in Antiquity and Christianity 4. Philadelphia: Fortress Press, 1988.
Messenger, John, "The Role of Proverbs in a Nigerian Judicial System." *Southwestern Journal of Anthropology* 15 (1959): 64–73. Repr.: pp. 299–307 in *The Study of Folklore.* Ed. Alan Dundes. Englewood Cliffs, NJ: Prentice-Hall, 1965.
Meyer, Wilhelm, *Die Handschriften in Göttingen.* 3 vols. Verzeichniss der Handschriften im Preussischen Staate I, 1–3. Berlin: Verlag von A. Bath, 1893–94.
Michel, Otto, *Der Brief an die Hebräer.* 6th ed. Kritisch-exegetischer Kommentar über das Neue Testament 13. Göttingen: Vandenhoeck & Ruprecht, 1966.
Mitchell, William E., *Mishpokhe: A Study of New York City Jewish Family Clubs.* New York: Mouton, 1978.
Moffatt, James, *A Critical and Exegetical Commentary on the Epistle to the Hebrews.* New York: Charles Scribner's Sons, 1924.
Morgan, Lewis Henry, *Systems of Consanguinity and Affinity of the Human Family.* Washington, DC: Smithsonian Institution, 1877.
Murphy, Roland E., *Wisdom Literature.* The Forms of the Old Testament Literature 13. Grand Rapids, MI: Wm. B. Eerdmans Publishing Co., 1981.
Murray, Gilbert, *The Five Stages of Greek Religion: Studies Based on a Course of Lectures Delivered in April 1912 at Columbia University.* Oxford: The Clarendon Press, 1925.
Müller, Paul-Gerhard, ΧΡΙΣΤΟΣ ΑΡΧΗΓΟΣ: *Der religionsgeschichtliche und theologische Hintergrund einer neutestamentlichen Christusprädikation.* Europäische Hochschulschriften, Reihe 23 vol. 28. Frankfurt and Bern: Lang, 1973.
Neusner, Jacob, *Method and Meaning in Ancient Judiasm.* Brown Judaic Studies 10. Missoula, MT: Scholars Press, 1979.
North, Helen, *SOPHROSYNE: Self-Knowledge and Self-Restraint in Greek Literature.* Ithaca, NY: Cornell University Press, 1966.
Nörr, Dieter, *Rechtskritik in der römischen Antike.* Munich: Verlag der Bayerischen Akademie der Wissenschaften, 1974.
O'Leary, De Lacy, *The Coptic Theotokia.* London: Luzac & Co., 1923.
Oden, Robert A., Jr., "Jacob as Father, Husband, and Nephew: Kinship Studies and the Patriarchal Narratives." *Journal of Biblical Literature* 102 (1983): 189–205.
Oliver, Andrew, *Beyond the Shores of Tripoli. American Archaeology in the Eastern Mediterranean 1789–1879.* N.p. [Boston]: Archaeological Institute of America, 1979.
Ortner, Sherry B., "Is Female to Male as Nature Is to Culture?" Pp. 67–87 in *Woman,*

Culture, and Society. Ed. Michelle Zimbalist Rosaldo and Louise Lamphere. Stanford, CA: Stanford University Press, 1974.

Ovid, *Metamorphoses.* 2 vols. Trans. Frank Justus Miller. 2d ed. rev. G. P. Goold. LCL. Cambridge, MA: Harvard University Press; London: William Heinemann Ltd., 1984.

S. *Pachomii vita Bohairici scripta.* Corpus scriptorum christianorum orientalium 89. Louvain: Secrétariat du CorpusSCO, 1965.

Pagels, Elaine H., *The Gnostic Paul: Gnostic Exegesis of the Pauline Letters.* Philadelphia: Fortress Press, 1975.

_____, "The Politics of Paradise: Augustine's Exegesis of Genesis 1–3 Versus That of John Chrysostom." *Harvard Theological Review* 78 (1985): 67–99.

_____, *Adam, Eve, and the Serpent.* New York: Random House, 1988.

_____, "Pursuing the Spiritual Eve: Imagery and Hermeneutics in the *Hypostasis of the Archons* and *The Gospel of Philip.*" Pp. 187–206 in *Images of the Feminine in Gnosticism.* Ed. Karen L. King. Studies in Antiquity and Christianity 4. Philadelphia: Fortress Press, 1988.

_____, "The Politics of Paradise." *New York Review of Books* 35,8 (1988): 28–37.

Paredes, Americo, and Richard Bauman, ed., *Toward New Perspectives in Folklore.* Austin, TX: University of Texas Press, 1972.

Parrott, Douglas M., ed., *Nag Hammadi Codices V, 2–5 and VI.* Nag Hammadi Studies 11. Leiden: E.J. Brill, 1979.

Pausanias, *Description of Greece.* 5 vols. Trans. W. H. S. Jones, H. A. Ormerod, and R. E. Wycherley. LCL. Cambridge, MA: Harvard University Press; London: William Heinemann Ltd., 1971ff.

Pearson, Birger A., "'She Became a Tree'—A Note to CG II, *4:* 89, 25–26." *Harvard Theological Review* 69 (1976): 413–15.

_____, "The Figure of Norea in Gnostic Literature." Pp. 143–52 in *Proceedings of the International Colloquium on Gnosticism, Stockholm, August 20–25, 1973.* Ed. Geo Widengren. Filologisk-filosofiska serien 17. Stockholm: Almqvist & Wiskell; Leiden: E.J. Brill, 1977.

_____, "The Figure of Seth in Gnostic Literature." Pp. 472–504 in *The Rediscovery of Gnosticism: Proceedings of the International Conference on Gnosticism at Yale, New Haven, Connecticut, March 28–31, 1978.* Vol. 2: *Sethian Gnosticism.* Ed. Bentley Layton. Studies in the History of Religions (Supplements to *Numen*) 41. Leiden: E.J. Brill, 1981.

_____, "Philo, Gnosis and the New Testament." Pp. 73–89 in *The New Testament and Gnosis. Essays in Honour of Robert McL. Wilson.* Ed. A. H. B. Logan and A. J. M. Wedderburn. Edinburgh: T. & T. Clark, 1983.

_____, "Jewish Sources in Gnostic Literature." Pp. 443–81 in *The Literature of the Jewish People in the Period of the Second Temple and the Talmud.* Vol. 2: *Jewish Writings of the Second Temple Period.* Compendia rerum judaicarum ad novum testamentum. Ed. Michael Stone. Philadelphia: Fortress Press, 1984.

_____, "Early Christianity and Gnosticism: A Review Essay." *Religious Studies Review* 13,1 (1987): 1–8.

_____, "Revisiting Norea." Pp. 265–75 in *Images of the Feminine in Gnosticism.* Ed. Karen L. King. Studies in Antiquity and Chrisitanity 4. Philadelphia: Fortress Press, 1988.

Peel, Malcolm, "The 'Decensus [sic] ad inferos' in the Teachings of Silvanus (CG VII,4)." *Numen* 26 (1979): 23–49.

———, "The Treatise on the Resurrection". Pp. 137–215 in *Nag Hammadi Codex I (The Jung Codex) Notes.* Ed. Harold W. Attridge. Leiden: E.J. Brill, 1985.

Peristiany, J. G., ed., *Honor and Shame. The Values of Mediterranean Society.* Chicago: The University of Chicago Press, 1966 (reprint 1970).

———, ed., *Mediterranean Family Structures.* Cambridge: Cambridge University Press, 1976.

Perkins, Pheme, "Peter in Gnostic Revelation." Pp. 1–13 in *SBL 1974 Seminar Papers.* Vol. 2. Ed. George MacRae. Cambridge, MA: Society of Biblical Literature, 1974.

———, *The Gnostic Dialogue: The Early Church and the Crisis of Gnosticism.* New York: Paulist Press, 1980.

———, "Logos Christologies in the Nag Hammadi Codices." *Vigiliae Christianae* 35 (1981): 379–96.

———, "Sophia and the Mother-Father: The Gnostic Goddess." Pp. 97–109 in *The Book of the Goddess Past and Present.* Ed. Carl Olson. New York: Crossroad, 1986.

———, "Sophia as Goddess in the Nag Hammadi Codices." Pp. 96–112 in *Images of the Feminine in Gnosticism.* Ed. Karen L. King. Studies in Antiquity and Christianity 4. Philadelphia: Fortress Press, 1988.

Peters, F. E., *The Harvest of Hellenism: A History of the Near East from Alexander the Great to the Triumph of Christianity.* New York: Simon and Schuster, 1970.

Peters, Melvin K. H., *A Critical Edition of the Coptic (Bohairic) Pentateuch.* 3 vols. SBL Septuagint and Cognate Studies 15, 19, 22. Chico, CA, and Atlanta: Scholars Press, 1983–86.

Peterson, David, *Hebrews and Perfection: An Examination of the Concept of Perfection in the 'Epistle to the Hebrews.'* SNTSMS 47. Cambridge: Cambridge University Press, 1982.

Pétrement, Simone, *Le Dieu séparé: Les origines du gnosticisme.* Paris: Editions du Cerf, 1984.

Pfister, Friedrich, "Herakles und Christus." *Archiv für Religionswissenschaft* 34 (1937): 42–60.

Philo, *Quod omnis probus liber sit:* cf. *Philonis Alexandrini opera quae supersunt.* Vol. 6. Ed. Leopold Cohn and Sigfried Reiter. Editio minor. Berlin: Georg Reimer, 1915.

Pickering, Mary Orne, *Life of John Pickering.* Boston: Privately printed, 1887.

Pitt-Rivers, Julian, "Honour and Social Status." Pp. 19–77 in *Honour and Shame. The Values of Mediterranean Society.* Ed. J. G. Peristiany. Chicago: The University of Chicago Press, 1966 (repr. 1970).

Plato, *Republic.* 2 vols. Trans. Paul Shorey. LCL. London: William Heinemann Ltd.; Cambridge, MA: Harvard University Press, 1987.

Plato. Vol. 4: *Laches, Protagoras, Meno, Euthydemus.* Trans. and ed. W. R. M. Lamb. LCL. Cambridge, MA: Harvard University Press, 1924.

Platt, Eliza, *Journal of a Tour through Egypt, the Peninsula of Sinai, and the Holy Land, in 1838, 1839.* 2 vols. London: Privately printed, 1841–42.

Plotinus. 5 vols. Trans. A. H. Armstrong. LCL. Cambridge, MA: Harvard University Press, 1966–84.

Poole, Lynn, "Cohen's First Eight Out of Egypt." *Art News* 47, 9 (January 1949): 38–39.

Porphyry, *Ad Marcellam.* In Kathleen O'Brien Wicker, ed. and trans., *Porphyry the*

Philosopher to Marcella. SBL Texts and Translations, Graeco-Roman Religions Series 28. Atlanta: Scholars Press, 1987.

Porphyrius, *Opuscula Selecta.* Ed. Augustus Nauck. Bibliotheca scriptorum Graecorum et Romanorum Teubneriana 43. Leipzig: B. G. Teubner, 1886.

Porphyry, *Vita Plotini.* In Richard Harder, trans., *Porphyrios, Über Plotins Leben und über die Ordnung seiner Schriften.* Band V. Hamburg: Felix Meiner, 1968.

Pratt, Norman T., *Seneca's Drama.* Chapel Hill, NC, and London: University of North Carolina Press, 1983.

Proclus, *Alcibiades I.* Trans. William O'Neill. 2d ed. The Hague: Martin Nijhoff, 1971.

Prusak, Bernard P., "Woman: Seductive Siren and Source of Sin?" Pp. 89–116 in *Religion and Sexism.* Ed. R. R. Ruether. New York: Simon and Schuster, 1974.

Quecke, Hans, *Untersuchungen zum koptischen Stundengebet.* Publications de l'Institut Orientaliste de Louvain 3. Louvain: Université Catholique de Louvain, Institut Orientaliste, 1970.

_____, *Die Briefe Pachoms: Griechischer Text der Handschrift W. 145 der Chester Beatty Library.* Texti Patristici et Liturgici 11. Regensburg: Pustet, 1975.

_____, Review of Burmester, *Koptische Handschriften. Orientalia* 46 (1977): 326–28.

Quispel, Gilles, "C. G. Jung und die Gnosis." *Eranos-Jahrbuch* 37 (1968): 277–98.

_____, "Gnosis and Psychology." Pp. 17–31 in *The Rediscovery of Gnosticism: Proceedings of the International Conference on Gnosticism at Yale, New Haven, Connecticut, March 28–31, 1978.* Vol. 1: *The School of Valentinus.* Ed. Bentley Layton. Studies in the History of Religions (Supplements to *Numen*) 41. Leiden: E.J. Brill, 1980.

Rad, Gerhard von, *Wisdom in Israel.* Nashville: Abingdon Press, 1972.

Rader, Rosemary, *Breaking Boundaries: Male/Female Friendship in Early Christian Communities.* New York: Paulist Press, 1983.

Reicke, Bo, *The Disobedient Spirits and Christian Baptism: A Study of 1 Pet. III, 19 and Its Context.* Acta Seminarii Neotestamentici Upsaliensis 13. Copenhagen: Munksgaard, 1946.

Rivers, William H. R., *Kinship and Social Organisation.* London School of Economics and Political Science, Studies No. 36. London: Constable, 1914.

Robinson, Gesine: see Gesine Schenke.

Robinson, James M., "Die Hodajot-Formel in Gebet und Hymnus des Frühchristentums." Pp. 194–235 in *Apophoreta. Festschrift für Ernst Haenchen.* BZNW 30. Ed. W. Eltester and F. H. Kettler. Berlin: Alfred Töpelmann, 1964.

_____, "Introduction: The Dismantling and Reassembling of the Categories of New Testament Scholarship." Pp. 1–19 in James M. Robinson and Helmut Koester, *Trajectories through Early Christianity.* Philadelphia: Fortress Press, 1971.

_____, "Gnosticism and the New Testament." Pp. 125–43 in *Gnosis. Festschrift für Hans Jonas.* Ed. Barbara Aland. Göttingen: Vandenhoeck & Ruprecht, 1978.

_____, ed., *The Nag Hammadi Library in English.* 2d ed. San Francisco and elsewhere: Harper & Row, 1981; 3d rev. ed., 1988.

_____, "Sethians and Johannine Thought. The *Trimorphic Protennoia* and the Prologue of the Gospel of John." Pp. 643–62 in *The Rediscovery of Gnosticism: Proceedings of the International Conference on Gnosticism at Yale, New Haven, Connecticut, March 28–31, 1978.* Vol. 2: *Sethian Gnosticism.* Ed. Bentley Layton. Studies in the History of Religions (Supplements to *Numen*) 41. Leiden: E.J. Brill, 1981.

_____, "Jesus—From Easter to Valentinus (or to the Apostles' Creed)," *Journal of Biblical Literature* 101 (1982): 5–37.

_____, and Helmut Koester, *Trajectories through Early Christianity*. Philidelphia: Fortress Press, 1971.

Rosaldo, Michelle Zimbalist, "Woman, Culture, and Society: A Theoretical Overview." Pp. 17–42 in *Woman, Culture and Society*. Ed. M. Z. Rosaldo and L. Lamphere. Stanford, CA: Stanford University Press, 1974.

_____, "The Use and Abuse of Anthropology: Reflections on Feminism and Cross-cultural Understanding." *Signs* 5 (1979–80): 389–417.

Rose, Herbert J., "Herakles and the Gospels." *Harvard Theological Review* 31 (1938): 113–42.

Rostovtzeff, M., *The Social and Economic History of the Roman Empire*. 2d ed. Oxford: The Clarendon Press, 1957.

Rothkrug, Lionel, "German Holiness and Western Sanctity in Medieval and Modern History." *Historical Reflections/Réflexions Historique* 15 (1988): 161–249.

Rousselle, Aline. *Porneia*. Paris: Presses Universitaires de France, 1983.

Rudolph, Kurt, *Gnosis. The Nature and History of Gnosticism*. Trans. and ed. R. McL. Wilson. Edinburgh: T. & T. Clark; San Francisco and elsewhere: Harper & Row, 1983.

Ruether, Rosemary Radford, "Mysogynism and Virginal Feminism in Fathers of the Church." Pp. 150–83 in *Religion and Sexism*. Ed. R. R. Reuther. New York: Simon and Schuster, 1974.

Ruppert, Fidelis, *Das pachomianische Mönchtum und die Anfänge klösterlichen Gehorsams*. Münsterschwarzacher Studien 20. Münsterschwarzach: Vier-Türme, 1971.

Sabine, George H., *A History of Political Theory*. 4th ed. Rev. Thomas L. Thorson. Hinsdale, IL: Dryden Press, 1973.

Sagan, Eli, *At the Dawn of Tyranny: The Origins of Individualism, Political Oppression, and the State*. New York: Alfred A. Knopf, 1985.

Sanders, Jack T., *The New Testament Christological Hymns. Their Historical Religious Background*. SNTSMS 15. Cambridge: The University Press, 1971.

Saville-Troike, Muriel, *The Ethnography of Communication: An Introduction*. Language in Society 3. Baltimore: University Park Press, 1982.

Schenke, Gesine, "'Die dreigestaltige Protennoia': Eine gnostiche Offenbarungsrede in koptischer Sprache aus dem Fund von Nag Hammadi." *Theologische Literaturzeitung* 99 (1974): 731–46.

_____, *Die Dreigestaltige Protennoia (Nag-Hammadi-Codex XIII)*, herausgegeben, übersetzt und kommentiert. Texte und Untersuchungen 132. Berlin: Akademie-Verlag, 1984.

Schenke, Hans-Martin, *Die Herkunft des sogenannten Evangelium Veritatis*. Göttingen: Vandenhoeck & Ruprecht, 1959.

_____, "Die neutestamentliche Christologie und der gnostische Erlöser." Pp. 205–29 in *Gnosis und Neues Testament: Studien aus Religionswissenschaft und Theologie*. Ed. Karl-Wolfgang Tröger. Berlin: Evangelische Verlangsanstalt; Gütersloh: Gerd Mohn, 1973.

_____, "Das sethianische System nach Nag-Hammadi-Handschriften." Pp. 165–73 in *Studia Coptica*. Ed. Peter Nagel. Berliner Byzantinische Arbeiten 45. Berlin: Akademie-Verlag, 1974.

_____, "The Phenomenon and Significance of Gnostic Sethianism." Pp. 588–616 in

The Rediscovery of Gnosticism: Proceedings of the International Conference on Gnosticism at Yale, New Haven, Connecticut, March 28–31, 1978. Ed. Bentley Layton. Studies in the History of Religions (Supplements to *Numen*) 41. 2 vols. Leiden: E.J. Brill, 1981.

——, "The Problem of Gnosis." *The Second Century* 3 (1983): 73–87.

——, and Karl Martin Fischer, *Einleitung in die Schriften des Neuen Testaments.* Vol. 2. Gütersloh: Gerd Mohn, 1979.

Schlier, Heinrich, *Christus und die Kirche im Epheserbrief.* Beiträge zur historischen Theologie 6. Tübingen: J.C.B. Mohr (Paul Siebeck), 1930.

Schmidt, C. L., "Der Descensus ad inferos in der alten Kirche." Excursus II in idem, *Gespräche Jesu mit seinen Jüngern nach der Auferstehung.* TU 43, Reihe 3 vol. 13. Leipzig, 1919. Repr. Hildesheim: Olms, 1967.

Schmitz, D. P., "La première communauté de vierges à Rome." *Revue Bénédictine* 38 (1926): 189–95.

Schottroff, L., *"Animae naturaliter salvandae:* Zum Problem der himmlischen Herkunft des Gnostikers." Pp. 65–97 in *Christentum und Gnosis.* BZNW 37. Ed. Walther Eltester. Berlin: Alfred Töpelmann, 1969.

Schulz, Fritz, *Classical Roman Law.* Oxford: The Clarendon Press, 1951.

Schweizer, Eduard, "The 'Matthean' Church." *New Testament Studies* 20 (1974): 216.

Scopello, Madeleine, "Jewish and Greek Heroines in the Nag Hammadi Library." Pp. 71–90 in *Images of the Feminine in Gnosticism.* Ed. Karen L. King. Studies in Antiquity and Christianity 4. Philadelphia: Fortress Press, 1988.

Seitel, Peter, "Saying Haya Sayings: Two Categories of Proverb Use." Pp 75–99 in *The Social Use of Metaphor: Essays on the Anthropology of Rhetoric.* Ed. J. David Sapir and J. Christopher Crocker. Philadelphia: University of Pennsylvania Press, 1977.

——, "Proverbs: A Social Use of Metaphor." *Genre* 2 (1969): 143–61. Repr.: pp. 122–39 in *The Wisdom of Many. Essays on the Proverb.* Ed. Wolfgang Mieder and Alan Dundes. New York: Garland Publishing, 1981.

Seneca, *Ad Lucilium epistolae morales.* 3 vols. Trans. Richard M. Gummere. LCL. London: W. Heinemann; New York: G. P. Putnam, 1917–25.

Shailor, Barbara, *The Medieval Book. Catalogue of an Exhibition at the Beinecke Rare Book and Manuscript Library, Yale University.* New Haven, CT: Yale University Library, 1988.

Shelton, Jo-Ann, *Seneca's Hercules Furens: Theme, Structure and Style.* Hypomnemata 50. Göttingen: Vandenhoeck & Ruprecht, 1979.

Simaika, Marcus, *Catalogue of the Coptic and Arabic Manuscripts in the Coptic Museum, the Patriarchate, the Principal Churches of Cairo and Alexandria and the Monasteries of Egypt.* Assisted by Yassa 'Abd al Masih. 2 vols. Publications of the Coptic Museum. Cairo: Government Press, 1939–42.

Simon, Marcel, *Hercule et le Christianisme.* Paris: Les belles lettres, 1955.

Le site monastique des Kellia (Basse-Egypte): Recherches des années 1981–83. Mission suisse d'archéologie copte de l'Université de Genève sous la direction de Rodolphe Kasser. Louvain: Peeters, 1984.

Smith, Jonathan Z., "The Prayer of Joseph." Pp. 253–94 in *Religions in Antiquity: Essays in Memory of Erwin R. Goodenough.* Ed. Jacob Neusner. Leiden: E.J. Brill, 1968. Repr. as pp. 24–66 in Smith, *Map is Not Territory.* SJLA 23. Leiden: E.J. Brill, 1978.

Smith, Richard, "Sex Education in Gnostic Schools." Pp. 345–60 in *Images of the*

Feminine in Gnosticism. Ed. Karen L. King. Studies in Antiquity and Christianity 4. Philadelphia: Fortress Press, 1988.

Smith, Terence V., *Petrine Controversies in Early Christianity.* WUNT, 2. Reihe 15. Tübingen: J.C.B. Mohr (Paul Siebeck), 1985.

Sotheby's, *Catalogue of the Valuable Library of the Late Rev. Henry Tattam.* London, 16 June 1868.

Spicq, Ceslas, *L'Epître aux Hébreux.* 2 vols. EBib. Paris: Gabalda, 1952–53.

Spitta, Frederich, *Christi Predigt an die Geister: Ein Beitrag zur neutestamentlichen Theologie.* Göttingen: Vandenhoeck & Ruprecht, 1890.

Stanton, G. N., "5 Ezra and Matthean Christianity in the Second Century." *Journal of Theological Studies,* NS 28 (1977): 67–83.

Stead, G. Christopher, *Divine Substance.* Oxford: The Clarendon Press, 1979.

Stroumsa, Gedaliahu A. G., *Another Seed: Studies in Gnostic Mythology.* Leiden: E.J. Brill, 1984.

Strout, Elizabeth, *Catalogue of the Library of the American Oriental Society.* New Haven, CT: Yale University Library, 1930.

Swain, Joseph W., *The Hellenic Origins of Christian Asceticism.* New York: Columbia University Press, 1916.

Tannehill, Robert C., *The Sword of His Mouth.* Semeia Supplements 1. Philadelphia: Fortress Press; Missoula, MT: Scholars Press, 1975.

Tardieu, Michael, *Trois mythes gnostique. Adam, Eros et les animaux d'Egypte dans un écrit de Nag Hammadi (II, 5).* Paris: Etudes augustiniennes, 1974.

Tattam, Henry, "A Catalogue of the Rev. H. Tattam's Coptic and Sahidic Manuscripts Purchased or Copied in Egypt." *Zeitschrift der Deutschen Morgenländischen Gesellschaft* 7 (1853): 94–97.

Tetz, Martin, "Athanasius und die Vita Antonii: Literarische und theologische Relationen." *Zeitschrift für die Neutestamentliche Wissenschaft* 73 (1982): 1–30.

Tischendorf, Constantin, "Rechenschaft über meine handschriftlichen Studien auf meiner wissenschaftlichen Reise von 1840 bis 1844." *Jahrbücher der Literatur/ Anzeige-Blatt für Wissenschaft und Kunst* 110 (April–June 1845): 1–19.

_____, *Reise in den Orient.* 2 vols. Leipzig: Verlag von Bernh. Tauchnitz jun., 1846.

_____, "Die Manuscripta Tischendorfiana in der Universitätsbibliothek zu Leipzig." *Serapeum* 8 (1847): 49–61, 63–78.

_____, *Anecdota Sacra et Profana ex Oriente et Occidente Allata.* Leipzig: Emil Graul, 1855.

Torjesen, Karen, "Controversies Over Women's Leadership in Early Christianity." Unpublished typescript.

_____, "Women's Virtues and Vices: Mechanisms for Social Control." Unpublished manuscript.

Trigg, Joseph Wilson. "Healing That Comes From God: The Alexandrian Response to the Third-Century Penitential Crisis." Ph.D. diss., The University of Chicago, 1978.

Tuckett, Christopher M., *Nag Hammadi and the Gospel Tradition: Synoptic Tradition in the Nag Hammadi Library.* Edinburgh: T. & T. Clark, 1986.

Tuki, Raphael, *Pi jōm nte ti metrefšemši n ni mustērion ethouab nem han jin hēbi nte ni refmōout nem han jinhōs nem pi katameros nabot.* Rome, 1763.

Turner, John D., trans., "Trimorphic Protennoia (XIII, *1*). Pp. 461–70 in *The Nag*

Hammadi Library in English. Ed. James M. Robinson. San Francisco and elsewhere: Harper & Row, 1977.

_____, "Sethian Gnosticism: A Literary History." Pp. 55–86 in *Nag Hammadi, Gnosticism, and Early Christianity.* Ed. Charles W. Hedrick and Robert Hodgson, Jr. Peabody, MA: Hendrickson, 1986.

Valantasis, Richard, "Third Century Spiritual Guides: A Semiotic Study of the Guide–Disciple Relationship in Christianity, Neoplatonism, Hermetism, and Gnosticism." Th.D. diss., Harvard University, 1988.

Vanhoye, Albert, *Situation du Christ: Epître aux Hébreux 1–2.* Lectio divina 58. Paris: Les Editions du Cerf, 1969.

Veilleux, Armand, *Pachomian Koinonia.* 3 vols. Cistercian Studies 45–47. Kalamazoo, MI: Cistercian Publications, 1980–82.

_____, *La liturgie dans le cénobitisme pachômien au quatrième siècle.* Studia Anselmiana 57. Rome: Herder, 1986.

Vetch, Robert Hamilton, "Turner, Sir Tomkyns Hilgrove (1766?–1843)." *Dictionary of National Biography* 57 (1899): 361–63.

Veyne, Paul, "The Roman Empire." Pp. 5–233 in *A History of Private Life.* Gen. ed. Philippe Aries and Georges Duby. Vol 1: *From Pagan Rome to Byzantium.* Ed. Paul Veyne and trans. Arthur Goldhammer. Cambridge, MA: Harvard University Press, 1987.

Virgil, *Georgica.* 2 vols. Ed. C. S. Jerram. Clarendon Press Series. Oxford: The Clarendon Press, 1892.

Vogels, Heinz-Jürgen, *Christi Abstieg ins Totenreich und das Lauterungsgericht an den Toten: Eine bibeltheologisch-dogmatische Untersuchung zum Glaubensartikel "descendit ad inferos."* Freiburger Theologische Studien 102. Freiburg, Basel, Vienna: Herder, 1976.

Werner, Andreas, "Die Apokalypse des Petrus: Die dritte Schrift aus Nag-Hammadi-Codex VII." *Theologische Literaturzeitung* 99 (1974): 575–84.

Werner, Martin, *The Formation of Christian Dogma: An Historical Study of Its Problem.* New York: Harper, 1957=*Die Entstehung des christlichen Dogmas.* Bern and Leipzig: Haupt, 1941; 2d ed. 1960.

Westcott, Brooke Foss, *The Epistle to the Hebrews.* 3d ed. London: Macmillan, 1909.

Westermann, Claus, "Weisheit im Sprichwort." Pp. 73–85 in *Schalom: Studien zu Glaube und Geschichte Israels.* Ed. Karl-Heinz Bernhardt. Stuttgart: Calwer Verlag, 1971.

Westermarck, Edward A., *Wit and Wisdom in Morocco: A Study of Native Proverbs.* London: George Routledge & Sons, 1930.

White, Harrison C., *An Anatomy of Kinship.* Englewood Cliffs, NJ: Prentice-Hall, 1963.

Wicker, Kathleen O'Brien, "First Century Marriage Ethics: A Comparative Study of the Household Codes and Plutarch's Conjugal Precepts." Pp. 141–53 in *No Famine in the Land. Studies in Honor of John L. McKenzie.* Ed. J. W. Flanagan and A. W. Robinson. Missoula, MT: Scholars Press, 1975.

_____, "Plutarch, 'Mulierum Virtutes.'" Pp. 106–34 in *Plutarch's Ethical Writings and the Early Christian Literature.* Ed. H. D. Betz. A Contribution to the Corpus Hellenisticum Novi Testamenti. Leiden: E.J. Brill, 1978.

Williams, Caroline Ransom, "The Place of the New York Historical Society in the

Growth of American Interest in Egyptology." *New-York Historical Society Quarterly Bulletin* 4 (1921): 3–20.

Williams, Ellen Reeder, *The Archaeological Collection of the Johns Hopkins University*. Baltimore and London: Johns Hopkins University Press, 1984.

Williams, James G., *Those Who Ponder Proverbs: Aphoristic Thinking and Biblical Literature*. Bible and Literature Series 2. Sheffield: Almond Press, 1981.

Williams, Michael Allen, *The Immovable Race. A Gnostic Designation and the Theme of Stability in Late Antiquity*. Nag Hammadi Studies 21. Leiden: E.J. Brill, 1985.

———, "Uses of Gender Imagery in Ancient Gnostic Texts." Pp. 196–227 in *Gender and Religion: On the Complexity of Symbols*. Ed. Caroline Walker Bynum, Stevan Harrell, and Paula Richman. Boston: Beacon Press, 1986.

———, "Variety in Gnostic Perspectives on Gender." Pp. 2–22 in *Images of the Feminine in Gnosticism*. Ed. Karen L. King. Studies in Antiquity and Christianity 4. Philadelphia: Fortress Press, 1988.

Wilson, John A., *Signs and Wonders upon Pharaoh: A History of American Egyptology*. Chicago and London: The University of Chicago Press, 1964.

Wilson, R. McL., "The Trimorphic Protennoia." Pp. 50–54 in *Gnosis and Gnosticism*. Ed. Martin Krause. Nag Hammadi Studies 8. Leiden: E.J. Brill, 1977.

Wimbush, Vincent L., *Renunciation towards Social Engineering (An Apologia for the Study of Asceticism in Graeco-Roman Antiquity)*. Occasional Papers of the Institute for Antiquity and Christianity 8. Claremont, CA: Institute for Antiquity and Christianity, 1986.

Winlock, H. E., and W. E. Crum, *The Monastery of Epiphanius at Thebes*. 2 vols. New York: Metropolitan Museum of Art, 1926. Repr. ed., New York: Arno, 1973.

Wipszycka, Ewa, "Les terres de la congrégation pachômienne dans une liste de payments pour les apora." Pp. 623–36 in *Le monde grec, pensée, littérature, histoire, documents. Hommages à Claire Préaux*. Ed. J. Bingen, et al. Brussels: L'Université Bruxelles, 1975.

Wisse, Frederik, "Stalking Those Elusive Sethians." Pp. 563–76 in *The Rediscovery of Gnosticism: Proceedings of the International Conference on Gnosticism at Yale, New Haven, Connecticut, March 28–31, 1978*. Ed. Bentley Layton. Studies in the History of Religions (Supplements to *Numen*) 41. 2 vols. Leiden: E.J. Brill, 1981.

———, "Flee Feminity: Antifemininity in Gnostic Texts and the Question of Social Milieu." Pp. 297–307 in *Images of the Feminine in Gnosticism*. Ed. Karen L. King. Studies in Antiquity and Christianity 4. Philadelphia: Fortress Press, 1988.

Wolfskeel, C. W., "Ist Augustin in 'De Immortalitate Animae' von der Gedankenwelt des Porphyrios beeinflusst worden?" *Vigiliae Christianae* 26 (1972): 130–45.

Wright, William, *Catalogue of Syriac Manuscripts in the British Museum Acquired Since the Year 1838*. 3 vols. London: British Museum, 1870–72.

Wüstenfeld, Ferdinand, "Coptisch-arabische Handschriften der Königl. Universitäts-Bibliothek." *Nachrichten der Akademie der Wissenschaften in Göttingen, philologisch-historische Klasse* (1878): 285–326.

Xenophon, *Memorabilia and Oeconomicus*. Trans. E. C. Marchant. LCL. London: William Heinemann; New York: G. P. Putnam's Sons, 1923.

Yamauchi, Edwin M., "Jewish Gnosticism? The Prologue of John, Mandaean Parallels, and the Trimorphic Protennoia." Pp. 467–97 in *Studies in Gnosticism and Hellenistic Religions Presented to Gilles Quispel on the Occasion of his 65th Birth-*

day. Ed. R. van den Broek and J. M. Vermaseren. Etudes préliminaires aux religions orientales dans l'Empire romain 91. Leiden: E.J. Brill, 1981.

Yankah, Kwesi, "Proverb Rhetoric and African Judicial Processes: The Untold Story." *Journal of American Folklore* 99 (1986): 280–303.

Zanetti, Ugo, *Les lectionnaires coptes annuels: Basse-Egypte*. Publications de l'Institut Orientaliste de Louvain 33. Louvain-la-Neuve: Université Catholique de Louvain, Institut Orientaliste, 1985.

Zwierlein, Otto, *Kritischer Kommentar zu den Tragödien Senecas*. Abhandlung 6. Mainz: Akademie der Wissenschaften und der Literatur, 1986.

Index of Ancient Literature

Old Testament and Apocrypha

New Testament

Old Testament Pseudepigrapha

New Testament Apocrypha

Nag Hammadi Tractates

Patristic Literature

Hellenistic and Classical Literature

Index of Modern Authors

192

Index of Subjects

virtue, 6, 14, 22, 93, 96–99, 101, 122
visions and revelations, 71

Wadi Natrun (Egypt), 146–61
water of life, 41
White Cloister, 141
will, testament, 30, 31, 142
Wisdom, wisdom, sage(s) (see also Sophia), 38, 46, 47, 50, 52, 57, 58, 60, 64–66, 75–88, 90, 100
Word (see also Logos), 54, 64

Xenophon, 17, 94, 95, 101

Yaldabaoth, 8, 19, 44
Yale University, Beinecke Rare Book and Manuscript Library, 154

Zoe, 10, 19, 21